Canadian Centre  s

Growing older,

The New Face of Retirement

Working longer

Monica Townson

Copies of this book may be purchased through
the CCPA online bookstore at **www.policyalternatives.ca**.

Library and Archives Canada Cataloguing in Publication
Townson, Monica, 1932–
Growing older, working longer : the new face of retirement / Monica Townson.

Includes bibliographical references.
ISBN 0-88627-473-7

1. Retirement—Canada. 2. Retirement—Government policy—Canada.
3. Older people—Employment—Canada. 4. Early retirement—Canada.
5. Pensions—Canada. I. Canadian Centre for Policy Alternatives II. Title.

HQ1063.2.C3T69 2006   306.3'8'0971   C2006-900811-6

Printed and bound in Canada. CAW★567 OTTAWA
Layout and cover design by Tim Scarth.

Canadian Centre for Policy Alternatives
Suite 410, 75 Albert Street, Ottawa, ON K1P 5E7
TEL 613 563-1341 FAX 613 233-1453 ccpa@policyalternatives.ca
http://www.policyalternatives.ca

Preface

It's not surprising that, as the leading edge of the baby boom generation reaches its late 50s, retirement has become a major preoccupation—especially when the springtime ritual of the RRSP season rolls around. A bombardment of ads encourages us to believe that, if only we follow the right advice and invest in the right plan, by the time we're in our 50s we'll be able to spend the rest of our lives lying on a sandy beach in the Caribbean, travelling around Europe, or relaxing on the golf course, without a care in the world. "Freedom 55," originally presented as a clever marketing slogan for a major insurance company, has now become the goal everyone is persuaded to aim for—that time when, free of the burden of work and economically secure, we'll have years of leisure ahead of us.

But there is now growing uncertainty about retirement—how and when it might happen, and what form it might take. More and more people will not be able to achieve their dreams of early retirement. Volatile stock markets and low interest rates have pushed workplace pension plans into deficit positions and undermined the value of individual retirement savings. Many people are no longer sure about just when they'll be able to stop working, or even if they'll ever be able to stop. And many of those who retired early are now going back to work—some for financial reasons, others because they prefer to keep active.

Governments around the world are trying to persuade people to postpone their retirement and go on working to ease pressure on pension plans as the big generation of baby boomers gets set to retire. But it's not just the cost of pensions that is fuelling the development of policy here. Workers who produce the goods and services the economy needs are essential to economic growth and prosperity. There is growing concern that, as the baby boom generation retires, fewer workers will be available to support the growth of the economy and produce the goods and services needed by all Canadians.

Canada is being urged by international bodies such as the OECD to get rid of early retirement incentives, to abolish mandatory retirement, and to take other measures to persuade people to go on working and to raise the age of retirement. The fear is that these efforts may become coercive and that people may be forced to go on working against their will.

At the same time, strong pressure is building to shift responsibility for retirement provision away from collective actions and programs and onto individuals, who will be expected to fend for themselves. There are already signs that this is happening as employers move away from defined benefit pension plans where a pension related to earnings and years of service is guaranteed, in favour of defined contribution plans and group RRSPs where retirement income depends on investment returns and no particular pension amount is promised.

Regardless of policy measures adopted by governments, there are already signs that people increasingly believe they will have to go on working longer or take some other kind of job after a formal retirement from a long-term "career" job. More and more workers are doing just that. In fact, we probably need a new word to describe what happens when workers grow old, because retirement has become a process: it's no longer a point in time when work stops and leisure begins.

This book will look at how what we used to call "retirement" is changing, and what it may mean. It will look at changes already under way and at the growing uncertainty about retirement. We'll discuss how the current retirement income system is coping. We'll consider new and more positive perspectives on the aging population in some detail and follow the demise of the early retirement dream. We will also discuss how older workers might be protected in this changing environment. The idea of "increasing choice" and giving people a "better range of alternatives" is receiving growing emphasis in policy development, but what does it mean and what could be the likely consequences? We will conclude with some consideration of where we might go from here.

My thanks go to Bruce Campbell, Executive Director of the Canadian Centre for Policy Alternatives, for his continuing support and encouragement as I worked on the book; to Ed Finn for his valuable editorial input and advice; and to Kerri-Anne Finn and everyone else in the Ottawa office of CCPA who helped in the editing and production of the book.

I am also grateful to John Myles, who read an early draft of the manuscript and offered helpful comments and advice. Responsibility for the opinions expressed in the book, and for any errors or omissions, is mine alone.

Monica Townson
Toronto, January 2006

An Uncertain Future

MOST OF US look forward to spending our golden years relaxing and enjoying life, playing with our grandchildren, maybe traveling to exotic places, or taking up that hobby we've been thinking about for so long. Just how much we can do in those retirement years will depend on income, health, and family situation. But almost everyone now has years of leisure after finishing a lifetime of work.

It wasn't always so. In the early 1900s, when farming was still a major source of employment, many people carried on working until poor health or death intervened.[1] Retirement was only possible for a tiny minority of people who had managed to get together enough savings to support themselves in old age—or whose families could support them when they were no longer able to work for pay. As recently as the 1950s, for instance, U.S. surveys showed only about 5% of retirees had stopped work voluntarily to enjoy more leisure. The rest had been forced to "retire" because they were laid off or were in poor health.[2] And many of them spent the rest of their lives in poverty.

Being able to spend senior years in leisurely comfort has been described by one writer as "one of the great achievements of the affluent democracies in the 20th century."[3] Essentially, the expansion of mandatory, universal pension schemes "democratized" access to retirement, so that it was no longer the privilege of the few.

Perhaps not surprisingly, with the leading edge of the baby boom generation reaching its late 50s, retirement has now become a major preoccupation—especially when the springtime ritual of the RRSP season rolls around. A bombardment of ads encourages us to believe that, if only we follow the right advice and invest in the right plan, by the time we're in our 50s, we'll be able to spend the rest of our lives lying on a sandy beach in the Caribbean, traveling around Europe, or relaxing on the golf course, without a care in the world. "Freedom 55," originally presented as a clever marketing slogan for a major insurance company, has now become the goal everyone is persuaded to aim for—that time when, free of the burden of work and economically secure, we'll have years of leisure ahead of us.

While some people may be able to achieve their dreams of early retirement, many more do not. Some were forced into early retirement when their employers decided to lay off workers during economic down-times. As well, volatile stock markets have pushed pension plans into deficit positions and undermined the value of individual retirement savings, so that many people are no longer sure about just when they'll be able to stop working, or even if they'll ever be able to stop. And many of those who retired early are now going back to work—some for financial reasons, others because they prefer to keep active. There's growing uncertainty about retirement—how and when it might happen and what form it might take. In fact, we probably need a new word to describe what happens when workers grow old, because retirement has become a process: it's no longer a point in time when work stops and leisure begins.

It could even be that early retirement is rapidly becoming just a fiction dreamed up by mutual fund companies and financial institutions to sell financial products at RRSP time. For instance, recent surveys have shown that high percentages of Canadians plan to go on working after taking a formal retirement, and many of those who took early retirement have returned to work in some capacity, even if not at the same kind of job from which they retired. One recent survey from Statistics Canada found that, while many people may say they want to retire early, less than one-quarter of people in their 40s and 50s plan to leave the work force before age 60.[4]

We can expect these trends to continue. In fact, governments will make sure they do. More and more jurisdictions have abolished mandatory retirement. Concerned about the growing cost of pensions as more and more people reach retirement age, governments in almost all the industrialized countries are now developing policies to encourage people to abandon their plans for early retirement and to keep on working to later ages. The United States is raising the age of eligibility for Social Security from 65 to 67, although the changes were announced 20 years ago and will be phased in over roughly the next 20 years. The United Kingdom government proposed age 70 as a "default" age of retirement, but then backed down and set the default age at 65—at least for now.

In Canada, a major federal government research initiative is looking at policies that might change the way people combine work, leisure, caregiving, and education over a lifetime instead of emphasizing only what policies are needed once they reach age 65. "Population Aging and Life-Course Flexibility" is what they've called the project. The aging population is no longer seen as a "crisis." Instead, officials say, "the coming retirement of the baby boom generation, if accompanied by good social policies, may provide an opportunity to make major social and economic gains."[5]

The view now is that tomorrow's generation of older people will be skilled and potentially productive in an economy based on knowledge and services. The growth of healthy life expectancy raises the possibility of increasing both time spent in work and time spent in leisure, with gains on both economic and social fronts. The process could eventually lead to a new definition of "retirement" and radical new policies that will change the way we look at the aging process.

This book will look at how what we used to call "retirement" is changing, and what it may mean. It will look at changes already under way and at the growing uncertainty about retirement. We'll discuss how the current retirement income system is coping. We'll consider new and more positive perspectives on the aging population in some detail and follow the demise of the early retirement dream. We will also discuss how older workers might be protected in this changing environment. The idea of "increasing choice" and giving people a "better range of alternatives" is receiving growing emphasis in policy development, but what does it mean and what could be the likely consequences? We will conclude with some consideration of where we might go from here.

Living longer and retiring earlier

The very idea of retiring in your 50s to live a life of leisure represents a remarkable turnaround in just a few generations. For instance, the first public pensions in Canada, introduced in 1927 through the Old Age Pensions Act, provided benefits only to people who had reached age 70. Our grandfathers—if they were lucky enough to have a company pension plan—could look forward to the proverbial gold watch once they reached age 65, after a lifetime of working for the same employer. And they went home to put their feet up. But they often didn't spend much time in retirement, because life expectancy was much lower then.

Our grandmothers, of course, generally didn't work outside their homes—at least if they were middle class. Busy with looking after their large families and keeping house, they didn't get to retire. Women from lower-income families generally have always had to combine those responsibilities with some kind of paid work—whether cleaning house or washing clothes for other families, or low-paid factory work or piecework in their own homes. They didn't get to retire either.

But life expectancy has increased significantly since grandmother was young. In 1921, a Canadian man who reached age 65 could expect to live another 13 years, on average. Women at age 65 in 1921 had an average 13.3 years still ahead of them.[6] Now, the life expectancy of men at age 65 has risen to 16.3 years, while women at age 65 can expect another 20.2 years on average.[7]

Ironically, while people are living longer, they are retiring earlier. In the 1970s and early 1980s, workers typically retired at age 65. But by 2001, the median age of retirement had dropped to 60.8.[8] Canada has just reached the cross-over point for men where lifetime years in and out of employment are about equal.[9] In 1970, Canadian men could expect to work 44 years of their lives and be doing other things—such as going to school, being unemployed, or retired—for another 26 years. Now, more time is spent out of employment than in it. The OECD suggests that, if current trends continue, by 2030 men would spend 35 years in paid work and 44 years not at work. In 1970, Canadian women could have expected to spend 19 years in paid employment and 58 years not in employment. By 2030, according to the OECD, women could spend 38 years in paid employment and 47 years out of employment.[10]

Early retirement could accelerate the process. Based on current life expectancy, anyone now thinking of retiring at 50 probably has more than one-third of their life still ahead of them. For instance, a 50-year old woman can expect to live another 33.2 years, on average, while a 50-year-old man probably has another 28.5 years to go.[11] That's a long time to be doing nothing.

Changing the culture of early retirement

While many observers believe there is now a general expectation of early retirement, it is important to note that early retirement is not always a voluntary choice. In the economic downturn of the early 1990s, for example, many employers laid off older workers as a way of downsizing their operations. Older workers may have been forced out of the work force even though they did not want to retire.[12] Some researchers suggest that the involuntary aspects of labour market withdrawal are often ignored in studies of retirement behaviour. In addition, older workers who keep working or return to the labour market may experience age discrimination, either by finding their job opportunities reduced, or having to accept lower-quality or lower-waged jobs. Protecting older workers from discrimination (discussed in more detail in Chapter 5) will have to be addressed if policy-makers hope to change the culture of early retirement.

One recent study, for instance, looked at individuals who turned 50 between 1976 and 1979 and followed their work patterns in the years leading up to age 65. Surprisingly, retirement as a self-reported event appeared to be relatively infrequent. Only about 51% of men and 30% of women in the selected age groups had retired from a job by age 65. In

An Uncertain Future

many cases, the job separation that ultimately ended a career must have been a layoff, an illness or disability, or a family-related event, according to this study. However, it must be noted that the workers who were the subject of this study would have turned 65 in the period from 1991 to 1994, part of which coincided with declining economic activity.[13]

Overall, the study found that about 60% of all job separations for both men and women in the age groups between 50 and 65 could be classified as involuntary. And the majority of those individuals found another job within 12 months. The authors of this study also say that the high rates of job change experienced within these age groups contradict the view that careers of older workers are characterized as either a process of gradual disengagement or a stable plateau preceding an abrupt final withdrawal. And, they say, "Since only a bare majority of men and a minority of women explicitly retired, many older workers seem to be interested in continued employment."

In the 1990s, some governments actively encouraged early retirement in an effort to free up jobs for younger workers and address the problem of high youth employment. The Quebec government, for instance, introduced a phased retirement scheme in 1997 which allowed people who would agree to reduce their hours of work to begin drawing on their workplace pension benefits, while continuing to contribute to the Quebec Pension Plan as if they were still working full-time. There's little evidence that such programs were successful in creating more job opportunities for younger workers. For one thing, younger workers generally do not have the same skills and experience as the older workers they are supposed to replace.

But there are signs that the culture of early retirement is changing. And it's likely to be helped along by public policies that will be designed to encourage people to stay at work longer—although some experts believe achieving the objective will not be easy. Sociologist and aging expert John Myles believes that institutions profoundly shape cultural preferences. "Once established," says Myles, "the expectation that 'normal retirement' occurs at age 55 or 60 may be extremely difficult to change."[14]

Nevertheless, phased retirement programs, intended to ease older workers out of the work force early, are now being abandoned. Sweden, one of the best-known practitioners of this type of policy, has dropped its well-known partial pension program and no new entrant has been allowed since 2000. And Quebec is now considering changes to the Quebec Pension Plan, outlined in a 2003 discussion paper called "Adapting the Pension Plan to Quebec's new realties."[15] Among other things, proposed changes would be designed to discourage early retirement. "Considering the rapid aging of the population and the new realities of the labour market," the Quebec government says, the Quebec Pension Plan must evolve so as to "make it more advantageous to remain employed."

In almost all industrialized countries, governments are looking for ways to ease the pressure on public pension programs. Having people retire later and keep up their pension contributions longer could be one way of doing that. The OECD has called for incentives for early retirement to be eliminated in favour of policies to encourage "active ageing."[16] Public pension programs, taxation systems, and social transfer programs should be reformed, the OECD says, to remove financial incentives to early retirement, and financial disincentives to later retirement.

In Canada, the Chief Actuary has suggested that the actuarial factors used to calculate early retirement pensions for people who claim their CPP benefits prior to age 65 are too generous.[17] An actuarial study of the plan, completed in 2003, found the formula currently being used effectively subsidizes early retirement and creates an incentive for individuals to opt for the CPP retirement pension at an early age (currently about 62, on average). The formula also penalizes those who want to continue working and claim their benefits after age 65, according to the study. The Chief Actuary said that, in the context of an aging population, where life expectancy at age 65 is expected to continue to increase and projected labour force shortages could induce older workers to stay at work longer, policy-makers will have to determine whether the legislated actuarial adjustment now in force should be changed or whether certain Plan provisions should be changed to restore cost neutrality.[18]

Peter Hicks, who was the first head of the federal government's Population Aging and Life-Course Flexibility research project, has expressed concern about "the significant real cost, both public and private, of supporting a much larger number of retirees, about sharing that cost across generations, and about the consequent need to make real changes in retirement ages and health care effectiveness."[19] He believes tomorrow's

An Uncertain Future

generation of older people will be skilled and potentially productive in an economy based on knowledge and services. According to Hicks, the growth of healthy life expectancy raises the possibility of increasing both time spent in work and time spent in leisure, with gains on both economic and social fronts."[20]

But it's not just the cost of pensions that is fuelling the development of policy here. Workers who produce the goods and services the economy needs are essential to economic growth and prosperity. There is growing concern that, as the baby boom generation retires, fewer workers will be available to support the growth of the economy and produce the goods and services needed by all Canadians.

Employers may soon be trying to address the looming shortage of younger workers as the baby boomers reach what used to be the traditional retirement age. They could do that by discouraging early retirement and trying to keep the older generation of baby boomers at work.

There's also the possibility that, as the population ages, employers may actively encourage those who took early retirement to come back to work. Analysts note that slow population growth has made the population 55 and over an important potential source of labour. But many of them have already left the labour force.[21]

One recent study looked at men in the 55-to-59-year age group and found that just over 78,000 men in this age group were not in the work force in 1976. By 2001, however, almost 220,000 men aged 55 to 59, representing 6.6% of the total labour force, were not active in the work force. The labour market would lose a wealth of experience and potential economic contribution if inactivity continues to rise among men in this age group, the author of this study said.

Uncertainty is increasing

All the evidence points to an uncertain future for Canadians as they get older. It's hardly surprising that people are worried that they will not have enough to live on in retirement. Some groups, such as recent immigrants, unattached individuals, and lower-income households, face particular challenges. There is widespread confusion about pension plans and how the retirement income system works. Many people don't understand the difference between a group RRSP, which doesn't guarantee any pension, and a defined benefit pension plan, in which the employee is entitled to a pension guaranteed by the plan sponsor related to earnings and years of service.

One recent survey from Statistics Canada revealed numbers of people who thought they had pension coverage at work when in fact there wasn't a pension plan at all.[22] Some who were in a group RRSP thought they belonged to a pension plan where retirement pensions are guaranteed. University graduates, unionized workers, workers in large establishments, and those employed in finance and insurance, and communications and other utilities, seem to be better informed than other workers. But recent immigrants seem to be having a particularly hard time understanding the system. Among recent immigrants who reported having a registered pension plan in their job, a solid 53% were in firms with no pension plan. While new immigrants are generally better educated than their Canadian counterparts, they may not be as familiar with labour market institutions in Canada. But the end result is that almost one recent immigrant

CHART 1 **Median age of retirement in Canada**

An Uncertain Future

in ten appears to be seriously misinformed about their coverage in an employer-sponsored retirement plan.[23]

Company pension plans that had been in surplus for many years faced deficits when the stock market tanked. Now they are having to make up the shortfall from current earnings so their pension plans will have adequate funding to finance the retirement of growing numbers of workers over the next few decades. Some employers in sunset industries already have more pensioners than current workers. And some companies, experiencing tough economic conditions, are even suggesting abandoning their defined benefit pension plans and switching workers to defined contribution arrangements, where the entire risk of providing a retirement income is shifted from the employer to the employee. Workers who had expected to get a decent and guaranteed pension at retirement may now find their retirement income depends on how well their investments perform. Those who counted on private saving through RRSPS to fund their retirement have seen the value of their investments drop, although by mid-2004 a recovery seemed to be under way. All these developments have increased uncertainty about retirement—especially for younger workers who have other priorities and for whom retirement may seem a very long way off.

It seems the majority of younger Canadians don't think the Canada Pension Plan will be there when they get to retirement.[24] Apparently they are not aware that the plan was substantially overhauled in 1998 and now has a reserve fund that is building up assets to help fund future pensions. As the former head of the CPP Investment Board pointed out, "They are still concerned that money may not be there for them when they retire—a myth promulgated during RSP time."[25] Confusion and uncertainty have proved a powerful selling tool for the promoters of mutual funds and RRSPS who try to attract investors by implying they will not be able to count on CPP pensions or government benefits in retirement.

Annual surveys of RRSP intentions, conducted by major financial institutions, seem to play on the uncertainty by asking respondents if they are confident the CPP will still be there when they get to retirement. Given the abysmal lack of knowledge about the plan and how it is funded, it is not surprising that so many express doubts. One recent survey by a major bank revealed that more than half of Canada's Generation

Xers—people between the ages of 25 and 39—are "not very confident" or "not at all confident" in the availability of the CPP when they reach retirement.[26]

So serious has the situation become that the former head of the CPP Investment Board had to call on the financial services industry to help "dispel the unsettling myth that the CPP may not be there for Canadians."[27] He pointed out that CPP pension reserves are segregated from general government revenues, so there is no fear of political interference in the plan. He also reminded his audience that the Chief Actuary of Canada has certified that the plan, as currently constituted, is sound for at least 75 years. He might also have added that, contrary to widespread popular belief, the CPP is not a federal government social program paid for by tax revenues. It is funded by contributions from employers and employees and administered by federal, provincial, and territorial governments. Changes can only be made with the approval of two-thirds of the provinces having two-thirds of the population—a formula that is even more restrictive than that required to amend the constitution.

But it seems the message is still not getting out. Media coverage has almost certainly added to the confusion and uncertainty by repeating the myths and creating an atmosphere of doom and gloom. Undoubtedly, it makes a better story to claim the CPP is going bankrupt—even if anyone who knows anything about pension funds will tell you that such a claim is nonsense.

Many people in their late 40s and 50s say they don't know when they're going to retire. But even those who say they plan to retire at a particular age may really only be making a best guess, given that they're still 10 or 15 years from their retirement transition. A lot can happen in the intervening period, and plans may be difficult to make in the face of such uncertainty.

The stock market correction through the early 2000s, for instance, may have forced near-retirees to adjust retirement plans to match returns on their investment income. There are already signs that this has begun to happen. People with lower personal and household incomes face more uncertainty about retirement timing. So do those without a pension plan. Greater uncertainty about planned retirement is more prevalent among self-employed individuals, and it is higher among immigrants than people born in Canada.

Statistics Canada's General Social Survey, conducted in 2002, looked at "near-retirees"—people aged 45–59—and documented many of these trends.[28] Almost one-fifth of those surveyed said they did not intend to retire—a finding that was greeted with skepticism by some in the financial community. But many of these people had lower household incomes, didn't own their own homes, and had lower levels of education. Saying they have no intention of retiring probably means they were worried about their financial ability to leave the labour force. For them, the idea of retirement probably seemed a distant and maybe even unattainable goal.

Almost one-third of the near-retirees felt they hadn't made adequate financial preparations to maintain their standard of living after they leave their jobs. Although no definition of "adequate" was provided, these findings were very similar to those of an earlier StatsCan survey that concluded about one-third of near-retirees may not be saving enough for retirement, because their post-retirement income would not be enough to replace 70% of their pre-retirement earnings, or to generate an income that is likely to be above Statistics Canada's low-income cut-off.[29]

Whether or not financial preparations for retirement were considered adequate was strongly associated with demographic characteristics and labour market experiences. For instance, women surveyed in 2002 were slightly more likely than men to say they expect their retirement income to be inadequate, or barely adequate, to maintain their standard of living. Recent immigrants were also more likely than persons born in Canada to believe they would not have enough to live on. In fact, other studies have found that declining earnings among recent immigrants will make it much more difficult for them to make ends meet and make them much more vulnerable to setbacks such as job loss or unexpected expenditures.

Individuals in poor health were almost twice as likely to view their retirement preparations as inadequate as were those who said their health was excellent. And people who were widowed, separated, or divorced were far more likely to feel financial preparations were inadequate, compared with those who were married or living in a common-law relationship.

In fact, unattached individuals—particularly women—in the older age groups may be particularly vulnerable as they approach the retirement transition.

There's an interesting difference between when Canadians plan to retire and when they would really *like* to retire. The 2002 survey asked respondents: "If you could choose, at what age would you like to retire?" Two-thirds of near-retirees said that, if they could choose, they would retire before age 60, and 88% said they would retire before age 65. Analysts interpret this to mean that many older workers would like to leave the labour force. But, while such a preference is widespread, the circumstances and constraints that people face often prevent it from being realized.

The age of retirement has stabilized

Perhaps another sign of the times is the finding that, over the past few years, the age of retirement has stabilized after more than a decade of decline (*see chart*). Twenty-five years ago, age 65 was the typical age of retirement for Canadian workers. After the Canada and Quebec Pension Plans introduced early retirement provisions in the mid-1980s, the median age of retirement—the age at which a typical worker retires—started to fall. By 1993, it had stabilized at around 62 for men, although the typical retirement age for women continued to fall to a low of 59.4 years in 1997.

Median age of retirement in Canada
Since then, the median age at which women retire has risen slightly and now seems to have leveled off at just over 60. That's probably not surprising, since CPP/QPP benefits are an important source of income for seniors, and these benefits may be claimed at age 60—although starting the pension prior to age 65 means an actuarially-reduced benefit. In the past few years, however, labour force participation among older Canadians has been increasing, as we shall see later in Chapter 5. That could mean the median age of retirement will start to rise.

The average retirement age dropped to 61.0 years in 1989 and to 60.4 years in 1994, when the average retirement age for women was 58.5 years,

An Uncertain Future

compared with 61.4 years for men.[30] In 1994, 31% of men and 43% of women had retired prior to age 60. Although the age of retirement fluctuated during the 1990s, after 1997 it increased slightly and it has stabilized since then.[31] Statistics Canada says the retirement age fluctuations in the 1990s may reflect government cutbacks and corporate downsizing. The popularity of early retirement incentives as a tool for workforce adjustment may also have influenced recent retirement behaviour, according to the agency.[32]

In the period from 1992 to 1996, 36% of all workers had retired prior to age 60. But, in the period from 1997 to 2001, the percentage retiring prior to age 60 had risen to 43%. There were noticeable changes during the 1990s in the proportion of those retiring at younger and older ages, as Table 1 shows.[33] The percentage under age 55 increased from 11% to 16%, while the percentage retiring between ages 55 and 59 increased from 25% to 27%. On the other hand, fewer people waited past age 65 (19% compared with 22%). About 7% waited until age 70 or later.

Statistics Canada points out that many factors influence the timing of retirement. Among the most important are the type of the last job held and the length of tenure. How long a person worked at a job prior to retirement is strongly related to retirement age. Long-term employees whose employer has a pension plan have had a chance to build

TABLE 1 **Distribution of ages at retirement**

Age group	1992 to 1996		1997 to 2001	
	'000	%	'000	%
Total	605	100	706	100
50 to 54	64	11	112	16
55 to 59	150	25	193	27
60 to 64	216	36	216	31
65 to 69	132	22	133	19
70 +	42	7	52	7

SOURCE Statistics Canada 2003d: 2.

up substantial pension entitlements and are more likely to take early retirement.

The sector where the person works also makes a difference. In the period from 1992 to 1996, employees in the private sector retired an average three-and-a-half years later than public sector workers.[34] Of course, this may also reflect the fact that almost all public sector workers belong to defined benefit pension plans, while few workers in the private sector have pension coverage. The gap between the two sectors increased even further over the period from 1997 to 2001. Self-employed workers tend to retire later, and they reach the decision to retire in a very different way from employees.

Going back to work again

Many studies have found that retirement does not necessarily mean an abrupt end to employment. The transition from work to full retirement can be interspersed with periods of employment. Some workers may retire from their job, begin to draw their pension, and yet work part-time either to supplement their pension or to pass the time. Some may retire and start their own business, taking advantage of the flexibility in work arrangements that comes with some businesses. Some may return to the labour market after a period of retirement.

And there are those who continue working, simply moving to a new full-time job. The 2001 Census of Population indicated that an increasing number of older workers are still employed.[35] For example, in 2001, 13.0% of men and 4.8% of women aged 65 or older had jobs. Between 1996 and 2001, while the population of seniors increased by 11%, the ranks of working seniors rose by 20%.

As well, more and more people are now going back to work after taking a formal retirement. And people who retired because they had access to early retirement incentives are twice as likely to return to the labour market as those without such a program.[36] A 1994 Statistics Canada survey found that people who returned to the labour market had initially retired at an average age of 57.9, compared with 60.6 years for those who did not return. Contrary to popular belief, for full-time as well as part-time employees, the return to the work force is based more on personal than financial reasons. In fact, the survey found that, of those retirees who reported returning to work, only 25% cited financial reasons, while 20% said they wanted to occupy their free time; 20% said it was their personal preference; and 35% gave other reasons.

Those who return to the work force are very likely to hold non-standard jobs, such as self-employment, part-time work, or temporary jobs. In fact, part-time paid work could be considered a transitional stage to a second retirement, when the individual continues to work, but has the benefit of more free time.[37]

Other studies show that a growing number of people whose career job has ended in fact continue to work. Almost half of workers aged 50–67, who had retired from a long-term career job lasting at least eight years between 1993 and 1997, were at work again within two years.[38] (This particular study is based on the Survey of Labour and Income Dynamics, or SLID—a longitudinal survey which follows the same people over a six-year period). Almost one-third had begun a new full-time job, and a smaller but significant portion (10%) had switched to part-time employment. More self-employed people returned to work, and they returned sooner than salaried workers did. For those aged 55 to 59, less than a third left a long-term job to begin another full-time job. Most of them did not work again within two years, suggesting that they could have taken early retirement. But about 11% of the under-60s switched from a full-time career job to a part-time job.

The findings of the StatsCan study are confirmed by other recent surveys commissioned by firms in the financial industry. They show that, while Canadians are still clinging to their dreams of early retirement, many now plan to go on working in some capacity after they retire. Although most working Canadians apparently don't know how much money they'll need in retirement, it seems a high percentage of those people plan to supplement their pensions by finding paid employment somewhere.

According to one survey, conducted by Decima Research for Investors Group, 72% of non-retired Canadians are strongly considering working after they "retire." That's a stark contrast with what retired Canadians are doing today, when only 23% said they are currently working.[39] The survey also looked at the retirement lifestyle expectations of Canadians. It showed that, while working Canadians envision spending their golden years going on winter getaways and pursuing their hobbies, today's retired Canadians say their lifestyle doesn't match this picture.

Winter getaways, often promoted as the retirement lifestyle choice for retired Canadians, are a standard dream of 62% of young Canadians, according to this survey. And 55% of the non-retired survey respondents expected to be able to spend a lot of time pursuing their hobbies during retirement. The reality is that only 30% of retirees today indicated they escape the worst months of Canada's winter. And only 35% of retired Canadians say they pursue their hobbies to any great extent.

Early retirement dreams—however unrealistic—also showed up in a survey conducted by SOM Opinions and Marketing for Desjardins Financial Security.[40] This survey found that only 16% of Canadians had a high degree of confidence in their ability to save for retirement, while 46% felt they would not be able to set aside enough money for this phase of life. But more than 40% of baby boomers—now aged 40 to 54—wanted to fully retire before age 55.

About 60% of survey respondents over 40 were interested in gradual retirement once they leave the work force, but very few of them want to return to work on a permanent basis once they retire. They are more likely to look for opportunities to work on their own terms, whether that be part-time consulting or turning a hobby into a business. Fifty-nine per cent planned to be self-employed and work about 20 hours a week so they can remain active.

Women and retirement

Much of the discussion about the changing nature of retirement overlooks the particular concerns of women. Several studies of retirement behaviour, for example, are based on male workers only, even though women now constitute more then 46% of the labour force. Although the vast majority of adult women now participate in paid employment, they are still generally expected to undertake a major caregiving role for their families. Child care years may affect their labour force activity early in their careers, but elder care will have a growing influence on the work patterns and retirement decisions of women in the work force as the population ages.

Among current seniors, about 22% of women compared with 3% of men have never worked outside their homes.[41] But almost all women retiring in the future will have spent considerable time in paid employment. For example, in 1999, only 5% of women aged 25 to 54 had never been employed. The percentage of adult women in paid employment has increased dramatically over the past three decades. In 1976, for example, about 50% of women aged 25 to 44, and 46% of those aged 45 to 54, had paying jobs.[42] By 2003, 76% of women aged 25 to 44 and 75% of those aged 45 to 54 were in paid employment. Even among women aged 55 to 64, 45% had paid employment in 2003, compared with only 30% of women in this age group who were working for pay in 1976.[43]

On average, women will spend many more years in "retirement" than men because they retire earlier and they live longer than men do. But because most women must combine both paid and unpaid work, they may never experience "retirement" in the same way men do. For example, an analysis of Statistics Canada's 1994 General Social Survey found that a large proportion of married women aged 60 to 70 defined their main activity as "housekeepers."[44] Among women aged 70 and over, 50% who were married declared their main activity as "housekeeping" and only 40% said they were "retired." Between 90% and 95% of men aged 65 or older who were no longer working at a job or business considered themselves "retired."

TABLE 2 **Women with jobs**

Percentage of women and men in paid employment in Canada

Year	People aged 25–44		People aged 45–54		People aged 55–64	
	% Women	% Men	% Women	% Men	% Women	% Men
1976	49.9	90.9	45.6	88.9	30.4	72.8
2003	76.1	86.1	75.0	84.5	45.0	61.4

SOURCE Statistics Canada 2000: 118; 2003f: 1.

Women's unpaid work and family responsibilities clearly continue even after they may have stopped working for pay. In fact, the 1994 Survey found that a considerable number of retired women had left work quite early to engage in unpaid activities. A significant proportion of retired women reported they had retired for "family reasons," whereas practically no men had done the same.[45] The average retirement age of women citing this reason for retirement was 48 years. Early retirement among women also reflects the fact that married women, who are generally younger than their spouses, may want to retire at the same time as the spouse does. The average age of women citing this reason was 59.2 years.

As the population ages, it is likely that more and more women will be called on to care for older and dependent family members. The increasing burden of eldercare will almost certainly affect the retirement plans of women who, unlike previous generations of women, will have been in paid employment for most of their adult lives. In 2002, nearly half a million Canadians 45 and over provided personal care to a senior and three-quarters of these caregivers were women.[46] More than half of personal care providers were 45 to 54 yeas of age, with proportions decreasing with age. And all indications are that eldercare is a very demanding role.

Female caregivers are also more likely than male caregivers to have to change their work patterns as a result of this unpaid work. For instance, the 2002 General Social Survey showed that 27% of female (compared with 14% of male) caregivers aged 45 to 54 had to change their work patterns—perhaps through working split shifts or leaving early and then making up the time later. Reducing hours of work was common for caregivers aged 45 to 54, and 20% of women compared with 13% of men reported having done so. Among caregivers aged 55 to 64, about 12% of women compared with 8% of men reported cutting down on the amount of time spent on paid work. Studies of women's caregiving activities have found that women are twice as likely as men to report missed promotional opportunities and four times as likely as men to report having left a job because of eldercare demands.[47]

All these working-time adjustments may affect women's ultimate retirement income and play a part in their retirement decisions. It is also important to note that policies designed to discourage early retirement may also have a differential impact on women. While women whose

An Uncertain Future

paid employment experience has been intermittent may—at least in theory—welcome the opportunity to continue working past the usual retirement age in order to augment low pension entitlements, their unpaid work for their families may make it impossible to continue in paid employment. As a result, they could find themselves doubly penalized: by having to continue working, but as unpaid caregivers in their homes; and by being unable to accumulate adequate retirement income to finance a withdrawal from their paid employment because early retirement is penalized in the pension system. Policy-makers will have to give special attention to these issues in any redesign of aging and retirement policies.

What is on the horizon?

Major changes in the nature of retirement are clearly well under way. Policy development now in progress will reflect those changes and probably try to put a positive spin on them. It is possible to identify several key themes now emerging:

> • **There is strong pressure to raise the age of retirement.** This could be achieved through some form of moral suasion—for example, offering incentives to workers to continue in paid employment. It could also be done by raising the age of eligibility for public pension programs, as the United States and other countries have done. It's worth noting here that, while the U.S. is raising its age of eligibility for Social Security to 67 from 65 over the next 20 years, many other countries, which had much lower ages of eligibility for their public plans, are only moving now to age 65. Some countries, such as the United Kingdom, which had lower eligibility ages for women than for men, are simply increasing the age of eligibility for women to match that of men—generally age 65.
>
> Aging expert John Myles believes the case can be made that the result of later retirement may be more benign than its alternative: reduced living standards for retirees and workers.[48] If the market is able to generate sufficient employment to absorb older workers and raise total employment levels, a potential payoff is greater economic growth and higher living standards for all. In any case, Myles points out that, since people

are and will be living longer, more working years does not mean fewer retirement years.

• **Mandatory retirement may be abolished in those jurisdictions that have not already taken this step.** Although there is no legislation in Canada that requires people to retire by age 65, Human Rights legislation in some jurisdictions prohibits age discrimination only up to age 65. As a result, human resources practices of employers, collective agreements, or pension plan provisions requiring employees to retire by age 65 do not contravene such legislation. Some provinces in Canada have already abolished mandatory retirement, and others are thinking of doing so. However, the Supreme Court of Canada has ruled that, while mandatory retirement contravenes the equality provisions of the Charter of Rights and Freedoms, it is saved by Section 1 of the Charter because it is "a reasonable limitation" in a free and democratic society.[49] Abolition of mandatory retirement is highly controversial and raises a number of issues relating to discrimination against older workers. We will return to this issue in Chapter 4.

• **Much more emphasis will be placed on the "life course" perspective.** In line with the new focus on active aging and the positive aspects of an aging population, policy development will emphasize a life course perspective that looks at different ways in which people might combine work, leisure, caregiving, and education over the course of their lives. The actual life course followed by Canadian women and men is already far from standardized. Yet, as aging expert Lynn McDonald points out, "Policy-makers persist in making policy according to an orderly life course of education, work, and retirement founded on the experience of the 19th century male industrial worker."[50] The federal government's Policy Research Initiative research project on aging, discussed in detail in Chapter 3 of this book, is trying to move away from this approach. It is based on a new life course perspective and will almost certainly come up with policy proposals that could be implemented over the longer term.

• **Shifting more responsibility onto individuals to provide for their own retirement.** This will involve much more than simply switching employees from defined benefit pension plans, where the employer or

An Uncertain Future

plan sponsor is on the hook to provide a pension related to earnings and years of service, into defined contribution plans or group RRSPS where the individual must bear the entire risk of providing a pension. Policy prescriptions increasingly mention giving older workers more "choice" and more "flexibility"—both code words, it would seem, for expecting them to fend for themselves much more than they do now.

For example, the OECD says that, "once poverty alleviation goals have been met, the total amount of an individual's retirement income should not be a goal of public pensions in isolation, but reflect individual choice based on all resources available on retirement, including earnings, private savings, or the use of assets such as reverse mortgages for housing."[51] The OECD also believes that "individuals should be free to choose how they allocate their time to work, unpaid work, and active and passive leisure activities. However," this organization says, "longer-term policy questions must arise if the consequence of public policy is to encourage ever-longer periods of passivity in the last third of life. Should such arrangements continue to have a high priority on the public policy agenda?"[52]

New public policies may establish a framework that will allow individuals to make different choices about how their own particular life course is ordered. But there will probably be a strong expectation that older people will continue to work well into their 60s and that they will have the necessary and up-to-date skills to do so.

• **Active aging will be official policy.** As the World Health Organization sees it, "years have been added to life, now we must add life to years." But active aging is not just about prolonging working life, it is a comprehensive way of organizing participation across the life course.[53]

Active aging, as the OECD defines it, refers to "the capacity of people, as they grow older, to lead productive lives in society and the economy. This means that people can make flexible choices in the way they spend time over their lives: earning, working, and partaking in leisure activities and giving care.[54] These choices are often constrained in ways that harm both individuals and society," according to the OECD. Constraints may include poor health or disability, or even lack of wheelchair access. But they may also include inflexibility in the workplace, where perhaps it is not possible to take time off for raising children, giving care to the elderly, or undertaking further education.

Other constraints may arise as a result of public policies that have not kept up with changes in demography, families, or employment, says the OECD. Educational arrangements may be aimed only at young people instead of allowing for lifelong learning. Social and labour market programming that encourages early retirement can also be a constraint.

Active aging policies must take a multi-dimensional approach. Alan Walker, professor of social policy at the University of Sheffield in the UK, says the policy challenge is to recognize the thread that links all of the relevant policy areas: employment, health, social protection, social inclusion, transport, education, and so on. An active aging strategy, he says, demands that all these elements are connected and become mutually supportive. The danger, however, is that this sort of approach will become coercive. That can be avoided, Walker believes, if policy takes an enabling and facilitating role and is responsive to age, gender, race, culture, and other differences.[55]

• **Special programs may be developed for older workers.** These might include special training programs or other employment initiatives to ensure that older workers have the updated skills they need to find or continue in work, and that there are real opportunities for them to continue in paid employment. Preventing discrimination against older workers will be essential if people are to be expected to work until later ages. The European Union, for example, issued an Employment Directive in 2000 that prohibits age discrimination in employment and vocational training.[56] However, it appears it still will not address the problem of pension plans that require retirement at a particular age. According to the Directive, differences in treatment in connection with age may be justified under certain circumstances if they relate to "legitimate employment policy, or labour market and vocational training objectives"—for example, some types of work involving heavy physical labour may not be suitable for older people.

The United Kingdom government, in a Consultation Paper outlining how it intends to comply with the Directive, points out that "mandatory retirement is only permissible under the Directive when it can be objectively justified."[57] However, the UK Government also says it intends to take advantage of the Directive's provisions that allow occupational pension schemes to set ages for admission or entitlement to retirement benefits. It points out that "a normal retirement age—that is, the date from which full scheme benefits are payable without actuarial enhancement—is necessary for the operation of defined benefit schemes, It is not the same as a mandatory retirement age." It proposes to address the problem by allowing people to draw their occupational pension while continuing to work for the same employer.[58]

• **Will inter-generational conflict be revived?** Conflict between the different generations over how public pensions were to be paid for was a big issue in the late 1990s when changes in the Canada Pension Plan were being contemplated. Pay-as-you-go plans, such as the CPP, are financed by contributions from the working age population. But, when the percentage of older people is increasing in relation to those of working age, contributions to these types of plans must increase to provide benefits for increasing numbers of retirees. It was suggested that younger Canadians would resent having to pay higher contributions to the plan to finance growing numbers of retired people.

Changes in the way in which the CPP is funded, implemented in 1998, were intended largely to address potential inter-generational conflict. The establishment of the CPP Investment Fund was made possible by a sharp increase in contribution rates over a brief period of time, generating surplus funds that could be invested to provide an additional source of income for the plan to help pay benefits when the baby boom generation would be retiring in about 20 years from now. In some respects, this was seen as requiring members of the baby boom generation to contribute more now to finance their own pensions payable down the road.

But discussion of inter-generational conflict issues among progressive scholars has always emphasized that a full accounting scheme of the allocation of retirement costs among the working and retired populations requires the inclusion of both the public and private side of the national ledger.[59] They have also pointed out that the well-being of future generations does not depend on the design of pension plans, but rather on the productive capacity—schools, hospitals, infrastructure, and so on—that one generation leaves to the next.[60]

However, scholars also emphasize that the relative size of economic differences between generations pales in comparison with those that exist within generations. For example, John Myles points out that raising the age of eligibility for public pensions will have the greatest effect on those without sufficient means to finance early retirement on their own and the least impact on those who do. Since health—life expectancy, disability—and wealth tend to be correlated, the equity problem is compounded. Similarly, the behavioural response to lower mandatory pensions will depend on income level, Myles notes. Low-income families are less likely than high-income families to compensate with more private saving.

A new social contract for older people

There is a growing consensus among progressive scholars that what is needed now is a comprehensive strategy to address issues raised by our aging population. In many countries, what should have been seen as a welcome demographic change has been transformed into a crisis of the welfare state.[61] The new direction must be to bring together and make the connections between pensions, employment, retirement, health, and citizenship and to join them together in the policy process. This is essential, says Alan Walker, if we are to move successfully towards an older society because, so far, the policy responses to the challenges created by population aging have been piecemeal and strongly compartmentalized in traditional policy domains and ministries.

There may be good reason to rewrite the retirement contract, but there is no need to abandon it.[62] However, there are very real risks in moving forward. In his 2002 paper on *A New Social Contract for the Elderly*, John Myles outlines them:

> The key issue is whether the progress made in democratizing retirement during the post-war decades is about to erode, and whether further democratization (e.g., equalizing retirement opportunities for

An Uncertain Future

men and women) is precluded. Does re-design mean convergence on some hypothetical neo-liberal model for the allocation of retirement wealth, one in which the rights of citizens contract while the importance of markets expands? Will, in short, the pressures of population aging on the public budget prove to be an additional source of dualism and polarization in the 21st century?[63]

But Myles also believes that the political constraint on policy-makers to reach reform through a "negotiated settlement" with a broad range of relevant actors makes radical demolition of the post-war retirement contract impossible. Myles argues that re-designing the retirement contract will require consideration of the three major components of the retirement income system: the age of retirement, the benefits structure, and the method of financing retirement incomes.[64] We will explore these issues in subsequent chapters of this book.

Notes

1 Rowe and Nguyen 2003: 55.

2 Myles 2002: 130.

3 Ibid.

4 Statistics Canada 2003c: 1.

5 Hicks 2003b: 12.

6 Statistics Canada 1999: 67.

7 Baxter and Ramlo 1998: 15.

8 Statistics Canada 2003d: 3.

9 OECD 2000: 112.

10 Ibid.

11 Baxter and Ramlo 1998: 15.

12 Rowe and Nguyen 2003: 55.

13 Ibid.

14 Myles 2002: 131.

15 Régies des rentes du Québec 2003: 28.

16 OECD 1998: 14.

17 Chief Actuary 2003: 38.

18 Ibid.

19 Hicks 2003b: 15.

20 Ibid. 3.

21 Habtu 2003: 3.

22 Morissette and Zhang 2004: 11.

23 Ibid. 15.

24 TD Bank Financial Group 2004: 1.

25 MacNaughton 2004: 7.

26 TD Bank Financial Group 2004: 1.

27 MacNaughton 2004: 7.

28 Statistics Canada 2003c: 1.

29 Maser and Dufour 2001: 27.

30 Monette 1996: 16.

31 Statistics Canada 2003d: 1.

32 Ibid.

33 Ibid. 2.

34 Ibid.3.

35 Duchesne 2004: 5.

36 Monette 1996: 26.

37 Ibid. 29.

38 Pyper and Giles 2002: 15.

39 Investors Group 2003: 1.

40 Desjardins Financial Security 2003: 4.

41 Statistics Canada 2000: 276.

42 Ibid. 118.

43 Statistics Canada 2004a: 1.

44 Monette 1996: 11.

45 Ibid. 17.

46 Cranswick 2003: 16.

47 Keating et al 1999: 62.

48 Myles 2002: 154.

49 Townson 1997: 25.

50 McDonald 1997: 395.

51 OECD 1998: 22.

52 OECD 2000: 105.

53 Walker 2003:29.

An Uncertain Future

54 OECD 2000: 126.

55 Walker 2003: 36.

56 European Union 2000: 1.

57 United Kingdom Government 2003: 21.

58 Ibid. 23.

59 Myles 2002: 144.

60 See Osberg 1998 for a full discussion of generational equity.

61 Walker 2003: 2.

62 Myles 2002: 132.

63 Ibid. 132–133.

64 Ibid. 153.

Year:		Month:					MORNING		AFTERNOON		OVERTIME	
							IN	OUT	IN	OUT	IN	OUT
	MORNING		AFTERNOON		OVERTIME							
	IN	OUT	IN	OUT	IN	OUT						
MON												
							WED			2:57 to 6:02		

2

The Pension Challenge

ANY DISCUSSION OF the changing nature of retirement must look at the role played by the retirement income system. Having adequate income for a retirement transition is crucial in determining whether a worker can end or reduce paid employment. But is the retirement income system up to the challenge of population aging? Changes were made to the CPP, effective at the beginning of 1998. In early 2004, Quebec held a public consultation to look at further changes in the QPP. Other pressures, now emerging, will have a major impact. Turbulent stock markets mean that many pension plans that enjoyed surpluses for years are now short of funds and may be downgraded or abandoned. Workers who counted on their own savings through RRSPS or money purchase pension plans could be faced with seriously diminished retirement savings affecting their plans for retirement. Bankrupt companies may try to abandon their defined benefit pension plans or convert them to defined contribution arrangements.

Governments may be under pressure to improve public pensions if workplace pension plans can't meet workers' needs. Canada gets high marks internationally for its retirement income system, which is seen as providing a good balance between public and private arrangements, as well as effectively reducing poverty among the elderly at relatively modest cost. But the design and structure of pension programs may also affect retirement decisions. In fact, according to the OECD:

> "It is becoming increasingly evident that public and private income-support programs designed for, or used by, older people have made work at later ages less financially attractive, and that public policies distort the retirement decision in other ways as well."[1]

For example, says the OECD, public pension schemes may discourage workers—especially, but not only, those who are low-paid or low-skilled—from continuing to work beyond the standard retirement age because they will not be able to accumulate additional benefits if they do.[2] In some countries, governments, by relaxing entitlement conditions for disability- or unemployment-related benefits, encouraged early retirement as a way of reducing unemployment. As well, the OECD notes, some defined benefit pension plans allow retirement earlier than the standard age, with little or no additional pension benefits accruing after this age. Tax systems that tax retirement income at preferential rates also distort the income/leisure trade-off in favour of more leisure, even when pension systems are actuarially fair for individuals, according to the OECD. And self-employed workers—who have more flexibility in choosing when to retire, and are often entitled to lower public pensions than employees—retire at significantly later ages than dependent employees, the OECD says.

The Organization for Economic Co-operation and Development (OECD) is a forum where governments of 30 democracies—including Canada—work together to address the economic, social and environmental challenges of globalization. It claims to be at the forefront of efforts to understand and help governments respond to new developments and concerns, such as corporate governance, the information economy and the challenges of an aging population. Based in Paris, the OECD is best known for its publications and its statistics. The organization says it "provides a setting where governments can compare policy experiences, seek answers to common problems, identify good practice and co-ordinate domestic and international policies."

Reforms recommended by the OECD and the European Union

In its landmark 1998 publication *Maintaining Prosperity in an Aging Society*, the OECD called for public pension systems, taxation systems, and social transfer programs to be reformed so as to remove financial incentives to early retirement and financial disincentives to later retirement. It also said retirement income should be provided by a mix of tax-and-transfer systems, funded systems, private savings and earnings.[3] The objective should be risk diversification, a better balance of burden-sharing between generations, and giving individuals "more flexibility" over their retirement decisions.

The central objective of reforms, as the OECD sees it, should be to ensure that the way societies transfer resources to a rapidly growing number of retired people creates neither major economic nor social strains.[4] This points to the desirability of speeding up the growth of output, according to the OECD, reducing the number of dependents by encouraging people to work longer, and ensuring that the transfer mechanisms operate efficiently.

The strong emphasis on the age of retirement in the OECD's approach reflects the organization's view that the age at which workers retire is of critical importance to both future material living standards and to fiscal pressures.[5] If people work longer, says the OECD, the output that can be shared among the population will be greater, the tax base will be larger, and there will be fewer dependent older persons receiving pensions. Reforms to pension systems and other social transfer programs that would ensure actuarial neutrality in the work-to-retirement transition would be a major step forward, the organization says, and would help ease the fiscal burden as well as reducing barriers to working longer in life and supporting a better allocation of societies' resources.

Principles for pension reform developed by the European Union illustrate the kind of dilemmas facing policy-makers in all the affluent democracies in the first half of the 21st century.[6]

The European Union's ten principles for pension reform[7]

1. Ensure that all older people enjoy a decent living standard, share in the economic well-being of their country and are able to participate actively in public, social and cultural life.

2. Provide access for all individuals to appropriate pension arrangements necessary to maintain the living standard of their choice after retirement due to old age or invalidity and that of their dependants in the event of death.

3. Achieve a high level of employment so that the ratio between the active and the retired remains as favourable as possible.

4. Ensure that pension systems and in particular early retirement and invalidity schemes and their interaction with tax-benefit systems, offer effective incentives for the participation of older workers; that workers are not encouraged to take up early retirement and are not penalized for staying in the labour market beyond the standard retirement age; and that pension systems facilitate the option of gradual retirement.

5. Ensure that public spending on pensions is maintained at a level in terms of percent of GDP that is compatible with the Stability and Growth Pact [the rules of the European Monetary Union that require members to maintain close-to-balance budgets].

6. Strike a fair balance between the active and the retired through appropriate adjustments to the levels of contributions and taxes and of pension benefits.

7. Ensure that private funded pension schemes will continue to provide, with increased efficiency and affordability, the pensions to which scheme members are entitled.

8. Ensure that pension systems are compatible with the requirements of flexibility, security and mobility on the labour market, and that non-standard forms of employment do not result in losses of pension entitlements and that self-employment is not discouraged by pension systems.

9. Review pension systems with a view to eliminating discrimination based on sex.

10. Make pension systems more transparent, predictable and adaptable to changing circumstances.

Canada has implemented reforms

Almost all the industrialized countries have been grappling with pension reform to cope with their aging populations. But there are significant differences between Canada and the European countries, and it is important to put the pension policy prescriptions advocated by the OECD and the European Union in context. According to the OECD, the demographic trends in Canada are not as dramatic as in some other countries; steps have already been taken to create a sound fiscal situation; and the labour market has the flexibility to respond to changes in the workforce.[8] The OECD says that one of the most important starting points for Canada is its multi-pillar system. The design of the system, which closely mirrors that advocated by the OECD, provides balance and flexibility.

Public pension programs in Canada play a relatively modest role in the entire retirement income system, compared with many of the European countries. As well, many European countries rely heavily on payroll taxes to finance old age pensions. For example, in 1991, combined employer/employee payroll taxes for pensions in OECD countries averaged 16.3%.[9] That included rates of 12.4% in the United States, 18.8% in the United Kingdom, 22.9% in Austria, 26.2% in Italy, 21% in Sweden, and 17.8% in Germany. Canada's payroll taxes for pensions, then at just 4.6%—the combined employer/employee CPP contribution rate—were by far the lowest of any OECD country except for Iceland. Unlike most of the other OECD countries, Canada's pension budget is divided more or less evenly between payroll taxes and general revenue financing.[10] As a result, Canada has perhaps not been subject to the kind of pressure for pension reform experienced in other OECD countries that were facing high and rising payroll taxes to meet current and future pension expenditures.

The Pension Challenge

Even after the 1998 CPP reforms, the combined employer/employee contribution rate has been fixed for the foreseeable future at 9.9% of covered earnings—a rate exceeded by almost all OECD countries back in 1991. That is still a very modest rate, but it reflects the fact that the CPP is still only a relatively modest part of the retirement income system. The basic pension guarantee, or first tier of the system—Old Age Security and the Guaranteed Income Supplement—are financed from the general tax revenues of the federal government.

In spite of the heated public debate that took place in the late 1990s, pension reform in Canada has not brought significant changes on the benefits side. In fact, during the federal, provincial, and territorial discussions on potential CPP reforms, Quebec made it clear it would oppose any significant benefit cuts, as did Saskatchewan and British Columbia, which then had NDP governments. Since changes to the CPP require the approval of two-thirds of the provinces having two-thirds of the population, this meant that the option of cutting benefits was effectively removed from the political agenda.[11] (Quebec has a vote on any changes to the CPP, even though Quebec residents participate in the Quebec Pension Plan rather than the CPP). But observers note that more significant—and unpopular—changes, such as an increase in the retirement age, were excluded from the agenda.[12] In any event, changes to the age of eligibility for CPP pensions are unlikely to have large effects on retirement behaviour except among lower-income earners, creating obvious equity problems.[13] Lower-income earners are much less likely to have other sources of retirement income, so must count on public pensions for the bulk of their financial support when employment earnings cease.

Privatization of the CPP by allowing people to divert their mandatory contributions to individual savings accounts, such as RRSPS, was also rejected in the 1997/98 reform package. The government said public consultations leading up to the reforms indicated a strong desire to see the CPP remain a public pension plan rather than privatized.[14] Most participants wanted the public system preserved, fearing that its many benefits would be lost if the plan was privatized. However, the government noted that a minority wanted the plan privatized and replaced by individual mandatory retirement savings plans.

Proposals to make radical changes in the first tier of Canada's retirement income system, replacing Old Age Security and the Guaranteed Income Supplement with an income-tested Seniors' Benefit, were abandoned in 1998 in the face of strong political pressure opposing the changes. In an about-face move, Paul Martin, who was Finance Minister at the time, claimed that, since the government's fiscal position had improved, there was now no need to reduce benefits paid to seniors.[15] Since then, relatively minor changes have been made in the third tier of the system, through increased contribution limits for Registered Pension Plans (RPPS) and Registered Retirement Savings Plans (RRSPS).

Béland and Myles conclude that ultimately, against the backdrop of the other affluent democracies, Canada has changed relatively little on the benefit side since the basic pension design was constructed in the 1950s and '60s.[16] Far from radically breaking from the historical path of the program, the 1997 reforms reaffirmed the contributory nature of the Canada/Quebec Pension Plan.[17] But pressure for more reforms continues—particularly from those who would like to see more market-oriented programs. Political changes at the federal level could well mean these pressures will receive more attention in Canada.

Continued pressure for change

Since the so-called aging crisis became a prominent policy issue in the mid-1990s, much of the analysis has focused on the impact of an aging population on public finances. Often overlooked is the impact of proposed reforms on the economic security of citizens as they pass through their retirement transitions into old age. The ongoing pressure for a more market-oriented system is no exception to this trend. Neo-liberal think-tanks and organizations continue to pursue an agenda of privatization of public pensions. Other institutions, including the International Monetary Fund, are still arguing for a reduction of public benefits. But there seems to be little concern about the potential negative impact of these proposals on the economic security of older people. Shifting the responsibility and risk of providing for retirement away from the state and onto individuals still seems to be the order of the day.

The Pension Challenge

According to the OECD, the need for further pension reforms is understood in general terms, but "there is less understanding of the solutions, such as working later, that will be needed."[18] Indeed, postponing retirement until later ages seems to figure prominently in proposals to deal with aging populations. It would appear that, while countries are being urged to cut back benefits, individuals will be expected to make up the difference by continuing to work.

Countries offering the lowest financial security for older citizens are often praised as having the best policies. For example, the Washington-based Center for Strategic and International Studies has calculated an Aging Vulnerability Index, which it describes as "the first attempt to develop a comprehensive measure of the old-age dependency change that is comparable across the developed countries."[19] In conjunction with pension consultants Watson Wyatt Worldwide, the first version of the index was published in 2003 and, according to the authors, "clearly shows that global aging is pushing much of the developed world toward fiscal and economic meltdown." They claim there is still time to avert the crisis, but "time is running short and the problem is worse than is generally supposed."

The solution, apparently, is to slash public pension benefits and encourage people both to work longer and save for themselves. These authors suggest the "challenge" will be particularly tough because, among other things, it will be "politically difficult" to reduce the "generosity" of public pension benefits. The vulnerability index covers 12 countries, including Canada, and assesses their vulnerability to rising old-age dependency costs. It ranks the countries and assigns them ratings from least to most vulnerable. Perhaps not surprisingly, the three countries deemed to have the lowest vulnerability are countries where the financial well-being of elders is probably least secure. But the three countries—Australia, the United Kingdom, and the United States—win the first three places, "thanks to their favourable demographics, their relatively inexpensive public benefit systems, and their well-developed private alternatives."[20]

A closer examination of the three countries chosen for their "low vulnerability" to population aging shows they are countries where retirement income systems depend largely on individuals fending for themselves. In other words, government finances may be "less vulnerable" to population aging because the risk has been shifted onto individuals who constitute the aging population. The devastating impact that market-oriented policy emphasis in some of these countries is having on the financial security of individuals preparing for their retirement transitions is also evident.

Australia's emphasis on private pension arrangements

Australia headed the list as the country least vulnerable to population aging on the aging vulnerability index calculated by the Center for Strategic and International Studies. But the Australian system has been described as "the clearest example in the industrial world of a retirement income system, 1) substantially dependent on funded individual accounts, and 2) without the social insurance mechanisms found in nearly all other industrial nations."[21]

While there is a basic guaranteed minimum old age pension, the retirement income system in Australia depends on compulsory private superannuation arrangements (the "Superannuation Guarantee" colloquially known as the "super")—in effect, a mandatory defined contribution savings program put in place in 1992, under which employers are required to contribute 9% of an employee's earnings. Pre-existing employer defined benefit pension programs are also adopting the SG's defined contribution format.[22] Public pensions are confined to a means-tested flat-rate benefit payable to eligible older people who are unable to adequately support themselves.[23] As well, individuals are not required to annuitize the account balances in their individual accounts at retirement. They receive a lump sum amount which could be consumed too slowly, thus restricting their standard of living, or too quickly, so they outlive their savings.[24]

John Myles and Paul Pierson explain that Australia's mandatory private pensions were "the end-product of a classical corporatist agreement between labour and government in which labour won new pension entitlements in exchange for wage moderation."[25] Observers note that, because the mandatory contributions to these plans were a direct substitute for wages, and because a centrally negotiated contribution figure had to be uniform across industries and firms, the plans to emerge from

The Pension Challenge

this initiative were overwhelmingly individual-account-defined contribution arrangements, with the funds invested collectively in employer or industry-wide funds, overseen by employer and employee trustees.[26]

More recently, there has apparently been a shift to greater employee choice and smaller funds, increasing the dispersion of individual results. According to some observers, the trend in Australia has been toward greater choice—and greater risk.[27] Myles and Pierson also note that, in the defined contribution design prevalent in Australia, future benefits depend entirely on contributions and returns on investments. Beneficiaries bear all of the risk, and future benefit changes can be "blamed on" (or credited to) markets rather than governments.[28]

According to the OECD, debate and analysis of population aging during the early 1980s revealed a strong view that "a sustainable social welfare policy which aims to provide adequate assistance to those most in financial need requires complementary policies to encourage self-provision among those who can afford to save for their own retirement."[29]

Pension concerns in the United Kingdom

In the UK, where the Blair government has continued down the "free market" path established by Margaret Thatcher, the "Third Way" approach has resulted in serious problems of what is euphemistically called "under-provision." To make matters worse, the UK pensions system has been wrestling with a major crisis as employers, faced with pension fund losses when the stock market tanked, have abandoned their defined benefit pension plans, often leaving workers without the pensions they had expected to get.

Pension provision in the UK is heavily dependent on the private sector and many people—especially those with low incomes—have not taken up the option of "providing for themselves." The UK system seems to have a bewildering array of options, many of them involving purchasing various kinds of private retirement savings products sold by insurance companies, or choosing whether or not to join an employer-sponsored scheme. Employers are allowed to opt out of the public pension system, as long as they provide an alternative plan to employees. But a 2002 government

Green Paper on pensions showed that many people were not providing adequately for their own retirement. And, because of a very weak public pension system, many faced financial hardship in old age.

So concerned was the Blair government that, in February 2004, it issued a discussion paper designed to encourage people to make more "informed choices for working and saving."[30] The government said it believes that, "given the right opportunity, people will plan ahead sensibly" if only the barriers to an informed choice are removed.[31] That was followed by the introduction of a Pensions Bill, aimed at pushing people further down the "post-welfare-state" road and getting them to make "better choices." As well, a key provision of the Bill was the establishment of a Pension Protection Fund intended to guarantee the pensions of workers whose employers go under.

As for public pensions in the UK, according to one expert, "few would argue that state pensions are in a mess. A major shake-up of the present system is what is needed, but the present government has shied away from this."[32] It seems the emphasis on individual responsibility for pension provision will continue. The government concludes its discussion paper with the hope that "these measures will help empower individuals to make their own decisions about retirement and the level of income they want in retirement."[33]

Social Security, deficits and privatization in the United States

In the United States, public pension programs have been a contentious issue for some years. Strong pressure has been applied to privatize Social Security and allow people to direct their mandatory Social Security contributions to individual private accounts, something like RRSPS in Canada. Privatization advocates have promulgated the usual mythology about Social Security, suggesting that it is "going broke," that younger workers will get nothing out of it, and that the best way to "solve the problem" would be to divert part of the contribution revenue into private accounts.

The Pension Challenge

Economist Paul Krugman, op-ed columnist for the *New York Times,* says the Bush plan for privatizing Social Security played well during the 2000 presidential election campaign.[34] But Krugman points out that Bush actually promised US$1 trillion in Social Security taxes to two different groups of people—telling younger workers that he will allow them to invest the money in personal accounts, while assuring older workers that it will be available to pay for their retirement.[35]

Like the CPP, Social Security benefits are funded by contribution revenue from employers and employees, but contribution rates in the U.S. have been deliberately set at a level where surplus funds will be generated. The surplus is accumulated in trust funds—one to cover old age benefits and one for disability insurance—and the funds are invested in special non-tradeable government bonds. The intention is that, if Social Security faces a shortfall in income as the baby boomers go through retirement, the trust fund assets will be used to supplement contribution revenue to pay the benefits.

At the beginning of 2004, the Social Security trust funds had assets of US$1.5 trillion or 306% of annual expenditures.[36] They were projected to increase to US$3.584 trillion at the beginning of 2013, or 442% of annual expenditures in that year. The 2004 report of the trustees said that the annual cost of Social Security is expected to exceed tax (or contribution) income starting in 2018, at which time the annual gap will be covered with cash from redeeming special obligations of the Treasury until these assets are exhausted in 2042. In other words, there will be sufficient funds to allow the continuation of full benefit payments on a timely basis until 2042.[37] By then, the leading-edge baby boomers—if they're still around—will be almost 100 years old. To allow the trust funds to remain solvent throughout the 75-year projection period used by the Social Security Administration—that is, through to 2079—the trustees suggested a range of options could be pursued, including increasing contribution rates, instituting small reductions in benefits, or transferring amounts from the government's general tax revenues to the trust fund.

But the security of Social Security is now threatened by the Bush administration's huge budget deficit, triggered by massive tax cuts totalling several trillion dollars over the next 10 years—not to mention the cost of the war in Iraq. Bush apparently intended to borrow from the Social Security trust fund to cover the cost of his tax cuts. In fact, in 2003, it was reported that $500 billion had already been siphoned off from the fund.[38] Borrowing from trust funds to cover the deficit could use up almost all the current trust fund surplus and jeopardize the future pensions of the big wave of people coming up to retirement in the next few years. A proposal from Federal Reserve Board Chairman Alan Greenspan to cut future Social Security benefits as a way of covering the budget deficit was met with strong public opposition. The president of the American Association of Retired Persons, for example, said the idea that Social Security should be a prime target to fix future budget deficits that are unrelated to the program is irresponsible.[39] "Social Security is designed as a self-sustaining program," he said, "and should be strengthened to ensure its long-term solvency." It should not be a resource for negotiations over the federal budget deficit, he said.

Bush's second term and the "Ownership Society"

Social Security privatization moved to the top of the domestic policy agenda after George W. Bush was re-elected for a second term in 2004. Fuelled by the deliberate falsehood that Social Security is in danger of imminent bankruptcy, Bush proposed to allow workers to invest part of their mandatory Social Security contributions in private accounts. He claims this would get the government off the hook for future benefits, as well as giving younger workers a more secure retirement. His arguments are nonsensical. Think about it. If Social Security really were broke, how would it help to take money out of the plan by diverting contribution revenues to private accounts? That would simply reduce the amount available to pay future Social Security benefits and increase the indebtedness of the government which will eventually have to pay them.

But there's a twist that doesn't seem to have been publicized much. Apparently, most of the balances in a worker's private account would be recaptured by the government when the worker retired in order to repay Social Security for the loss of revenue it incurred when a worker elected to direct some of his or her payroll taxes from the Social Security Trust Fund to a private account. In effect, people opting for the private accounts

The Pension Challenge

would get no net gain from the accounts unless their accounts produced a return higher than 3% above the inflation rate. If the return on their private accounts produced a return lower than 3% above the inflation rate, people would lose money as a result of the private accounts. And that would be on top of the other Social Security benefit cuts—such as price indexing instead of wage indexing—to which they were subjected.

In fact, while Bush pointedly promises no cuts for retirees or near-retirees, his plan would result in a 30% cut in guaranteed benefits for today's 25-year-old workers. And private accounts would make up less than half the loss, according to calculations by the Center for Economic and Policy Research.[40] For many workers, the private accounts plan would not offset any of the reductions in Social Security benefits that would be part of the plan. For these workers, their entire private account balance would be recaptured by the government when they retired.[41]

As for whether younger workers would get a better return on their contributions by investing them in the stock market, that idea is based on the assumption that high rates of return—6.5% to 7% above the rate of inflation—will continue indefinitely into the future. Dean Baker, co-director of the Center for Economic and Policy Research in Washington, has pointed out that, given the much slower projected rates of profit growth and the fact that price-to-earnings ratios in the stock market continue to be far higher than the historic average, it will be impossible for stock returns to be as high in the future as they were in the past.[42]

Baker also notes that the promoters of privatization have one other standard trick to promote fear about Social Security's future. They point out that, beginning in 2018, Social Security will be forced to rely on income from the Trust Fund to pay benefits. But that's the way it was planned to be. The 1983 Social Security Commission, chaired by Alan Greenspan, deliberately designed a system that would build up a surplus—taxing more than was necessary to pay benefits—so that the income from the surplus could be used to help pay the costs of the baby boomers' retirement. Drawing on the trust fund, says Baker, is no more a problem for Social Security than it is for any pension fund to use some of its accumulated assets to pay benefits to retirees. Indeed, that is exactly what is supposed to happen.[43]

Bush's plans to privatize Social Security are based on neo-liberal ideology, not on any kind of economic imperative. As Harold Meyerson, editor-at-large of *The American Prospect,* has pointed out, the plans to privatize Social Security have been devised by people who are ideologically committed to its destruction. "When Milton Friedman was calling for privatization a half-century ago," says Meyerson, "it wasn't because he feared the system would run out of money when the boomers retired. (The boomers were at that point just midway through being born). It was because he was a committed advocate of *laissez-faire* capitalism."[44] Meyerson explains the strategy like this:

> ...The advocates for privatizing Social Security have for the past quarter-century been housed at the Heritage Foundation and the Cato Institute—the nation's leading institutions of economic libertarianism. But, since 1983—when a commission appointed to augment Social Security's solvency declined to consider privatization, though it was appointed by Ronald Reagan and headed by Ayn Rand-acolyte Alan Greenspan—they have understood that the only way to realize their libertarian hearts' desire was to convince the American people that the system was teetering on bankruptcy.[45]

Progressive economists and commentators have done much to expose the deception and fraudulent claims about Social Security made by the Bush administration, but they don't get much coverage in the mainstream media. In fact, Mark Weisbrot, co-director of the Center for Economic and Policy Research, suggests that media mis-reporting of the Social Security issue has been almost as bad as the failure to expose the false claims used to justify the invasion of Iraq. Reporting false or unsubstantiated allegations over and over, without countervailing facts, says Weisbrot, "makes it easier for politicians to pursue a 'big lie' strategy—to deliberately repeat false information until it is accepted as truth."[46] For Bush to say, as he did in early 2005, that, "without changes, this younger generation of workers will see a UFO before they see a Social Security check," should have the same credibility as the statement, "Elvis Presley is alive, I just talked to him yesterday," says Weisbrot.[47]

And in case anyone thinks "it couldn't happen here," the *Globe and Mail* ran an editorial in February 2005,[48] praising Bush's plan for Social

The Pension Challenge

Security, and suggesting Prime Minster Paul Martin should have followed the Bush example. *Globe* editorial writers apparently swallowed the Bush mythology and propaganda about Social Security heading for bankruptcy and repeated what was the similar prevailing mythology about the CPP, just prior to the 1996–97 reforms, when privatizing Canada's public pension plan was also a hot topic. "Whether or not his plan flies in the end, Mr. Bush is at least proposing solutions," said the *Globe*. Just what "problem" still needed fixing in Canada's public pensions program, the editorial didn't say. But it accused Paul Martin, when he was Finance Minister, of avoiding "pension troubles by taking the easy way out," when he raised CPP contribution rates. Of course, the *Globe* failed to note that CPP combined employer/employee contribution rates have been capped at 9.9% for the foreseeable future, while the U.S. contribution rates to Social Security were already at 12.4% of contributory earnings—and contributory earnings for Social Security are set at a level more than double the equivalent CPP contributory earnings level—even before Canada started on its CPP reform debate.

But Bush apparently is pushing ahead with his plan to redirect Social Security contributions to private accounts and to remake the United States as an "Ownership Society." According to the Cato Institute, an Ownership Society —

> ...values responsibility, liberty, and property. Individuals are empowered by freeing them from dependence on government handouts and making them owners instead, in control of their own lives and destinies. In the Ownership Society, patients control their own health care, parents control their own children's education, and workers control their retirement savings.[49]

In other words, an extreme version of the neo-liberal agenda, where government no longer has a role, where individuals are expected to fend for themselves, and where collective responsibility for all citizens, and particularly the most vulnerable, is abandoned. The philosophy of Roosevelt's New Deal, which provided the genesis of Social Security, apparently no longer applies. Bush's plan, says the Labor Research Association, "abandons decades of federal programs designed to pool the risks that workers face and provide financial protection for all." The administration's approach to Social Security reform, says this organization, also ignores the inability of the elderly to risk any portion of their benefits or to live on reduced benefits. Social Security accounts for 42% of the income of the elderly, on average, but, for the lowest quintile, Social Security accounts for 91% of total income.[50]

But Bush's idea, according to Robert Kuttner, co-editor of *The American Prospect,* is that American workers aspire to be owners—owners of stock for their retirement, owners of homes, owners of businesses, owners of good health insurance, and owners of the skills that they need to navigate changes of jobs and careers. But it's a "bait and switch" tactic, says Kuttner. "How does Bush propose to create the "Ownership Society?" he asks. "Mainly through more tax credits. If people don't have reliable health care, there will be tax-favoured savings accounts to buy health insurance. If they need more secure retirement, there will be new tax incentives to set aside savings. If jobs are precarious, there will be tax credits to purchase retraining when your job moves to China." The fact that workers must have a decent income before they can take advantage of tax credits seems to have been overlooked. Decent wages and benefits and real government help are the part that Bush's Ownership Society leaves out, says Kuttner. "To Bush, ownership means the lone individual is made the sole owner of the problem. Lost your job? Better get yourself some new skills. Corporation cancelled your pension? Better sock away more savings. Company health insurance plan raising premiums and co-pays? Congratulations—you're an owner."[51]

Meanwhile, as the U.S. gets kudos from the Center for Strategic and International Studies for being one of the countries least "vulnerable" to population aging pressures, analysts point to a growing gap between rich and poor when it comes to adequacy of retirement income. Among households headed by a person approaching retirement, the percentage unable to replace half of their pre-retirement income once they retire rose sharply from 29.9% in 1989 to 42.5% in 1998.[52] The share was even higher among African Americans and Hispanic households, at 52.7%. Only households with wealth holdings of above US$1 million saw consistent increases in their wealth, after inflation. Growth in retirement wealth tended to be the province of white households, who saw a 6.1% increase in average retirement wealth between 1989 and 1998—a period

The Pension Challenge

of strong economic growth and a 24% rise in stock prices. Black and Hispanic households experienced a 19.9% drop.[53]

According to economist Edward Wolff, the growing system of voluntary accounts in the United States has produced greater inequality between rich and median households, and declining retirement wealth for the typical household. As well, he says, the contraction of traditional defined benefit pension plans and their replacement by defined contribution plans appears to have helped rich, older Americans but hurt a large group of lower-income Americans.[54] (The plan sponsor of a defined benefit plan guarantees a retirement pension related to earnings and years of service. In a defined contribution plan, pension contributions are accumulated in a fund and used to purchase a pension at retirement. The amount of the pension depends on investment returns, and no particular pension amount is guaranteed). Social Security, which pools contributions in order to ensure a retirement income floor for all participants, is the one segment of the retirement income system that distributes its wealth universally. Far from reducing Social Security, Wolff says one possibility for improving the adequacy of retirement income for the typical household would be to improve Social Security benefits.

Analysts believe that replacing the Social Security system would fundamentally change the experience of retirement in the United States. In particular, making what has been a secure source of income subject, to a significant degree, to the inconsistent performance of market investments instead of lifetime work history, would have a substantial effect on retirees. It is generally agreed that the majority of elderly in the U.S. can't afford to gamble their retirement income now or in the future. Ending up on the losing side of this bet would have a devastating impact on their quality of life.[55]

Pension reform pressures in Canada

Some commentators seem to think that efforts to privatize Social Security in the United States will inevitably spill over into Canada and that pressure to privatize the CPP will be revived. That seems highly unlikely—especially given the major reforms implemented in 1997–98.

But neo-liberal aficionados still keep trying. For example, an article in the *Financial Post* in March 2005 argued that CPP reform should have embraced private retirement savings accounts rather than shore up the existing plan with higher contributions and an investment reserve fund. (Apparently an argument along the same lines as that presented in the *Globe and Mail* editorial mentioned earlier). Apart from the fact that even a dedicated neo-liberal federal government would risk a major public backlash if it now tried to undo the 1997 CPP reforms in favour of private accounts, even high-profile members of the pension industry have taken issue with the privatization agenda.

For example, Keith Ambachtsheer, a respected author and long-time pension consultant, former president of the Association of Canadian Pension Management, took on the author of the *Financial Post* article and argued that the CPP reforms were in fact "well designed and executed, and that it is our workplace pension system that now needs a major overhaul."[56] The author of the article, said Ambachtsheer, offers three reasons for his stated views: 1) Private accounts would produce much higher real returns than the 4.5% goal of the CPP Investment Board. 2) The World Bank strongly supports private accounts. And 3) Private accounts are immune to political meddling. But Ambachtsheer challenges all three reasons. He says: 1) While the author of the article says private accounts in other jurisdictions realized 8% to 10% real returns in the 1980s and 1990s, he fails to note that periods of high returns are invariably followed by periods of far more modest returns. Looking ahead from today, the board's 4.5% return target (net of inflation and expenses) is in fact quite ambitious. 2) The World Bank advocates a 100% private accounts approach only for developing economies without national pension plans; it in fact holds Canada up as the reform poster child for developed economies that do have national pension plans. 3) Private accounts may be immune from political meddling, but not from private meddling. In many instances around the globe, says Ambachtsheer, unsuspecting retirement account holders are charged outrageous fees of 2% to 3% annually by for-profit intermediaries.

In any event, Canada ranks fourth on the Center for Strategic and International Studies aging vulnerability index—just low enough to push it into the medium vulnerability category. The ranking undoubtedly reflects the relatively modest scale of public pensions in Canada compared with those in most other industrialized countries. But, according to the study, Canada faces a less favourable demographic future than the other countries.[57] It also starts out with "a larger public sector, no plans for future cuts in public pensions, and a high rate of projected growth in health care benefits"—all of which, of course, are assumed to be negative features.

The study acknowledges that Canada, alone among the 12 countries measured in the Index, has announced plans to pursue a policy of prefunding some public pension benefits (a reference to the establishment of the CPP Investment Fund). But the authors of the study say that, "while Canada may succeed where others have failed, the projected level of 'prefunding' is small relative to the projected size of its dependency burden. Even if factored into the Index, it would not alter Canada's overall ranking."[58]

All of this implies that Canada needs to go much further in reforming its pension system if it wants to avoid fiscal disaster. But the findings are at variance with Canadian studies indicating Canada will not have a problem accommodating its aging population, even with no change in the design of current programs. For example, Frank Denton and Byron Spencer of McMaster University's Program for Research on Social and Economic Dimensions of Population Aging (SEDAP) say that expressions of apprehension about the effects of population aging typically relate to the demand side of the economy, and in particular to public expenditures on health care and old age security systems. Usually ignored is the fact that those same demographic forces will tend to reduce expenditures in some areas, such as education, employment insurance, and correctional services.[59] Also ignored, say these authors, is the fact that CPP/QPP and OAS transfer payments are taxable. Hence the net cost of these programs may be significantly less than it appears to be if only benefit payments are considered.

The projections of these authors indicate that, when a comprehensive view is taken of the impact of population aging on government expenditures, the demographically induced rate of growth of total expenditure is likely to be the same as the overall rate of growth of the population. As well, they say, when projected expenditures are compared with the projected productive capacity of the economy, "it seems likely that the total expenditure for all budgetary categories will be a smaller percentage of GDP in 2031 than in 1991, even though there will be large increases in expenditure on health care and social security."

Other Canadian researchers have made similar arguments. Retired people do continue to pay taxes, including income tax, sales taxes and GST, and property taxes. As the baby boomers retire, not only will more taxpayers be in the older age groups, but higher percentages of tax revenue will come from people in these age groups. The baby boomers have been described as "the trillion dollar generation." And there's evidence the myth is not far off the mark. By the end of 2001, Canadians had accumulated more than $1 trillion in retirement savings.[60] While some of those assets may be destined to fund the eventual retirement of younger people, boomers, now in their 40s to late 50s, likely account for much of the accumulated savings. As they move into retirement and start drawing down these savings, taxes will have to be paid on the amounts withdrawn, generating considerable tax revenue for the government. It has even been suggested that funding for elderly benefits such as OAS and GIS, as well as health care, could be financed largely by transfers within the older generation itself, rather than through transfers from younger people to older.[61]

Actuary Robert L. Brown, Director of the Institute of Insurance and Pension Research at the University of Waterloo, argues that, instead of looking at registered pension plans (RPPS) and RRSPS as a drain on tax revenues today because of the tax deductions they trigger, they should be regarded as a source of future tax revenues when the funds are withdrawn.[62] He also points out that the extra pension income dollars of tax revenue will come at exactly the same time when the baby boomers will need extra government support to pay for their increased health care delivery. In fact, Brown argues, these two cash flows can be combined to create the perfect macroeconomic immunized portfolio. In other words, increased health care costs associated with a much greater older population can be offset with the increased tax revenues generated when pension plans and RRSPS are cashed in by the boomers. Brown also suggests that rising per capita health care costs could be accommodated by allowing the RPP/RRSP system to expand at the same pace.

The Pension Challenge

Brown notes that the 1997/98 reforms have established the long-term sustainability of the CPP. He suggests the increased cost of first-tier benefits such as OAS and GIS could be managed by gradually increasing the age of eligibility for these benefits to match increases in life expectancy. While this raises a number of other issues, he says it's an idea worthy of a full policy debate—something it has not had to date.[63]

The International Monetary Fund weighs in

Meanwhile, in March 2004, the International Monetary Fund entered the debate with a report on "selected issues" prepared as the basis for a periodic consultation with Canadian officials. A chapter on Canada's pension system emphasizes the familiar "post-welfare-state" approach, although perhaps not quite as dogmatically as some other reports have. While acknowledging that the Canadian pension system appears sound, the IMF says "there may be scope for further reforms ahead of the retirement of the baby boom generation."[64] Its suggestions include strengthening the private pension pillar, including by reviewing the structure of retirement savings vehicles and strengthening governance of corporate pension schemes. In fact, in May 2005, the federal Department of Finance issued a consultation paper designed to solicit ideas to improve the legislation governing federally-regulated defined benefit plans, with comments due by September 2005.[65] And the Régie des rentes du Québec was conducting a similar exercise in the summer of 2005.

However, unlike some of the other reports, the IMF report acknowledges that, over the longer term, care will be needed to ensure that the support provided by the basic public pension system is kept at adequate levels to avoid a rise in old age poverty.[66] It also notes that, because OAS benefits are indexed to cost-of-living increases rather than wages, the income replacement value of these benefits would be expected to decline over time. In other words, seniors will fall further and further behind the rest of the population.

The IMF approves recent increases in contribution limits for RRSPS and suggests possibly adding tax-pre-paid savings plans (TPSPS) to the mix. These savings plans, proposed by the corporate-funded C.D. Howe

Institute in 2001, would allow people to accumulate private savings tax-free. Although no tax deduction would be allowed for contributions, interest and capital gains on the investments would not be taxed either, so the entire amount saved could be withdrawn tax-free at retirement. The C.D. Howe Institute advocated such plans and claimed they would represent a move towards consumption-based taxes, whereby only income that is consumed is subject to tax, while income that is saved is tax-free.[67] Advocates of consumption taxes claim that consumption is a drain on the economy, while savings contribute to economic growth and should therefore be subsidized. But consumption taxes generally penalize lower-income earners, who have no leftover income to save and must spend almost everything they earn to support themselves.

Supposedly, these tax-prepaid plans would help lower-income Canadians save for retirement because they would not be denied income-tested public benefits when the funds in their TPSP plans were withdrawn. The assumption, of course, ignores the possibility that lower-income families just don't have the spare cash to invest in private retirement savings plans. And if they are unable to do so when they can get a tax break on their contributions—as they can with RRSPS—they are unlikely to be able to save when the promised tax break will not materialize until several decades down the road when they reach retirement age.

Of course, higher-income individuals who are best able to save—and who are perhaps more likely to have well-developed investment expertise—would get the biggest tax breaks because the capital gains and interest on their investments would not be taxable. It is suggested that tax-prepaid plans would be particularly attractive to higher-income earners who have already used up all their permitted RRSP contribution room. There has been some suggestion that there might be a limit on the permitted amount of annual, and perhaps lifetime, contributions to TPSPS. Proposed limits have ranged from $5,000 or $10,000 a year to an amount comparable to the RRSP contribution limit. According to the federal government's 2004 budget, Ottawa is continuing to examine the possibility of introducing TPSPS and, at budget time in March 2004, the federal Finance Department had finished a round of consultations with the investment industry—which would, of course, benefit considerably from the introduction of such plans—and with tax experts. The

The Pension Challenge

newly formed Conservative Party proposed T P S P S as part of its election platform during the 2004 federal election campaign, naming them Registered Lifetime Savings Plans, and proposing an annual contribution limit of $5,000.

Commenting on the failed attempt to abolish O A S and G I S in favour of an income-tested Seniors' Benefit, the I M F report says it remains important to explore options for simplifying the existing system and targeting benefits more directly at the neediest group of elderly. It advocates merging the programs into one and income-testing benefits based on family income—a key feature of the old Seniors' Benefit proposal that raised so much opposition because of its impact on women's economic autonomy.

The CPP has been secured

Following extensive debate and public consultations, Canada made major changes in the way the C P P is funded in 1997/98. Until that time, the plan had been essentially a pay-as-you-go plan. Contributions from employers and employees were used to fund benefits for those who were retired or who became disabled. Legislation required the federal, provincial, and territorial finance ministers, who administer the C P P, to review the plan every five years and to set contribution rates at a level high enough to cover all benefits to be paid and to maintain a reserve of two years' worth of benefits. This contingency reserve was invested in long-term non-negotiable provincial government bonds.

Inevitably, with an aging population, higher contributions were needed from those in the work force to fund benefits for a growing number of retired. But the finance ministers had already anticipated this and had established contribution rates for 25 years in advance, setting them to increase gradually over time. When the finance ministers met in 1995 to begin their regular five-year review of the rate schedule, as required by law, they had received projections from the Chief Actuary, which he was required by law to produce as the basis for their discussions. His report indicated that, to meet the requirements of the law, contribution rates would have to be increased at a faster rate than he had projected in his previous report. The Chief Actuary projected that, if rates were increased right away, instead of waiting until 2015 when they were scheduled to go up again, combined employer/employee contribution rates would likely have to go up to 13.91% of contributory earnings in 2030, rising to 14.07% in 2050 and reaching a peak of 14.4% in 2100.

Contributions to the CPP are based on a percentage of earnings, within certain limits, known as "contributory earnings"—in other words, the earnings on which a worker's contribution is based. For example, in 2006, workers contribute 4.95% of earnings above $3,500 (known as the Year's Basic Exemption or YBE) and below $42,100 (known as the Year's Maximum Pensionable Earnings or YMPE). The YMPE is roughly equivalent to the average wage. The employee's contribution is matched by an equal contribution from the employer. Self-employed individuals must pay both the employer and the employee portions.

The finance ministers decided that combined contribution rates of close to 14% of contributory earnings in 35 years' time would be unacceptable. Strong lobbying from the business community and others persuaded them that combined employer/employee contribution rates could not be allowed to exceed 10% of contributory earnings. After exploring various options for cutting benefits and adjusting contributions, they decided to move to a system of partial funding of the plan. (They also implemented a number of changes that effectively reduced some benefits). By increasing contribution rates sharply over a six-year period, they would be able to generate surplus funds which could be invested in the capital market. Future earnings on the fund could then be used to supplement contribution revenue so that no further increases in contribution rates would be required.

They established a combined employer/employee contribution rate of 9.9%, to be phased in by 2003. (Contribution rates in 1996, at the start of the reform debate, were at 5.6% of contributory earnings). Known as the "steady-state" rate, this contribution rate would be maintained indefinitely. Since it would be more than enough to pay all benefits, surplus revenue would be directed to the newly-established CPP Investment Board, operating at arm's length from the government, which would invest the funds. At the beginning of 2004, the investment fund had about $65 billion invested and the fund was expected to reach about $160 billion within a decade.[68]

Following the hyperbole of the World Bank and a variety of neo-liberal commentators, think-tanks and politicians, media coverage of the pension reform debate of the late 1990s was hysterical. There was talk of an "aging crisis," of a "demographic time bomb," and of an "age war over pensions." People were questioning whether Canada could "afford" its aging population, and there were calls for privatization of public pensions, shifting the risk of providing for retirement onto individuals and absolving society, through its governments, of the responsibility for providing basic social security and public pensions for all its citizens.

Ultimately, most of these arguments were rejected and what might be thought of as a typical Canadian compromise was found. By moving to partial funding of the CPP, Canada was able to retain the CPP as an important public social insurance program and to restore confidence in the future sustainability of the plan—at least, that was the intention. However, as we saw in Chapter 1, many younger people still do not believe the CPP will be there when they reach retirement. It seems media coverage of the so-called aging crisis, around the time the CPP reforms were being put in place, still lingers in the minds of many people. And the annual marketing campaigns of financial institutions trying to sell RRSPS play on those fears to sell their products. It is hardly surprising that many younger people are confused about their future retirement, when faced with such deliberately created uncertainty.

Most people still don't understand how the CPP is funded. Media coverage of the plan continues to be misleading and negative. Quarterly losses on the investment fund, for example, get banner headlines so that many people believe their CPP retirement pensions are at risk. In reality, however, quarterly ups and downs of the CPP's investment portfolio are generally irrelevant to the long-term sustainability of the plan. Former Investment Board president John MacNaughton tried to explain the plan's long-term time frame. "It is important to note how we are different from other pension plans," he said. "The single biggest difference is that our investment horizon is extraordinarily distant. The reserve fund we are building is not expected to contribute to the payment of benefits for approximately 17 years—and it will continue to grow for decades beyond the start date."[69] In effect, earnings on the investment fund will not be needed to pay benefits until 2021. Until that date, contribution revenue will be more than enough to cover the cost of benefits. Because of its long-term time frame, MacNaughton said, "we don't get too excited when we have a great quarter and not too glum when we don't."[70]

As well, the Chief Actuary's projections for the plan are encouraging—although this, too, receives very little media coverage. Following the same practice used for the United States Social Security Administration, CPP legislation requires a 75-year projection period. Projections are based on past trends and future assumptions for three key variables—demographic, economic, and investment markets—and involve consultations with experts in these fields. In addition, the Chief Actuary's projections and actuarial assumptions are reviewed by a panel of independent actuaries.

In his 21st Actuarial Report, released in November 2004 and assessing the state of the plan as at December 31, 2003,[71] he said not only is the CPP sustainable in the long term, but cash inflows are projected to exceed outflows over the entire projection period (the next 75 years)—long after the boomers have retired and long after their children and grandchildren have retired, too. The report, required under the CPP Act, served as the basis for the federal and provincial finance ministers' statutory three-year review of the CPP in 2005, when they were required to consider whether any changes in contribution rates or benefit levels are needed. Given the positive actuarial report, further changes seem unlikely this time around.

What's more, the Chief Actuary says, "The pool of assets generated over the projection period provides the plan with the capacity, through investment earnings, to absorb a wide rage of unforeseen economic or demographic fluctuations, which otherwise would have to be reflected in the legislated contribution rate." In fact, better than anticipated economic experience over the period from 2001 to 2003—especially on labour force participation and employment data—combined with amendments since the last report, have put downward pressure on the "steady-sate" contribution rate, he says. While other factors have offset those trends, the steady state rate—the lowest combined employer/employee contribution rate sufficient to sustain the plan without further increase—remains at

The Pension Challenge

9.8%, he says, the same as when he last reported in December 2001. Since the legislated contribution rate is set at a combined employer/employee rate of 9.9% of contributory earnings, in effect, the CPP is doing even better than expected.

The Chief Actuary says he expects the CPP to be able to meet its obligations throughout the projection period, even though there will be a substantial increase in benefits paid as a result of the aging population. The good news prompted Finance Minister Ralph Goodale to claim that "Canada is one of the few countries in the world with a rock-solid public pension system." Canadians can continue to have confidence in the CPP "and count on it as an important part of their retirement savings," says Goodale.

Among other key findings of the report:

• With the 9.9% legislated contribution rate, the assets are expected to increase significantly over the next 17 years, with the ratio of assets to the following year's expenditures growing from 3.1% in 2004 to 5.6% by 2021.

• Total assets are expected to grow from $68 billion at the end of 2003 to $147 billion by the end of 2010.

• During the period 2004 to 2021, contributions are more than sufficient to cover the expenditures. Thereafter, a proportion of the investment earnings is required to make up the difference between contributions and expenditures. In 2050, the proportion of investment earnings is 29%.

• Investment earnings, which represent 14% of revenues (i.e., contributions and investment earnings) in 2004, will represent 27% thereof in 2020. In 2050, investment earnings will represent 32% of revenues. "This clearly illustrates the importance of the investment earnings as a source of revenues to the plan," the report says.

The actuarial report is based on several key assumptions on demographics, retirement rates, and rates of return on investments, including:

• Life expectancy will continue to increase. By 2025, for example, a woman who reaches age 65 could expect to live another 22.3 years, compared with 21.4 in 2004. Life expectancy of men at age 65 could increase from 18.4 years in 2004 to 19.6 in 2025.

• Over the next couple of decades, more people may postpone their retirement until a later age, but the differences don't seem to be that significant. Among those who were aged 60 in 2004, 56.6% of men and 65.4% of women were expected to claim their CPP retirement pensions before age 65. For people aged 60 in 2030, 55.5% of men and 64.1% of women were projected to claim CPP benefits prior to age 65.

• Labour force growth will weaken as the working age population expands at a slower pace. Growing labour shortages after 2010 may force higher real wage growth and that may help keep people in the labour force who might otherwise retire.

• Real rates of return on CPP assets are assumed to be 4.4% in 2004, rising to 5% for 2005 and 2006, then falling gradually to 4.2% by 2015 and 4.1% by 2025.

It's worth repeating here that the CPP is *not* a federal government program. It is administered by federal, provincial, and territorial finance ministers, and the amending formula is more stringent than that required to amend the constitution. As well, CPP pension reserves are segregated from general government revenues, so there is no fear of political interference.

Growing concern about workplace pension plans

Many workers who belong to registered pension plans (RPPS) in their workplaces are also concerned about the future security of their pension plans. While many workplace pension plans experienced surpluses in the stock market boom of the 1990s, the surpluses quickly turned to deficits when the stock market tanked in the early years of the 21st century. Forced with having to make up pension shortfalls out of current earnings, some employers have begun to reconsider the wisdom of having a defined benefit plan at all. Many are looking for cheaper alternatives,

The Pension Challenge

such as defined contribution pension plans or group RRSPS, which shift
responsibility and risk from the employer to the employee.

The pension crisis in the UK

In the UK, for example, in 2001/02, employers rushed to abandon their
final salary pension plans—a form of defined benefit pension plan—pro-
voking a pension crisis that caused considerable alarm. Some shut down
their defined benefit plans completely, switching existing pension plan
members to defined contribution arrangements that will likely give them
considerably less than they'd expected to get at retirement. In one case,
employees threatened to sue the employer for breach of contract because
it intended to close its final salary pension scheme to existing members
as part of a three-year restructuring intended to boost its share price.[72]
In another case, employees were given just three months' notice that the
employer's final salary scheme was being terminated and they were being forced to join new employees in the company's defined contribution
plan instead.[73]

Pension experts and actuaries in the UK commented on how quickly
employers moved away from final salary pension plans following the
market downturn. They also pointed out that many of the employers
who were switching their workers into defined contribution plans were
contributing far less to those plans than they had put into their final
salary plans. Of course, lower contributions to DC plans could mean
much lower pension income for employees. According to Amicus, the
UK's largest manufacturing union with over one million members in
both public and private sectors, a typical money purchase (DC) scheme
will generate a pension around 40% lower at age 60 than a typical final
salary scheme.[74]

Amicus and the Trades Union Congress charged that final salary
schemes started to disappear mainly because contribution holidays for
employers were over. But Amicus also notes that, while it's now a common tactic for employers in the UK to close their final salary schemes
to new entrants, while offering "inferior schemes" for new employees,
"today's new starters will become the majority of tomorrow's workforce

and employers will over time be confronted with demands for better pensions from that workforce."[75]

The British Trades Union Congress (TUC) has led the fight for decent pensions in the UK and has undertaken actions in support of better pensions. A major TUC demonstration in June 2004, for instance, highlighted key issues that are important not only for British workers, but for those in other countries—including Canada—now being faced with increasing pressure for more changes and downgrading of financial security for workers approaching their retirement transition. Included in the TUC demands were these points:

- The basic state pension to be linked to earnings to provide a secure foundation on which everyone can build a pension;

- Urgent action to help women who face much lower pensions in retirement, including making it much easier for women who take career breaks to build up a full state pension;

- Compensation for those who have lost out in recent occupational pension fund collapses and who will not be covered by the new Pensions Protection Fund [introduced by the UK government in its 2004 Pensions Bill]; and

- More choice on retirement, not higher retirement ages.

Summing it up, the TUC General Secretary said: "Politicians of all parties have yet to appreciate the depth of our pensions crisis and are avoiding the really radical action that is needed if large numbers of today's workers are not to face poverty in retirement.[76] Fewer and fewer are members of good traditional occupational schemes, and pensions mis-selling [a scandal involving fraudulent practices of insurance companies selling individual retirement savings plans], growing student debt, and the high cost of housing have put people off making alternative arrangements."

The Pension Challenge

Workers' pensions in Canada are threatened

As we noted earlier, the UK pension system relies heavily on private pension arrangements. Because there is no compulsory public pension scheme comparable to Canada's CPP, employer-based defined benefit pension plans in the UK are even more important as a source of predictable retirement income for employees than they are in Canada. There is also a different regulatory environment in Canada. But defined benefit plans in Canada have been facing similar problems to those of the UK—particularly where companies operate in the old industrial sectors—often referred to as "sunset" industries. Some companies with older, long-term employees find that, as their older workers retire, they have only a small number of existing members to fund a scheme which is supporting a large number of pensioners or deferred members (who will retire in the future).

This is particularly true of companies that have gone through a downsizing where large numbers of workers were laid off or terminated. Some observers say these companies may now have pension costs out of all proportion to the size of their current payroll. Even where companies switch to defined contribution plans, replacing their old defined benefit plans, their liabilities for past benefits for employees and ex-employees may now be overwhelming. All of this, of course, greatly increases the uncertainty for workers about their future financial security as they approach their retirement transitions.

There has been much debate in Canada about the "funding crisis" faced by defined benefit pension plans as a result of the stock market downturn in 2000–2002. The Bank of Canada reports that aggregate funding positions of Canadian pension plans moved to a net deficit in 2002 from a roughly neutral position in 2001 and a net surplus at the end of 2000.[77] By early 2004, markets had improved and the value of pension fund assets was starting to increase again. However, many pension plan sponsors are now faced with making extra payments into their pension plans to cover the deficits they have accumulated. And some may be having second thoughts about the value of having a defined benefit pension plan. Many of these plans are negotiated through collective bargaining, and unions which have fought to establish the plans will certainly fight to see they are maintained. But recent high-profile cases have shown that the fight will not be easy. They also highlight the fact that workers who thought they could look forward to a decent pension on their retirement may have those hopes dashed by unforeseen circumstances.

The situation of Air Canada is a case in point. Air Canada sank into insolvency in 2003 and applied for protection under the Companies' Creditors Arrangement Act (CCRA) so it could restructure its operations. Hong Kong billionaire businessman Victor Li's Trinity Time Investments Ltd. offered to come to the rescue and buy into the company. But Li made it a condition of his offer that Air Canada change its defined benefit pension plan to a defined contribution plan. Current employees would have the option of remaining with the existing defined benefit plans or switching to a new defined contribution plan and be given a bonus equivalent to 10% of their base salary if they switched. All new employees would automatically be enrolled in the defined contribution plan—in effect creating a two-tier pension plan. The Air Canada pension plan had a surplus of $915 million in 2001, and the company took contribution holidays starting in 2001 and continuing into 2002 and 2003.[78] By 2004, however, the pension plan reportedly had a deficit of $1.2 billion.[79]

TABLE 3 **Percentage of paid workers in registered pension plans**

Year	% Men	% Women	% Total
1992	48.1	41.6	45.1
1993	46.8	41.9	44.6
1994	45.3	41.1	43.4
1995	44.0	40.6	42.4
1996	43.4	40.3	42.0
1997	42.9	39.9	41.5
1998	41.9	39.1	40.6
1999	41.9	39.3	40.7
2000	41.8	39.3	40.6
2001	40.9	39.2	40.1
2002	39.9	39.2	39.6

SOURCE Statistics Canada 2004e.

The Pension Challenge

After making significant wage concessions, the various unions representing the employees refused to agree to the downgrading of their future pension benefits. But these workers have no protection if the company goes under. Their pensions may be lost completely. Air Canada falls under federal jurisdiction, and there is no fund to guarantee the pensions of employees whose employer fails. The NDP has called on the federal government to provide a federal pension insurance program, similar to the one in place in the United States, funded by small employer contributions from corporations under federal jurisdiction, such as banks, airlines, and telecommunications companies.[80] It has also urged the federal government to introduce legislation to ensure that employees and their pension plans are the preferred creditors in the event of corporate bankruptcies. Under the current system, workers who are owed wages and pension benefits rank low down on the list of creditors in the event of corporate bankruptcy.

In Ontario, there is a Pension Benefits Guarantee Fund (PBGF), financed by contributions from employers who sponsor pension plans in the province, and designed to provide pension benefits up to a limit of $1,000 a month for each worker when a plan sponsor goes bankrupt. But workers in Ontario are not always protected, either. Stelco Inc. obtained bankruptcy court protection in January 2004, claiming pension and retiree benefit obligations as a main reason for its bankruptcy. The company demanded wage cuts and reductions in pension and benefit payouts in order to survive. But Stelco took a contribution holiday in the early 1990s, saving millions of dollars in contributions that should have been made to the pension plan. Then the plan was hit with the collapse of equity markets in 2000–2002. By the beginning of 2004, the Stelco defined benefit pension plan had a deficit of $1.25 billion. Normally, the deficit would have been covered by the PBGF, but there was only $230 million in the fund. Just like the workers at Air Canada, the pensions of Stelco workers were then also at risk. The United Steelworkers, which represents the Stelco workers, believed the company was using the court process to slash collective agreements on wages and benefits.[81]

Unions have called for government protection of pensions and workers' rights when a company seeks bankruptcy protection.[82] And workers may have leverage where pension plans have been bargained. Non-unionized workers are clearly in a much more precarious position. Most workers in Canada, however, are not covered by workplace pension plans. In fact, pension plan membership has been declining over recent years. Among women who had paid jobs, coverage has dropped from 42% in 1992 to 39% in 2002. In the same period, coverage of men in paid employment dropped from 48% in 1992 to 40% in 2002 (*see Table 2*).

Are defined benefit plans doomed?

Although by the beginning of 2004 the value of pension plan assets had begun to increase again, some observers believe the pension shortfalls triggered by the stock market decline of 2000–2002 have soured employers on the wisdom of providing defined benefit pension plans for their employees. At the end of 2003, a well-known senior actuary with a major Canadian pension consulting firm actually advised employers to get rid of their defined benefit plans, claiming such plans were no longer feasible.[83] His comments caused a firestorm and prompted the president of the Canadian Labour Congress to call on the consulting firm that employs the actuary—as well as providing consulting advice to trade union clients—to dissociate itself from his comments.[84] Employers who don't have a pension plan should not start one, this actuary said, and those who feel they must have a plan should make it a defined contribution plan. For those who already had a defined benefit plan, he suggested the possibility of winding up the plan, settling the benefits, and offering larger salaries to the employees in lieu of future accruals. However, he admitted that, where such plans had been negotiated through collective bargaining, such options would likely be impossible. He also acknowledged that defined benefit pension plans have done a good job for pension plan members, but it would appear his views were focused on the dangers he foresaw for corporations that sponsor such plans, and their shareholders. It seems remarkable that such high-profile people in the pension community should offer very public advice that ignores the impact of their comments on the future financial security of workers, but much of the current lobbying to change the pension system seems to take the same approach.

The Pension Challenge

Although most workers in pension plans belong to defined benefit plans, the percentage in defined contribution plans has been increasing. In 1991, for example, 8.8% of pension plan members belonged to defined contribution plans, while 89.8% were in defined benefit plans. By 2000, 14.0% were in defined contribution and 84.1% were in defined benefit.[85] By the beginning of 2003, the percentage of pension plan members in defined benefit plans had dropped to 82%, while the percentage in defined contribution plans had edged up to 15%.[86] Unfortunately, there is no information on the percentage of workers who had group RRSPS at work. However, it is important to note that such plans do not guarantee a pension at retirement. In fact, there is nothing to prevent them from being used for other purposes long before the holder reaches the normal retirement age.

In spite of claims to the contrary, it does not seem that there has been widespread conversion of defined benefit plans to defined contribution plans—at least not yet. But observers suggest the practice is prevalent in some industries. Many Alberta-based oil and gas companies, for example, have apparently closed their defined benefit plans to further pension accruals and have moved employees into DC plans or group RRSPS. However, some experts suggest corporations who already have defined contribution plans may now be deeply concerned about how they will deal with employees who have lost so much money because of the market downturn. Employees in DC plans who are approaching retirement may have been heavily invested in equities and then suddenly their pension plummeted by 10% or 15%, so now they can't afford to retire. There are also suggestions that worse news on DC plans is still to come as the impact of the financial market meltdown works its way into the pension system over the next several years. Other observers believe many members of DC plans will not have accumulated enough assets in their plans to last throughout their retirement years. They would then be forced to rely on public income support programs. Of course, the same concerns apply to those who have counted on RRSPS to fund their retirement and have seen the value of their savings drop when markets declined.

For advocates of the "Third Way" approach to retirement income provision, emphasizing private provision of retirement income, these developments provide salutary lessons. Apart from anything else, they demonstrate the importance of having a basic underpinning of public pensions to secure the financial well-being of individuals as they move through their retirement transitions and beyond.

Retirement decisions and the design of the pension system

Decisions individuals make about retirement are clearly influenced by the availability of pension income or other financial support if they stop paid employment. But analysts argue that the design of some pension plans may actually encourage workers to stop working early. For example, defined benefit pension plans are required to establish a "normal retirement age" at which pension plan members are entitled or expected to retire—generally the age at which pensions are first paid without any reduction.

Early retirement, with an actuarially reduced benefit, is generally permitted for those who are within 10 years of the normal retirement age. But those who meet certain requirements for age and years of service may retire early with an unreduced benefit. The plan member must have reached age 60; or have at least 30 years' service; or the member's age plus years of service must total 80. Pension legislation permits early retirement with unreduced benefits at an earlier age for people in certain occupations considered particularly strenuous and stressful and therefore involving public safety. In these cases, the age criterion is reduced to 55; the 30-year eligibility is reduced to 25; and the age-plus-years-of-service is reduced from 80 to 75. The occupations are firefighter, police officer, air traffic controller, commercial airline pilot, and the military. Interestingly, the occupations are all male-dominated. Nurses, who are predominantly women, asked to be added to the list when their union appeared before the House of Commons Finance Committee holding hearings on a bill to change the tax treatment of pensions and retirement savings in 1990, but their appeal was rejected.

Although many pension plans allow employees to continue working and accruing benefits past the normal retirement age, it is often not worth their while to do so—at least from a pension point of view. The pension accrual gained by working an extra year will probably be worth less than

The Pension Challenge

the one year of pension that will be lost by continuing to work—especially for older workers who may have many years of service. Of course, there may be other reasons for continuing to work: for instance, the employee may not be able to live on the amount of the pension and would prefer to keep on working and getting paid a salary. In any event, income tax laws require the pension plan to start paying out pension benefits by the end of the year in which the employee turns 69.

Critics have also charged that the CPP encourages early retirement because the formula used to adjust benefits is too generous to those who claim benefits prior to age 65, and not generous enough to those who want to continue working past age 65. (A CPP retirement benefit may be claimed at any age between 60 and 70. For those claiming the benefit between age 60 and 65, the amount of the benefit that would be payable at age 65 is reduced by 0.5% for each month before the month of the individual's 65th birthday. Benefits claimed between age 65 and 70 are increased by 0.5% for each month after the person's 65th birthday). If these provisions were cost-neutral to the plan, the net cost of the provision should be the same, regardless of whether contributors take the retirement benefit at age 65 as opposed to any other age between 60 and 70 inclusive. That is, the timing of any plan member's retirement benefit uptake should be neither advantageous nor disadvantageous to plan members taken as a group.

According to a 2003 study of the CPP actuarial adjustment factors conducted by the Office of the Chief Actuary, "the generosity of the current legislated actuarial adjustments creates an incentive for individuals to opt for the CPP retirement pension at an early age (currently about 62 on average)." [87] As we noted in Chapter 1, the Chief Actuary also said that, in the context of an aging population, where life expectancy at age 65 is expected to continue to increase and projected labour force shortages could induce older workers to stay at work longer, policy-makers will have to determine whether the legislated actuarial adjustments now in force should be changed, or whether certain plan provisions should be changed to restore cost neutrality.

Under current rules, individuals who claim a CPP retirement pension before age 65 must demonstrate they have substantially ceased working—although it appears the federal government is reviewing that provision so that people could start their pension but continue to work. There is no such requirement for those who claim benefits after age 65, although they cannot continue to make contributions once they start receiving benefits. The Chief Actuary suggested possible changes might be needed to require working beneficiaries to pay contributions or ending the contributory period at age 65 for everyone, regardless of when they start benefits. Under current rules, the average earnings on which the retirement pension is based are calculated over the person's "contributory period," defined as the period from age 18 to the date when the benefit begins.

The province of Quebec has already proposed changes to the actuarial adjustments used in the Quebec Pension Plan.[88] Although it has proposed that the reduction of 0.5% a month between ages 60 and 65 remain the same, the pension of a person who waits until after age 65 to claim QPP benefits would be increased to 0.7% for each month between the 65th birthday and the month in which the application for benefits is made, up to age 70. The Quebec government says this and other changes it proposes would make working past retirement age more attractive to individuals who continue working.

The IMF study, referred to earlier, also notes that Canada's public pension system "contains a number of disincentives to work beyond the early retirement age."[89] But it also admits that Canada's public pension system "appears to be relatively neutral, with some estimates suggesting that only about 20% of the trend decline in average retirement age is explained by public pension incentives."[90]

The OECD report on *Maintaining Prosperity in an Aging Society* also places heavy emphasis on reducing the disincentives to work longer in public pension programs. But it also advocates a shift in company pension plans from defined benefit to defined contribution. Shifting the risk of providing a retirement income onto individuals, it says, is "an important element in promoting greater choice in the decision to retire." It would appear that, once the burden of providing for retirement is shifted to individual workers, it will then be entirely up to them whether they can afford to stop working for pay. That will then be their "choice." But the OECD does at least admit that "the problem with defined contribution plans is that they transfer risk to individuals. They therefore make most sense in

The Pension Challenge

a system where risks of low income are covered by other programs and where there are real opportunities to work later in life."[91]

The vulnerability of elders

Ironically, "Third Way" approaches to pension provision—described in detail in the next chapter—also seem to rely heavily on reducing benefits from public pension plans so that people will be forced into saving more for themselves, or more probably having to work until later ages before they can afford to stop paid employment completely. The OECD apparently believes that, with reduced pay-as-you go benefits, many families will seek to top up their pensions with private savings for retirement.[92] It also argues that "lower public pensions may lead to spontaneous changes in other pillars, offsetting the detrimental impact on the income of older people." As for younger people, as mentioned earlier, they will need to understand that the solution to all this will be working later, says the OECD.[93]

The OECD also argues, along with other neo-liberal commentators—including those in Canada—that many old people don't really need the money they receive from public pensions. There is evidence, says the OECD, that "retired people do not consume the resources at their disposal, but give money to children and grandchildren during their retirement years and as bequests."[94] But anecdotal evidence in Canada suggests many older people continue to save because they are worried about unforeseen emergencies, such as illness, emergency household repairs, or cost increases such as higher property taxes and user fees for services. The OECD argues that older people can always tap into their assets to support themselves in retirement—for instance, by taking a reverse mortgage on their homes, or selling their businesses if they're self-employed.[95] This cavalier attitude to the financial security and well-being of elders is astonishing.

A "reverse mortgage" is an arrangement whereby, in exchange for holding a mortgage on an individual's home, a lender offers a lifetime annuity that pays monthly benefits to the individual. However, no mortgage payments have to be made. Instead, the mortgage debt accumulates, with interest, until the home is sold or the owner dies, at which point, the debt becomes due and payable. The no-payment provision means the debt with interest compounds rapidly, but lenders generally guarantee that, if the total debt exceeds the value of the home when the home is sold, no additional payment will be required. This feature, however, is the key reason why reverse mortgages are only available in communities where house prices are strongly expected to continue increasing in value. It is also why lenders offering reverse mortgages generally will only lend amounts that represent a small portion of the total market value of the home.

While this type of reverse mortgage—more correctly called a "reverse annuity mortgage"—is widely available in the United States and some other countries, it is not well-known in Canada. None of the major banks in Canada offers reverse mortgages, although some will refer potential borrowers to the Canadian Home Income Plan Corporation , a private corporation based in Vancouver, which is the only place Canadians can arrange a reverse mortgage. Many financial advisors do not recommend reverse mortgages to their clients because of the rapid compounding of the debt.

It should also be noted that the OECD's analysis—like that of many other neo-liberal commentators—of how seniors might be able to support themselves in retirement is based on a married couple living in a mortgage-free home. Increasing numbers of elders do not fit this pattern. For example, older women on their own may have gone through a divorce and ended up without a home, or may still have many more years of mortgage payments to make. As well, a significant proportion of older Canadians do not own their own homes. In Canada, older women on their own have one of the highest poverty rates of any group in the population. In 2001, for example, 45.6% of unattached women aged 65 or older had incomes below Statistics Canada before-tax low-income cut-off—the measure generally used by social policy analysts to indicate poverty.[96]

Canada's public pension system has done a remarkable job in improving the financial security of seniors. Sociologist and aging expert John Myles says Canada's old age security system appears to have achieved an enviable position. Canadian expenditures on income security for seniors are modest by international standards, and are projected to peak at levels well below those anticipated by most other western nations in the next

The Pension Challenge

[now the current] century. In spite of this, says Myles, low-income rates among Canadian seniors measured by the usual "relative" international standard (persons with adjusted incomes less than 50% of the median) are now among the lowest in the OECD, even when compared with the egalitarian Sweden.[97] In the mid-1970s, low-income rates among Canadian seniors were still well above those of their American peers.[98] And the first truly comparative studies of low-income rates among seniors for the early 1980s placed Canada at the lower end of the international league tables.

Myles says the maturing CPP and the continued development of private pension plans fuelled these developments. These two pension sources provided 45% of the disposable income of seniors in 1995, compared with 21% in 1980.[99] But he also says that, while the income gains among low-income seniors have been substantial, it would be "extremely difficult" to make a case for the claim that Canadian seniors have become "too rich." Virtually all of the gains have been at the lower end of the income distribution.[100]

Another study of the incomes of older Canadians, by Bob Baldwin and Pierre Laliberté of the Canadian Labour Congress, came up with similar results. This study emphasizes that the improvement in the income situation of older Canadians is, in significant measure, "a triumph of public policy and programs."[101] The authors emphasize that OAS/GIS and the CPP/QPP have become important building blocks around which workplace pensions and individual savings efforts have been planned. They also note that, while the CPP/QPP is generally associated with earnings replacement rather than the provision of a minimum income floor, its role in increasing the incomes of low-income Canadians is striking.[102] These authors make the point that their research provides little support for the notion that the incomes of the elderly are too high and therefore should be subject to a general reduction. Not only are they modest by current standards, say these authors, but they are somewhat vulnerable to reduction in the years ahead.

The research of these authors was designed to establish a basis for considering whether the aging of the population will bring with it an ever-growing portion of the population living on substandard incomes.

But in response to the push to get people to work longer, Baldwin and Laliberté say this:

> Although the point should not have to be made, it would not be a forward step if the alternative to public pension benefits to which people have to resort is paid employment. Some of the background work for the OECD seems to ignore this basic point. In the Canadian context, it is hard to imagine a substitution process that would result in a benefit structure that would be as effective or equitable as the OAS/GIS and CPP/QPP. During the period that led to changes to the Canada Pension Plan, there was no public forum for the airing of these issues.[103]

Will further changes be made?

According to sociologist and pension expert Alan Walker, there can be little doubt that pension expenditure has been stabilized on the basis of the institutional reforms implemented to date. But Walker believes the appetite for reform is nowhere near being assuaged.[104] He says there is a new conventional wisdom among policy-makers in Europe that further change is required to ensure financial sustainability. There are still strong pressures for pension reform coming from international economic agencies and from vested interests in the private pension world, Walker says.

At this point, Canadian governments are not likely to undertake a major overhaul of the retirement income system. It's possible, however, that further changes could be made to address particular issues. It would be relatively simple to eliminate perceived disincentives for early retirement in the CPP, for example—either by following the approach now being considered by Quebec for the QPP (as discussed earlier) or by instituting the kind of changes suggested by the Chief Actuary, noted above.

Quebec is proposing other changes to the QPP, including basing the retirement pension on a standard contributory period of 40 years instead of the current system which allows an individual to exclude up to seven years of lowest earnings from the average earnings calculation on which the pension is based. Essentially, the pension would be 25% of the person's

The Pension Challenge

total earnings divided by 40. In other words, the more the person earns during a lifetime, the higher the pension could be. The effect would likely be to encourage people to work longer and therefore build up a bigger pot of earnings on which to base the pension.

Quebec is also proposing to limit the benefit paid to a surviving spouse of a QPP contributor. In the case of a surviving spouse who is not retired, the surviving spouse pension would only be payable for three years, instead of for life as under the current system. But the amount of the pension would be higher and the spouse's account would be credited with 60% of the earnings entered in the QPP under the name of the deceased for each year of their life together. It is not clear what the impact of this change might be on the incomes of older women left on their own. At the moment, as we saw earlier, a high percentage of these women have incomes below the poverty line.

In presenting its proposals, the Quebec government said it was aiming to "strengthen the flexibility in the different forms of retirement."[105] Considering the rapid aging of the population and the new realities of the labour market, the government said, the Quebec Pension Plan must evolve. In fact, according to the government, instead of maintaining a set of measures (early or late retirement, right to an early pension if the individual has reached a phased retirement agreement, increase in the pension of a retiree who returns to work), the new provisions would allow a worker to choose his or her own form of retirement. In this way, the worker could:

• take phased retirement or work full-time then retire definitively;

• claim a pension at the beginning of phased retirement or at the definitive end of his or her career; or

• work or not work after pension payments have started.

No way would be more advantageous than another. All pensionable earnings—that is, earnings on which the worker made a contribution—would contribute to increasing the pension.

There is no indication so far that federal, provincial, and territorial finance ministers will make similar moves to change the CPP. But it would not be surprising to see at least some of the proposed Quebec changes eventually mirrored in the CPP. Discouraging early retirement will probably be a priority—especially given the recent comments of the Chief Actuary about disincentives to working past 65.

As far as workplace pension plans are concerned, there are now attempts to harmonize pension legislation among the 11 pension jurisdictions in Canada. But these efforts do not seem likely to come to very much in the near future, and their impact will be more on how pension plans are administered than on benefits provided. Perhaps of more interest is the suggestion by a major pension consulting firm that employers may want to consider phasing out early retirement benefits—although it described this possibility as "in the radical change neighbourhood of the spectrum." It was suggested that sponsoring companies should look at this sooner rather than later, since "it takes a long time to phase them out." According to these consultants, if the provisions become necessary in the future, they can be restored with the stroke of a pen.[106]

Further moves by governments to encourage private provision of retirement income could also be implemented. The federal government has been under continuing pressure to increase the contribution limits for RRSPS, and limits were increased in the 2004 budget and again in 2005. The introduction of Tax-Paid Savings Plans, discussed earlier, is also a possibility—one highly favoured by the financial community as well as proposed by the Conservative party in the 2004 federal election campaign.

Changes in the age of eligibility for CPP retirement benefits do not seem to be on the policy agenda at this point. This option was rejected during the major funding reforms of the late 1990s, but there is an important aspect of the CPP pre-funding that is sometimes overlooked. As Bob Baldwin and others have pointed out, pre-funding of pension plans may be able to reduce pension contributions, but it does not change either total pension expenditures or the share of GDP claimed by pensioners.[107] Pre-funding simply changes the source of income from which pensions are paid by supplementing wage-based contributions with investment income. As we have noted, the push to persuade people to work longer is driven largely by the desire not to lose the productive capacity of large numbers of workers who are now retiring early. If more older workers would continue in employment, they would maintain the economic out-

The Pension Challenge

put needed to support the growing number of older people. As a result, working longer is still likely to be an issue of growing importance over the next decade or so.

At this point, it seems likely that further reforms will not be made until the completion of the federal government's research project on the aging population, now under way as part of its Policy Research Initiative, discussed in the following chapter. The path being taken in this research suggests a radically different approach to policy-making for an aging population, with important implications for retirement income policies and programs and for how retirement is viewed. We will discuss those possibilities in the following chapter.

Notes

1 OECD 1998: 43.

2 Ibid.

3 Ibid: 19.

4 Ibid: 18.

5 Ibid: 41.

6 Myles 2002: 134.

7 European Union 2001: 5–8.

8 OECD 2000: 55.

9 World Bank 1994: 367–368.

10 Béland and Myles 2003: 4.

11 Ibid: 24.

12 Ibid: 21.

13 Ibid: 25.

14 Government of Canada 1997: 21.

15 Battle 2003: 26.

16 Béland and Myles 2003: 3.

17 Ibid: 21.

18 OECD 1998: 18.

19 Jackson and Howe 2003: iv.

20 Ibid: iii.

21 Sass 2004: 2.

22 Ibid. 1

23 OECD 2000: 52.

24 Sass 2004: 12.

25 Myles and Pierson 2001: 305–333.

26 Sass 2004: 7.

27 Ibid. 9.

28 Myles and Pierson 2001: 305–333.

29 OECD 2000: 52.

30 United Kingdom Government 2004: 31.

31 Ibid: 1.

32 Mercer Human Resources Consulting 2003.

33 United Kingdom Government 2004: 31.

34 Krugman 2003: 135.

35 Ibid: 143.

36 United States Social Security Administration 2004: 2.

37 Ibid: 3.

38 Dean for America 2003.

39 American Association of Retired Persons 2004b.

40 Baker and Rosnick 2004: 2.

41 Furman and Greenstein 2005: 4.

42 Baker 2005: 3.

43 Ibid. 2.

44 Meyerson 2005: 1.

45 Ibid.

46 Weisbrot 2005: 1.

47 Ibid: 2.

48 Globe and Mail 2005.

49 Cato Institute 2003: 1.

50 Labor Research Association 2005: 2.

51 Kuttner 2003: 2

52 Wolff 2003: 1.

53 Ibid: 2.

54 Ibid: 52.

55 Ettlinger and Chapman 2005: 3.

56 Ambachtsheer 2005: 1.

57 Jackson and Howe 2003: 22.

58 Ibid: 6.

59 Denton and Spencer 1999: 23.

60 Statistics Canada 2003f: 1.

61 Wolfson and Murphy 1997: 86.

62 Brown 2002b: 1.

63 Ibid 27.

64 International Monetary fund 2004: 64.

65 Department of Finance 2005: 1.

66 Ibid.

67 Kesselman and Poschmann 2001: 2.

68 MacNaughton 2004: 3.

69 Ibid: 7.

70 Ibid: 6.

71 Chief Actuary 2004: 11.

72 Ananova News Service 2002: 1.

73 Accountancy Age.com 2002: 1.

74 Amicus 2002b: 1.

75 Amicus 2002a: 6.

76 Trades Union Congress 2004: 1.

77 Bank of Canada 2003: 8.

78 Le Pan 2003: 2.

79 Partridge 2004: B10.

80 New Democratic Party 2004: 1.

81 Erwin 2004: 1.

82 CUPE 2004: 1.

83 Hamilton 2003: 11.

84 Georgetti 2003: 2.

85 Statistics Canada 2003e: 59.

86 Statistics Canada 2004e: 12.

87 Chief Actuary 2003: 38.

88 Régie des rentes du Québec 2003: 29.

89 International Monetary Fund 2004: 62.

90 Ibid: 66.

91 OECD 1998: 61.

92 Ibid: 60.

93 Ibid: 58.

94 Ibid: 56.

95 Ibid: 62.

96 Statistics Canada 2004b: 2.

97 Myles 2000: 1.

98 Ibid: footnote 4.

99 Ibid: 6.

100 Ibid: 1.

101 Baldwin and Laliberté 1999: 52.

102 Ibid.

103 Ibid: 58.

104 Walker 2003: 11.

105 Régies des rentes du Québec 2003: 28.

106 Mercer Human Resources Consulting 2004: 1.

107 Baldwin 2004a: 4, footnote 3.

Year:			Month:					MORNING		AFTERNOON		OVERTIME	
								OUT	IN	OUT	IN	OUT	
	MORNING		AFTERNOON		OVERTIME								
	IN	OUT	IN	OUT	IN	OUT							
MON													
						WED			2:57 to 6:02				3

New Perspectives
On the Aging Population

WHILE UNCERTAINTY about retirement and concern about their future financial security still seems to be widespread among Canadians, in official policy-making circles there is now a new mood of optimism about the aging population. Talk about the so-called "aging crisis" and the "coming generational war over pensions" has faded away. Questions about whether Canada can afford its rapidly aging population are now seldom heard. An aging population is now seen as a good news story—not only in Canada, but around the world. Experts say the new mood is a remarkable turnaround in just a few short years. But it is not clear just why this has happened. Nor is there much evidence about the basis for the new optimism. However, there now seems to be more emphasis on older people as an untapped resource. If they could be encouraged to continue working for longer, it could both improve the financial basis of pension programs and expand the productive capacity of the economy to provide the goods and services needed by an aging population. And that, according to some, could provide an opportunity for major social and economic gains.[1]

In Canada, as we noted earlier, the federal government is involved in a project, under its Policy Research Initiative (PRI), looking at *Popu-*

lation Aging and Life-Course Flexibility, that could eventually present new policy approaches for the aging population.[2] The Clerk of the Privy Council created the organization known today as the Policy Research Initiative in 1996. It was originally designed to strengthen the federal government's ability to identify, understand, and address medium and longer-term cross-cutting policy research issues. It is organizationally affiliated with the Privy Council Office (PCO) and receives administrative support from the PCO. Under its current incarnation, PRI has three main areas of focus:

- deepening research on emerging horizontal issues and integrating the results into the government's policy agenda;

- devising means for building a capable policy research workforce; and

- creating the infrastructure to support horizontal policy research collaboration. ("Horizontal" projects refer to issues that cut across several different policy areas or federal departments).

The PRI currently has five horizontal research projects: 1) Population Aging and Life-Course Flexibility; 2) New Approaches for Addressing Poverty and Exclusion; 3) Social Capital as a Public Policy Tool; 4) North American Linkages; and 5) Sustainable Development (Freshwater Management). The PRI also has a mandate to identify data needs and priorities for future policy development through the Policy Research Data Group, an interdepartmental committee charged with addressing emerging data gaps linked to medium to longer-term challenges.[3]

The PRI ageing project was initiated under the direction of Peter Hicks, a Canadian who was closely involved in the OECD's aging project when he was with the organization's Directorate for Education, Employment, Labour, and Social Affairs in Paris. That work culminated in the OECD's landmark 1998 publication *Maintaining Prosperity in an Aging Society*. Perhaps not surprisingly, it appears the work of the PRI project has been heavily influenced by the OECD's approach to population aging. The PRI project was expected to report by the end of 2005, but it looks as if the work will now be extended beyond that deadline. The research is looking at a range of scenarios, using modelling techniques, to see what happens when work and other activities of life—everything from caregiving, further education, leisure and volunteering—are distributed in different ways over the course of life.

Hicks, who was subsequently appointed Assistant Deputy Minister, Strategic Direction at Social Development Canada, set out his vision on *Preparing for Tomorrow's Social Policy Agenda* in a comprehensive paper published by the Ottawa-based Social Research and Demonstration Corporation in late 2002, outlining new priorities for policy research and development that emerge from an examination of the economic well-being of the working-age population. He cited three forces he felt were likely to dominate policy-making in five years' time (that is, by 2007): a continuation of the competitiveness and social cohesion pressures that have resulted in today's preoccupation with life-long learning; a new concern about a decline in the percentage of total population that will be employed; and a new shift towards incentives to later retirement. His paper proposed new types of policy development work "that could begin now in order to prepare for such an agenda." It may be assumed that the work being done through the PRI aging project is based on his analysis.

At this point, it is not clear how influential the work of this aging project will be in shaping public policy on retirement and the aging population. But Hicks suggests that policies affecting the work-retirement transition will be at the centre of the medium-term policy agenda. He believes the task will be to find a new balance between the long-term goal of life-course flexibility and the medium-term goal of encouraging more time spent at work and in learning. He suggested that preparatory work is needed—presumably now being undertaken by the PRI project—so that, "when the time is ripe," there could be quick publication of a consultation paper (possibly a Green Paper) on moving to later and more flexible transitions from work to retirement.[4]

Over the past couple of decades, population aging has been receiving increasing attention in most of the industrialized countries. Increases in life expectancy, combined with declining fertility, have resulted in a growing percentage of the population moving into older age groups. But, as many people have pointed out, both increased life expectancy and declining fertility would generally be considered desirable developments. Better health and economic circumstances have enabled people to live longer—a development that most people would regard as a remarkable

New Perspectives On the Aging Population

achievement—while reduced fertility has long been a goal adopted to combat world over-population. As Peter Hicks points out, "The key question, therefore, is not why we now see aging as good news, but why it was seen as bad news a decade ago."[5]

Hicks attributes much of the aging panic of the 1990s to a growing realization in many countries that the financing of their public pay-as-you-go pension plans had not fully taken account of the consequences of the retirement of the baby-boom generation. The World Bank's 1994 publication *Averting the Old Age Crisis* helped crystallize those views, Hicks says, and its analysis and proposals became central elements in a polarized debate.[6]

But the World Bank's neo-liberal analysis advocated a market-based system, with heavy emphasis on privatization, holding up the Chilean system as a model. (In 1981, Chile, under the dictatorship of Augusto Pinochet, privatized its public pension system literally overnight, without any public consultation, replacing it with a system of mandatory private individual savings accounts). The International Labour Organization (ILO) was at the opposite end of the spectrum from the World Bank in the debate, starting from the premise that old age provision is a collective social duty and that, with reform, there were fundamental merits in continuing a larger role for public pay-as-you-go pensions.[7]

As Hicks describes it, by the end of the 1990s, the positions of the World Bank and the ILO came closer together, with increasing emphasis on pragmatic approaches in line with national needs—something that had always been applied in practice anyway, according to Hicks. Emphasis was increasingly placed on the importance of having a multi-tiered approach, rather than on the particular design of the various tiers. Other bodies such as the OECD also stressed the importance of having multiple sources of retirement income, and countries—including Canada—began developing their own responses to the issue of their aging populations. Canada's approach, as we saw earlier, has received kudos from the OECD as the kind of multi-tier system that countries should espouse.

Aging policy goes beyond pensions

While the 1990s were the decade when pensions were the main focus, by 2000 policy-makers seemed to be moving to a much broader agenda in thinking about their aging populations. It was not so much that they had solved all the problems of pensions and retirement income—although some seemed to act as if they had—but that they seemed to be interested in widening the policy debate beyond pensions, to consider much more radical changes. While the outcome could be to put a much more positive spin on aging and the aging population, that does not seem to have been the objective. Putting a lid on the costs of aging populations and maintaining generational equity were apparently two of the fundamental reasons for moving beyond pension reforms—or, as the OECD put it, "the overriding importance of curbing the growth of spending on public pensions, health and long-term care."[8]

In contrast, the approach taken by the United Nations, which has held two World Assemblies on Aging, seems to be much more altruistic and focused on the welfare of older people rather than on how to minimize the cost to society as the number of older people increases. In its report of the Second World Assembly on Aging, held in Madrid in 2002, the UN noted that —

"When aging is embraced as an achievement, the reliance on human skills, experiences and resources of the higher age groups is naturally recognized as an asset in the growth of mature, fully integrated, humane societies."[9]

As well, the UN said,

We recognize that concerted action is required to transform the opportunities and the quality of life of men and women as they age and to ensure the sustainability of their support systems, thus building the foundation for a society for all ages.[10]

As Peter Hicks explains it, the solutions for population aging are not special rights for older people, which would have the effect of ghettoizing them. Instead, aging should be treated as a life-course, society-wide issue as much as an older persons issue.[11] The thinking that forms the

New Perspectives On the Aging Population

basis for this approach was also developed in a 2001 UN publication *The World Aging Situation: Exploring a Society for All Ages.* And it was made official in a resolution adopted by the General Assembly in December 2003 as a follow-up to the 2002 Madrid Plan of Action, emphasizing the need "to set national and international priorities and to select appropriate approaches to ensure that countries achieve a society for all ages."[12]

The approach of the OECD seems to be something along the same lines, but perhaps somewhat narrower in focus. In his preface to the OECD's 1998 report *Maintaining Prosperity in an Aging Society,* the Secretary-General of the OECD (also a Canadian) outlined the approach and what he saw as the urgent need to address the issue of aging. Here's what he said:

> ...Meeting the challenge of aging populations will require comprehensive reform that addresses the fiscal, financial, and labour market implications of aging, as well as the implications for pensions, social benefits, and systems of health and long-term care. The goal must be to harness the skills and experiences of older people and to ensure adequate living standards for them without placing an unfair burden on younger people.

> Successful reforms will bring large rewards. They would avoid major fiscal problems, improve living standards and the quality of life, and result in a more equitable, cohesive society. The temptation to delay action is strong, but the message that the OECD seeks to communicate as widely as possible on behalf of its Member governments is that solutions will be much more difficult and painful if needed reforms are postponed.[13]

Time is of the essence, according to the OECD. Since the main demographic pressures will emerge in about 10 years' time (that would be around 2010), societies have "a very limited window of opportunity to put reforms in place."[14] The OECD set out seven principles to guide these reforms.[15] Many of these relate to recommended reforms to pension systems, but some relate to broader objectives. According to Peter Hicks, the OECD's principles "mirror quite closely recent policy thinking in Canada."[16] Of course, it is not without significance that Hicks, who was one of the leaders of the OECD aging project, initiated the federal government's research project on Population Aging and Life Course Flexibility.

These are the seven OECD principles:

1. **Public pension systems, taxation systems and social transfer programs should be reformed to remove financial incentives to early retirement, and financial disincentives to later retirement.** Many countries, including Canada, have already made changes to their pension programs. But the OECD points out that public pension systems interact with other social transfer programs and multiple reforms are needed "to accomplish the basic objective of providing an incentive structure that will increase the time spent at work." That could slow or reverse trends towards ever-longer periods of healthy life being spent in retirement, according to the OECD.[17]

Hicks says the first principle broadens the policy emphasis from financing pensions to the more fundamental macro-economic question of living standards.[18] The material living standards of tomorrow's working and retired people will depend on the goods and services produced by those who will be working at the time. While changes in retirement income financing might alter the relative living standards of workers compared with retirees, he says, "only later retirement could have a large effect increasing living standards for both."

2. **A variety of reforms will be needed to ensure that more job opportunities are available for older workers and that they are equipped with the necessary skills and competencies to take them.** If people are going to be expected to work longer, measures will have to be taken to increase the employability of older workers, the OECD says. Such measures would include increasing the priority given to life-long learning for all; developing policies to help older workers find jobs; and removing discrimination against hiring older workers. A key challenge, says the OECD, will be to gain a stronger empirical understanding of the linkages among learning, skills, productivity and wages as workers grow older.[19]

This second principle seems to dovetail neatly with what appears to be the key objective of the PRI's aging project emphasizing "life-course flexibility." According to Hicks, the policies the OECD refers to are main-

New Perspectives On the Aging Population

ly those addressed to lifelong learning and a "workforce for all ages" rather than those addressed to older workers alone.[20] Certainly, that seems to be the approach being adopted by the PRI project, discussed later in this chapter. It would also reflect the United Nations emphasis, mentioned earlier.

3. **Fiscal consolidation should be pursued, and public debt burdens should be reduced. This could involve phased reductions in public pension benefits and anticipatory hikes in contribution rates.** The OECD sees this not only as a call to urgent action on pensions before the main effects of population ageing take hold in 2010, but the development of agendas to contain health care costs and improve effectiveness.[21] It should be noted that, by the time the OECD was issuing its seven principles, Canada had already implemented reforms to the CPP that increased contribution rates and established the CPP investment fund, thus moving to a system of partial funding for the plan.

But the emphasis on debt reduction has now surfaced again. For example, in early 2004, David Dodge, Governor of the Bank of Canada, was making comments about the need to reduce the ratio of public debt to GDP still further, "to give us the flexibility to meet the demands of our aging population."[22] And the federal government's fiscal policy is still emphasizing debt reduction as a key priority. While a full discussion of this issue is beyond the scope of this book, it may be worth mentioning work that has been done to explode some of the myths about the potential costs of our aging population.

For example, several of the studies produced by McMaster University's program for Research on Social and Economic Dimensions of an Aging Population (SEDAP) have looked at the economic costs of population aging. In a 1999 study on this subject, Frank Denton and Byron Spencer concluded that:

Expressions of apprehension about the effects of population aging typically relate to the demand side of the economy and in particular to public expenditures on health care and old age security systems. Usually ignored is the fact that those same demographic forces will tend to reduce expenditures in some areas (such as education, employment insurance, correctional services) and also that CPP/QPP and OAS transfer payments are taxable and hence the cost of them may be significantly less than it appears to be if only the benefit payments are considered. In total, CPP/QPP, OAS and GIS and health care expenditures account today for about a quarter of total (consolidated) government expenditures in Canada for all levels of government considered. Also largely ignored in the public debate is the impact of population change on the supply side or productive capacity or the economy, and hence on the ability of the economy to generate tax revenue to support higher expenditure levels."[23]

It may also be important to note that, following the 1997/98 reforms of the CPP, the Chief Actuary says the plan is sustainable, as is, for at least the next 75 years. The peak year of retirement for the baby boom generation will be around 2030. The boomers have accumulated more than a trillion dollars in retirement savings[24] which they will start to draw down when they retire and which will then become taxable. Not only will older Canadians then constitute a much higher percentage of all taxpayers, but older people will be paying income taxes, sales taxes, GST and property taxes. More tax revenues of all kinds will come from older Canadians. Analysts note that increased costs for public pensions and health care will be accompanied by substantially increased income and sales tax revenues from this same set of baby-boom birth cohorts.[25] Some even suggest that, under some projected scenarios, the future elderly may generate enough tax revenue to pay fully for the projected increased costs of their future public pensions and health care. In other words, increased costs could be covered by a transfer within the older generation rather than a transfer from the younger generation to the older.

Denton and Spencer also said that—

When projected expenditures are compared to the projected productive capacity of the economy, it seems that the total expenditure for all budgetary categories combined will be a smaller percentage of GDP in 2031 than in 1991, even though there will be large increases in expenditures on health and social security. (Our projections relate to the effects of population change only; there well may be non-demographic influences that will raise or lower future expenditures, but that is another matter).[26]

4. Retirement income should be provided by a mix of tax-and-transfer systems, funded systems, private savings and earnings. The objective

New Perspectives On the Aging Population

is risk diversification, a better balance of burden-sharing between generations, and to give individuals more flexibility over their retirement decision. As we noted earlier, Canada gets high marks for its adherence to this fourth principle—at least as far as risk diversification and a mix of tax and transfer systems goes. But the OECD's focus is very much on giving people "choice" and "flexibility": which are often used as code words for shifting responsibility from the state onto individuals. In explaining this fourth principle, the OECD even suggests phasing out or targeting subsidized privileges for seniors, such as discounts on public services, and consideration of reducing excessive preferential tax treatment of occupational pensions and individual retirement savings plans.

5. In health and long-term care, there should be a greater focus on cost-effectiveness. Medical expenditure and research should be increasingly directed to ways of reducing physical dependence, and explicit policies for providing care to frail older people should be developed. The central challenge here, says the OECD, will be to ensure that these expenditures are effective and aimed at the most pressing problems.[27] Many countries now are moving on from pension reforms to consider the implications of aging for health and long-term care.[28]

6. The development of advanced-funded pension systems should go hand-in-hand with that of strengthening of the financial market infrastructure, including the establishment of a modern and effective regulatory framework. Canada, as noted earlier, has already moved towards a partially advance funded system for the CPP. As well, if more reliance is to be placed on private pension arrangements, it would be important to strengthen financial market infrastructure and improve the regulatory framework—especially in light of recent problems with pension plans in Canada, discussed in Chapter 2. In mid-2005, both the federal and Québec governments were holding consultations on pension regulation and defined benefit pension plans, presumably as a prelude to changes in the regulatory framework for these plans.

7. Strategic frameworks should be put in place at the national level now in order to harmonize these aging reforms over time, and to ensure adequate attention to implementation and the build-up of public un-

derstanding and support. The OECD explains that, taken one at a time, all of these reform directions would be desirable, quite apart from any aging considerations. But taken collectively, they represent a considerable new challenge for government policy-making—a challenge that resides in the policy-making process as much as in the specific content of each reform.[29] As well, given the long time frames involved and the complexity of the issues, there will also be a challenge in "building public understanding, engagement, and viable political support."

It is this seventh principle that appears to form the basis for the PRI's project on aging and life course flexibility. The end result of this research may well be a framework for a very different approach to the aging population. But a comprehensive plan would have to be phased in over time. According to Peter Hicks, much of the adjustment process regarding aging populations will take place automatically as a result of market forces. But many smaller reforms will likely be needed to help counter a deeply embedded culture of early retirement. In a sense, it may be a question of adopting what another political scientist describes as the concepts of "layering and conversion."[30] Layering involves accommodating and adapting to the logic of the pre-existing system by adding new programs rather than dismantling the old and, thus, working around those elements of the existing system that cannot be changed. Conversion occurs where existing programs are redirected to a new logic.

The approach to these reforms, says Hicks, requires a strategic plan to ensure that separate activities in many policy areas will reinforce each other. It may be remembered that, 10 years ago, in his 1994 budget, Paul Martin, who was then Finance Minister, had this to say about the aging population:

> As Canadians live longer and healthier lives, the roles and needs of seniors will change. In the months ahead, we will be releasing a paper that will look at what an aging society will need in terms of services; and what changes are required to the public pension system to ensure it is affordable.[31]

The promised paper on aging, focusing on "the needs of seniors" and intended to "examine the challenges and opportunities posed by Cana-

New Perspectives On the Aging Population

da's aging society,"[32] never materialized. Instead, the attention of policy-makers turned to cutting the cost of public pensions. The report that will emerge from the PRI project on aging—perhaps some time during 2005/06—will almost certainly present a very different perspective on the issue of Canada's aging population than would have been developed in any aging paper drafted in the mid-1990s. But the underlying focus of the latest report may still be on controlling the costs of population aging, albeit by much more varied and complex measures.

Changing the social architecture

There is growing pressure to restructure Canada's social architecture, redesigning social programs to take account of the impact of globalization, the knowledge-based economy, and other changes in the economy and society. For example, in early 2004, the Canadian Policy Research Networks Inc. (CPRN) launched an ambitious series of nine Social Architecture Papers designed to look at how the world has changed since Canada's social programs were established, and what new model is needed for the future. In an introduction to the series, CPRN President Judith Maxwell said that, since 1980, governments have tinkered with many of the policies put in place in the first two decades after the Second World War. They have recognized the existence of new realities and tried to address them. But she believes that Canada now needs to go back to first principles.[33]

Jane Jenson, until mid-2004 director of CPRN's Family Network, who conceived and directed the Social Architecture Papers, argues that, in light of the new realities of Canada in 2004, the roles and responsibilities of market, family, state, and community need to catch up.[34] In relation to the aging society, Jenson points out that key issues involve more than just pensions. Active aging is now an important issue. A social architecture seeking to promote an active aging model, says Jenson, will need to address labour markets (how to ensure greater flexibility, if longer employment is the goal) and housing markets (to ensure appropriate housing options), as well as the community (so dependent on the volunteer work of active seniors).[35] She also believes a well-designed social architecture will be sensitive to the complexities of aging and intergenerational equity. "It will be one that can adopt a life-course analysis and thereby demonstrate social interdependencies more than conflicts," Jenson says.[36]

In another paper in the series, Bruno Palier, a permanent Research Fellow of the Centre national de recherche scientifique in France and a researcher at Centre d'Étude de la Vie Politque Française of the Fondation nationale des sciences politques in Paris, notes that reforms in various European countries reflect an attempt to adapt welfare regimes to new macro-economic norms, putting more emphasis on the market and sound public finances, employment, and so on.[37] Palier says that, although European countries have taken different approaches to social policy reforms, they share important common trends: to make social policies more employment-oriented and to institute supply-side social policy instruments.[38] He notes two general trends that characterize all the policies implemented in the European countries: 1) the desire to limit government social expenditures and the redefine the role of the state, and 2) the re-alignment of social programs with the circumstances of the labour market.[39]

In the post-Keynesian world of the late 1980s and 1990s, Palier says, there was a growing demand for the role of the state to be downgraded since it was perceived as too costly and inefficient, and for a reallocation of social responsibilities towards other social forces, such as the market, the family, or community associations.[40] He also notes that, regardless of whether policies implemented throughout Europe were totally new or whether they simply reformed existing programs, they were based on an approach to social protection whose function was no longer to protect individuals against risk, but to change their behaviour.[41]

Other policy institutes in Canada are exploring the implications of a new social architecture, but from a somewhat different perspective. For example, work at the Canadian Council on Social Development (CCSD) used as a starting point the kind of ideas found in a 2001 report on *A New Welfare Architecture for Europe*, commissioned by the President of the European Union. The findings of the report are presented and discussed in the 2002 book *Why We Need A New Welfare State*, edited by Gosta Esping-Andersen with Duncan Gallie, Anton Hemerijck, and John Myles. In 2002, CCSD held a seminar jointly with CPRN to discuss major themes of the report and their relevance to Canada. And in early 2003, as part of its ongoing work on changing the social architecture, it held an invitation-only working conference on Strategies to Ensure Economic Security for all Canadians, at which discussion emphasized a life-cycle approach.[42] In 2004, it had a project under way to look at what kind of Canada citizens would like to see in the 21st century, and it was calling for a national debate on the new Canada Social Transfer, instituted on April 1, 2004.[43]

The "Third Way" or the post-welfare state

In developing the case for a new social architecture for Canada, Jane Jenson notes that Canada, like many other countries, faces a moment of fundamental choice. She says that —

> The social knowledge that informed both the first three decades after 1945 and the years of neo-liberal politics that followed is being re-evaluated. Whereas for Keynesians, social policy was a support for widespread well-being, for neo-liberals social spending was a burden, to be minimized as much as possible. Now, a third position is taking hold. We recognize that social policy makes contributions to well-being in the knowledge-based economy and society, but also that there can be no simple return to previous policy formulae, precisely because so many socioeconomic situations are profoundly different from what they were in the post-1945 decades.[44]

As Béland and Myles describe it, the old welfare state constructed between the 1930s and 1970s emphasized protecting people *from the market*. The new approach, which has also been characterized as "The Third Way," following the approach of New Labour in the UK, emphasizes programs that provide incentives and help people to succeed *in the market*.[45] As one analyst describes it, a neo-liberal revolution in economics defined the Thatcher era, but it was Tony Blair who completed the revolution in the social arena.[46] New Labour's adoption of the Third Way was characterized by the maintenance of a broad safety net, active support to provide opportunities for the unemployed, and talking up the need for unemployed individuals to be responsible in taking opportunities for self-reliance.[47]

Sociologist Ken Battle, President of the Ottawa-based Caledon Institute of Social Policy, refers to this new social policy model as the "post-welfare state."[48] According to Battle, the post-welfare state model is based on a critique of key social programs—especially UI and welfare—that sees them as costly, inefficient, and ineffective. The new model seeks mechanisms that are more effective and better suited to the changing economic, social, and political realties of the new century. Instead of "civilizing capitalism," as the old welfare state approach did, the post-welfare state, says Battle, is seen as "nurturing capitalism" by providing social and educational infrastructure that enhances economic growth and investing in human capital.

But the Third Way approach has been strongly criticized by those scholars who were given the task of developing the ideas in the European Union's report on *A New Welfare Architecture for Europe*. Gosta Esping-Andersen says that the Third Way of the 1990s heralded the arrival of a second grand formula for the post-industrial Good Society. No doubt it succeeded better in catching the mood of the times, Esping-Andersen says, in large part by retaining some of the more credible and popular aspects of neo-liberalism, including its accent on individual responsibility and a more competitive reward structure, while fusing these with a concomitant public responsibility. But, contrary to the extreme transparency of neo-liberalism, says Esping-Andersen, the Third Way is broadly viewed as "an emperor with no clothes."[49]

In a stinging critique of the Third Way approach, Esping-Andersen explains that—

> First and foremost, it proposes one sharp break with the past: rather than tame, regulate, or marginalize markets so as to ensure human welfare, the idea is to adapt and empower citizens so that they may be far better equipped to satisfy their welfare needs within the market. At its core, it is a supply-driven policy attempting to furnish citizens with the requisites needed for individual success. Hence, its flagship policies are training and life-long learning. The assumption seems to be that the social risks and class inequalities that emanate from mar-

kets can be overridden if we target policy so all compete on a more
equal footing.[50]

During the 1990s, according to Béland and Myles, the major targets
for "Third Way" reforms in Canada were unemployment insurance and
child benefits.[51] Changes in eligibility rules for what used to be called UI
were made much more restrictive, greatly reducing coverage rates among
the unemployed, while income-tested child benefits for the working poor
were greatly expanded to enhance work incentives. But these authors say
that pension policy and population aging only get on the radar screen
of "Third Way" advocates when they are widely perceived to be reducing
employment levels, either by encouraging early retirement or by driving
up payroll taxes. And neither feature has figured prominently in Canadian policy debates, they say.

However, the policy dialogue in Canada now seems to be placing
a growing emphasis on discouraging early retirement and providing
incentives for people to work longer. With its focus on life-long learning, individual responsibility, equality of opportunity, and providing
"choice" and "flexibility," it would appear the work of the PRI ageing
project will be based on the post-welfare state model or "Third Way."
For example, a key objective of the project is to examine how particular
policy instruments might complement market forces in moving in "desirable directions." As well, according to Peter Hicks, "People's confidence
in government policy to protect them is down." He suggests the lack of
confidence in government has "great importance to policy" and may
reflect value shifts about the roles of individual, market, and state. It is
these shifts that have not yet been reflected in the public policies now
under review, Hicks believes.[52]

The life-course perspective

Integral to the new approach to aging policies is a focus on the "life-
course" perspective, defined by sociologists Victor Marshall and Margaret Mueller as "a set of principles that, taken together, offer a more
realistic and comprehensive way of looking at the aging of individuals

and cohorts."[53] These two authors offer some insights from the life-course perspective in a 2002 CPRN Discussion Paper *Rethinking Social Policy for an Aging Workforce and Society*. As they explain, the life-course perspective brings to the fore issues that econometric or individual choice models either ignore or deem irrelevant. By explicitly linking the individual and societal levels of analysis, the life-course perspective helps to counter a demographic determinism that assumes "demography is destiny." It may be worth noting here that "demographic determinism" has fuelled much of the debate about Canada's aging population and got a huge boost with the publication in 1996 of the highly popular book *Boom, Bust and Echo* co-authored by economist and demographer David Foot.

But Marshall and Mueller also point out that much of public policy has been organized around the concept of a standardized life-course. It has primarily been the organization of education and work and the development of the welfare state that have been responsible for structuring life into distinct stages based on chronological age.[54] Retirement as a major social institution, they believe, has effectively created a separate age category in the overall age structure. But, while there is nothing inevitable about such things as a "normal" age for retirement, in effect, institutional arrangements, such as public and private pension plans, laws and legal judgments on age discrimination, mandatory retirement, and so on, have established 65 as the usual age of retirement. That then becomes the standard against which people see retirement as early, on time, or late.[55]

It is important to note that the idea of a standardized life-course never did apply to women. Because of their caregiving and other unpaid work, women have different patterns of paid and unpaid work than men do. Their unpaid work may have a major impact on other sequences in their life-course, such as education and retirement. As we noted in Chapter 1, the orderly life-course that policy makers seem to regard so favourably seems to be based on the experience of the 19th century male industrial worker.

Other authors note that the modern welfare state is founded on a particular model of the entire life-course and not just the period of life after 65 that we now call "old age." John Myles and Debra Street say this is a model that developed slowly in the early years of the 20th century

New Perspectives On the Aging Population

and only came to maturity after World War II. It had little to do with the actions or desires of the elderly and a great deal to do with the strategies of employers, workers, and governments for managing the distribution of risk over the economic life course.[56] Other studies have suggested that older workers are often used as a balancing factor to regulate labour supply. As we noted earlier, many employers have restructured or downsized their operations by easing out older workers. In fact, some observers suggest this form of downsizing is the main reason the retirement age of older men in Canada has been declining.

Myles and Street argue that, while "conservative" strategies to deal with an aging population have emphasized privatization of the pension function and greater emphasis on providing income-tested benefits to the low-income elderly, new "progressive" alternatives have advocated a redesign of the welfare state to allow for a more flexible model of retirement and the economic life-course more generally.[57] The new approach, these authors say, takes the position that, rather than focusing on the demand side, public dollars should be directed toward investment in skills and education, technology development, and other supply-side strategies that help workers and families adjust to the effects of globalization and technical change. Such investments, it is hoped, will generate a new round of economic growth, which in turn will create the government revenues required to pay down debt.[58]

The supply-side approach could have major significance for how society views retirement. Myles and Street note that proponents of this approach argue that —

> Instead of investing in stability (the "social security" welfare state) we now need to invest in change (the "social investment" welfare state). This means a work life punctuated by frequent job changes and, necessarily, constant retraining. In such a world, retirement and "old age," as we know it, could well disappear. The older population is healthier than in the past and potentially able to continue working well beyond age 65. Instead of an extended period of retirement after age 60 or 65, it is pointed out, the retirement years could be redistributed over the entire life-course for periods of retraining, child-rearing, and even leisure.[59]

Policy-makers in Canada now seem to be adopting a similar vision. According to Peter Hicks, the work-retirement transition is central to the medium-term agenda. And policies must support the medium-term goal of increasing the total time over life that is devoted to work, learning, and more flexibility over life in caregiving, with the increase in learning being primarily in the middle years of life and in early childhood; with more flexibility in how caregiving, including both child care and elder care, is mixed with work and learning; with most of reallocated time coming from a reduction in leisure in retirement. In other words, Hicks notes, "the freed-up leisure in retirement could not be simply reallocated to leisure at other stages of life."[60]

However, moving to a more flexible view of the life-course, which seems to be the direction now favoured by policy-makers, is not without its dangers. Marshall and Mueller argue that greater flexibility in the life-course is (at least) a two-edged sword. They say flexibility allows workers to piece together their own working biographies, or, more accurately, it requires them to try to do so. Flexibility is championed as appropriate for life in the "risk society" in which little is certain and the institutional supports for the life-course are reduced, these authors say. But, given the problem associated with instability and uncertainty, to what extent should we be promoting the "risk society"?[61]

The question goes to the heart of the so-called "Third Way" approach to social policy. On the face of it, no one could disagree with the sentiment expressed by the National Advisory Council on Aging in a 1999 publication that, "Ideally, people of all ages should be able to arrange their lives in a more flexible way, take development or transition leave, and enjoy leisure throughout their lives."[62] The danger is that, where support systems are lacking, "flexibility" and "choice" can result in insecurity and even poverty.

Trying to define the view of a more flexible life-course presents huge challenges to policy-makers. As Myles and Street point out:

> To many, the flexible life course appears to be one punctuated not by "time out" for education or leisure, but by insecurity and large fluctuations in income. Flexibility means more "contingent labour" without the benefits (including pension coverage) associated with traditional

New Perspectives On the Aging Population

full-time employment. If the industrial life-course brought rigidity and security, the post-industrial life-course threatens to bring flexibility and insecurity. The challenge to policy-makers, it would seem, is to create a welfare state that brings flexibility and security.[63]

Population Aging and Life Course Flexibility

It is not clear yet how the PRI project on life-course flexibility and population aging will respond to that challenge. Essentially, the project is trying to see what can be done to encourage people to allocate their activities in different ways over the course of their lifetimes. Instead of having many years of hard work and no time for anything much else, followed by years of "leisure" with not enough to do, people would somehow be able to allocate their work and leisure more evenly over the course of their lives.

Just how that might be done is a concept that may be difficult to grasp. Underlying the push to greater life-course flexibility, however, seems to be a view that long years spent in "retirement" are somehow being "wasted." And later retirement is essential to the project. According to Peter Hicks, "In the absence of a shift to later retirement, there will be continued growth in the extraordinarily large pool of leisure that has been building up among retirees, where it is mainly passive, unhealthy, and often unwanted—and a growing source of social exclusion."[64]

For example, Statistics Canada's 1996 General Social Survey found older people spent an average of eight hours a day in leisure activities—mainly watching television.[65] Two hours were spent socializing, and only one hour in active leisure. Interestingly enough, retired people said they were generally satisfied with life. But studies by the OECD suggest people would still prefer to continue working if appropriate jobs were available.[66] That suggests job quality is the key to getting people to work longer.

Advocates of a flexible life-course approach argue there would be many potential gains if people had the choice to spread work, learning, caregiving, and leisure more rationally over their lives.[67] They also believe that public policies have resulted in long-standing and entrenched social norms relating to retirement. However, according to Peter Hicks, "That which public policy creates, public policy can ultimately undo."[68] And that is clearly the objective of the research on aging and the flexible life-course he was directing. Hicks admits, however, that it will not be easy to find quick solutions and that careful policy research will be needed to understand the far-reaching social and economic effects of changes in the distribution of time spent at work and other activities of life over the course of life.[69]

There are also indications that policy-makers will be faced with quite a challenge when it comes to explaining their approach and getting the general public on side. For example, focus groups held by PRI in 2004 and designed to solicit views on life-course flexibility and Canada's aging population seemed to indicate some confusion about the idea. For example, when asked about their personal interest in the concept of working later in life to have more time off earlier, most responded with questions about how the mechanics or implementation of the concept would work.[70] Apparently, the concept of the flexible life-course seemed to hold the greatest appeal to people of upper socioeconomic status (SES), particularly those in their prime working years. According to a PRI report, "They more easily grasped its personal and societal significance and generally felt the trade-off made sense at a number of levels." It is perhaps a telling comment that:

> The concept held less appeal for lower SES participants, particularly the pre-retirement segment. Those who were attracted to it put forward the same reasoning as other supporters. Those who were not interested, or who in some cases opposed the idea, could not see how they personally would benefit and still harboured concerns about a possibly hidden government agenda to keep older people in the workforce more or less forcibly.[71]

Based on the results of the focus group testing PRI concluded that:

> Encouraging people to remain in the labour force later in life (either by working past retirement or by "borrowing" time earlier in life) receives mixed reactions as a policy response to Canada's aging population. It

New Perspectives On the Aging Population

seems clear that the policy, whether tied to work-family life flexibility earlier in life or not, is less appealing and resonant when presented as a response to the potentially negative labour market impacts of an aging population. Conversely, reaction is much more positive and people are more open to the concept when this and other related options are based on the rationale of giving Canadians greater choice and helping them to achieve their career and life goals. In short, this policy should not be positioned as reacting to a crisis as people will logically assume that inherent in crisis response is some form of sacrifice.[72]

That, too, is a revealing comment and highlights the kind of approach government might make to convince people to go on working.

The PRI project on aging and life-course flexibility involves several federal government departments, the main ones being Human Resources and Skills Development Canada, the Department of Finance Canada, and Statistics Canada. Their work is directed at acquiring a better understanding of the potentially complex effects of moving to a flexible life-course approach, the kinds of policy changes that may be required, and the experience of other countries in addressing similar challenges.[73]

The project has three components[74]:

1. There will be a detailed quantitative examination of a range of scenarios where work and other activities of life are distributed in different ways over the course of life. This examination will include scenarios similar to current arrangements and others that represent what Hicks describes as "more desirable alternatives." A combination of different modeling techniques (both macroeconomic modeling and the LifePath micro-simulation model at Statistics Canada) is being used to examine a range of economic, fiscal, labour market, and social consequences of these scenarios. The analysis will also look at the different effects of population aging on different economic sectors.

2. The work plan also includes an assessment of how market forces and existing policies are likely to lead toward different life-course patterns. Individuals and labour markets are always adjusting to change such as the age structure of the work force, and the research is intended to as-

sess where policy initiatives can help—or impede—the natural process of adjustment.

3. Researchers will also consider how current policies might present barriers to change and what new policies might be needed—including pension and other transfer policies, immigration policy, labour market and learning policies—to complement market forces in moving in "desirable directions."

Hicks believes that, if people had a true choice and there were jobs available, they would probably choose to extend their working life, although not necessarily continuing in the same jobs they'd had up to that point. They would develop a better balance between work and other activities over their lifetimes, he says, and perhaps phase into retirement gradually, rather than concentrating all their leisure at the end of life after taking a formal retirement. In fact, he believes recent Statistics Canada surveys (referred to in Chapter 1) show signs this has already started to happen. But he emphasizes the focus of the aging project is on gradual change over a long-term time frame. "We're trying to set long-term directions for incremental policy changes that everybody understands," says Hicks, not radical reforms in the next few years.[75]

Just the same, the baby boomers are already very close to their retirement transition. The leading edge of the generation born between 1947 and 1966 will start going through some form of retirement by about 2010. That doesn't leave much time to change the policy focus and shift to a different mind-set. But, even in that short period of time, unanticipated change can affect the policy agenda. For example, privatization of public pensions was very definitely high on the agenda for neo-liberal commentators and think-tanks when pension reforms were being discussed in the mid-to-late 1990s. Stock markets were booming and many people seemed to believe investment returns would continue increasing almost indefinitely. But when the market tanked at the end of the decade, it became much more difficult to convince people that sacrificing public pensions for individual savings accounts was such a good idea. It is also surprising how many projections—from doom-and-gloom scenarios to inter-generational transfers—seem to assume "everything else being equal." Of course, other things never remain equal. Public programs

New Perspectives On the Aging Population

may change, investment returns may drop, or the age of retirement may stabilize—which may be why we should view many such projections with a healthy dose of skepticism.

Hicks believes "the so-called aging crisis of the 1990s tells us much about the role of projections in policy-making."[76] He suggests the social, economic, technological, and environmental pressures that drive policies cannot be predicted with any certainty for more than a handful of years into the future. The lesson to be learned, he says, is that we should be modest in our expectations about projecting too far into the future. While we shouldn't refuse to make such projections, he says, "Good management of the risks of an uncertain future lies not so much in our projection capacity, but in our capacity to design a set of flexible policy instruments that can adapt to future pressures as they emerge."[77]

The first phase of the PRI project on population aging and life-course flexibility culminated with a conference in December 2004 on new approaches to social policy. Then, using a framework developed during 2004, the project team was preparing a serialized project report. The first paper was to focus on older workers and the labour market. This document was to present the likely economic, fiscal, labour market, and distributional consequences associated with the retirement of baby boomers and the aging of the population. It was also to assess the potential of various approaches to help respond to these consequences, including providing workers with a real choice for working later in life. According to PRI, "Such choices could be facilitated by reducing barriers that may prevent individuals from working later in life, or by re-balancing the financial incentive structure."[78] Subsequent papers were to look at work and family issues with a report due in the fall of 2005, and report on *A Labour Market for All,* scheduled for the winter of 2005/06.[79]

A new policy agenda for the aging population

Essentially, the new policy agenda is attempting to bring together a wide range of issues and policies so that individual life-courses can be configured in different ways. How can learning be spread over a lifetime, for instance, instead of being concentrated at the beginning? How could spells of leisure be interspersed with work or learning or caregiving, instead of being mainly concentrated at the end of a life when a person enters "retirement"? What kinds of policies and programs are needed to contribute to a more flexible life-course—for example, education policies, labour market policies, tax policies, pension policies, and so on? Fundamental to the debate is the view that older people should not be separated from other age groups and treated as a special target for policy reform.[80] In the ideal world envisaged by the United Nations, we would build the "society for all ages."

But encouraging "active aging" is also fundamental to the new approach. And public policy will be designed to foster active ageing by removing the constraints on life-course flexibility, and especially by persuading people to work longer.[81] The current emphasis on addressing population aging through policies to promote life-course flexibility will almost certainly have an important impact on the way we think about retirement and aging transitions. But adopting a new policy agenda to implement reform would require a really strong political commitment to implement change over a fairly long time-frame, and such commitment seems unlikely in the current political climate.

Even where political commitment is proclaimed, that "commitment" often does not get translated into concrete actions. A perfect example is the federal government's long-standing "commitment" to a national child care program. First advocated more than 35 years ago by the Royal Commission on the Status of Women, successive federal governments over the years have promised a national child care strategy but have never delivered on their promises, as women in paid employment know only too well. Even now, when a so-called national system of early learning and childcare has been announced, it still does not seem to be operational.

Myles and Street, in their 1995 paper *Should the Economic Life Course be Redesigned?* conclude that some variant of the status quo will be necessary well into the future.[82] They say that, as workers, employers and governments develop new strategies to cope with new economic realities, a different sort of welfare state will emerge and, with it, a different form for the economic life-course. But they also say that whether this also means a new and more diverse social construction of "old age" remains in question.

New Perspectives On the Aging Population

And when it comes to official policies on aging that involve a sweeping change in mind-set, there are other challenges. In its 1998 report on *Maintaining Prosperity in an Aging Society,* the OECD sounds an ominous warning. Commenting on the need to mobilize governmental capacities relevant to the aging issue, it says a key challenge will be to avoid "capture of the issues by those most directly affected rather than reflecting broader national interests."[83] No doubt that is why policy-makers working on the life-course flexibility project seem to believe they will have a tough selling job to do.

Developing the strategic framework

Nevertheless, pieces of the strategic framework are already falling into place. High on the list are specific measures that now seem to be getting much attention in social policy circles. For example, asset-based social policies are now being seen as a way to provide poor families with a way out of poverty, but also potentially as another way to help individuals support more flexible life-course arrangements. Lifetime accounts are a way of implementing the asset-based approach and could be used by individuals over the course of their lives to fund learning, spells of unemployment, child care or elder care, or retirement. Tax policies—for example, the proposed Tax-Prepaid Savings Plans (TPSPS) referred to in Chapter 2—that are supposed to help lower-income people save for their own retirement could be another weapon in the arsenal.

It is not a coincidence that all of these initiatives are very much in the spirit of Tony Blair's Third Way, discussed earlier. Replacing a social insurance program, such as Employment Insurance, with a system of individual accounts would indeed be a radical departure, and one likely to be strongly resisted if it were ever to be seriously suggested. But advocates of this approach may see it as a logical continuation of policies based on "hand-ups rather than hand-outs" and a focus on "responsibilities" to balance rights.[84] In any event, the foundation for all these initiatives seems to be to shift responsibility away from society as a whole onto individuals, thus providing them with "choice" and "flexibility."

Asset-based policies

Public programs to support older people, and other social programs such as unemployment insurance, have traditionally focused on income transfers from governments to those requiring support. But in the post-welfare state or Third Way, such policies are seen as fostering dependency. The new approach now being promoted in social policy circles is based on helping people accumulate assets—not just financial assets, but assets in the form of human capital, housing, information resources, community resources, social capital, and so on.[85] Having these assets enables people to become more self-reliant, or so the theory goes. That fits very well with Third Way market-oriented ideas, and would be particularly suited to facilitating a flexible life-course, according to the advocates of this approach.

For example, assisting in the accumulation of human capital through policies that promote life-long learning would prepare people for a longer working life and for the possibility of interspersing work with other activities over the course of a lifetime. Housing can provide security in old age and may influence independent living and long-term care as people grow older. People who acquire "social capital"—another popular concept in current social policy thinking—may be better prepared for old age. ("Social capital," loosely defined, refers to social support networks individuals may have, their contacts and involvement with the community in which they live, and so on). It is even suggested that information is an asset and should be thought of as "a separate product line of government."[86] Hicks argues that "More than income, it might be thought of as a universal social policy product." A cynic might argue that, if people are going to be forced to rely more and more on their own resources, information may well be the most important issue for their well-being.[87]

Asset-based social policies are generally promoted as a way of lifting people out of poverty. The philosophy behind this approach is the view that "income meets immediate needs, but assets help build futures."[88] Proponents of asset-based social policies also emphasize that they are intended to supplement essential income support strategies, not to replace them. But the possibilities of substitution are clearly there. Some participants at a recent conference on asset-based social policies sponsored by the Policy Research Initiative apparently believed that asset-based policies offer a different look at poverty and provide a more strategic approach for thinking about the long-term future of social policy. For example, they asked, "Would an asset-based stakeholder account—a kind of guaranteed lifetime account that combined income and assets—be a good replacement for the traditional utopian goal of a guaranteed annual income?"[89]

Canada already has some experimental programs to promote asset accumulation by poor families, administered through Social and Economic Development Innovations (SEDI). SEDI describes itself as a national charitable organization dedicated to enabling poor, unemployed, and under-employed people to become self-sufficient. It advocates Individual Development Accounts (IDAs) to help low-income families and individuals build savings by matching each dollar saved over time with a savings credit.

SEDI is currently involved in a demonstration project funded through the Applied Research Branch of Human Resources Development Canada (HRDC) known as *learn$ave*, operating at various sites across Canada. A total of $35 million over nine years has been earmarked for the project, which is part of the branch's work on measures to enhance life-long learning. Low-income participants enrolled in the program receive from $2 to $5 of federal funds for each $1 saved (up to $1,500 in savings) over a 1-to-3-year period. The funds can be used to finance a learning opportunity through adult education, training, or micro-enterprise start-up.

Similar programs using IDAs are now in effect in the United States and the UK. And in Canada, the 2004 federal budget took the idea one step further by proposing a Canada Learning Bond to kick-start education saving for low-income families. Starting in 2004, a lump sum payment of $500 would be provided to children in these families, who would be able to receive payments of up to $2,000 throughout their childhood. Advocates of asset-based programs directed at poor people make the point that middle- and higher-income people who have more disposable income are able to benefit from asset accumulation incentives such as Registered Education Savings Plans (RESPs) and RRSPS. Asset-based programs such as IDAs simply offer similar opportunities to those with lower incomes, or so the argument goes.

Asset-based policies directed at the poor could obviously be expanded and adapted to provide an opportunity for more people to acquire assets at different stages in their lives.[90] For example, one of the objectives of the UK government's asset-based policies is developing savings products suitable for each stage in a person's life-cycle.[91] As the scale of saving increases, proceeds from one product may be rolled into the next, helping people to progress up the savings ladder. It is almost a given that we will hear more about asset-based policies as aging policy moves to an even greater emphasis on the flexible life-course.

Lifetime accounts

Advocates of the flexible life-course approach seem to be intrigued by the idea of lifetime accounts, which they believe could be used over the course of a person's life to finance retirement, learning, spells of unemployment, child care or elder care—or virtually any purpose that is now served by point-in-time income policies. And, according to Peter Hicks, "They can be used to privatize existing public policies or to strengthen collective social cohesion, depending on design features."[92]

Lifetime accounts are, in effect, a mechanism by which asset building can take place. Canada already has various kinds of lifetime accounts, RRSPS being the most obvious example. Tax incentives are provided to encourage people to save for retirement through RRSPS over the course of a lifetime and to draw on the funds once they reach old age. Under certain conditions, funds in an RRSP may also be used without tax consequences to fund the purchase of a home or to pay for higher education—both forms of asset building that might also be described as asset-based policies. Registered Education Savings Plans (RESPS) are another form of lifetime account through which the government provides tax incentives to support individual savings to finance the education of children.

Advocates of the privatization of public pensions have suggested thatindividual savings accounts, such as RRSPS, might replace public

New Perspectives On the Aging Population

pensions, thus absolving society generally of the responsibility of supporting its older citizens and shifting that risk and responsibility onto the individual. Similar proposals have been made in relation to unemployment insurance. The suggestion here is that, instead of contributing to a public social insurance program to protect themselves against job loss, individuals could contribute to a personal ("lifetime") unemployment insurance account. Funds could be withdrawn if the person becomes unemployed. There could also be features that would allow the person to borrow from the account if accumulated funds were not high enough to cover the expenses—for example, if a spell of unemployment came early on in a person's career when not much had been accumulated in the lifetime unemployment account, with the loan being repaid later.

There is a wide range of possible designs of lifetime accounts. For example, there could be limits on what the funds could be used for. (It may be worth noting here that, while RRSPS are intended to help people save for retirement, there is no restriction on the use of funds for other purposes. Some people use them as a source of emergency cash, perhaps in times of job loss or other unforeseen circumstances. The only requirement when funds are withdrawn is that they be included in taxable income). Individuals or families might establish accounts (although provisions would have to be made for changing family relationships, as they are now with spousal RRSPS when a relationship ends). Governments might match individual or family contributions to the accounts. In fact, this already happens in Canada where the federal government will add a matching contribution to an RESP within certain limits. Government subsidies to the accounts might be paid during periods of leave, education, caregiving, and so on, when the individual cannot continue contributions but is drawing on the funds in the account. Matching government contributions to the accounts could also be designed to provide higher benefits to those with lower incomes. The possibilities seem to be almost endless.

It is easy to understand the attraction of lifetime accounts to the proponents of the flexible life-course approach. With funds in such an account, individuals would then be free to choose how they spent their accumulated savings: whether on financing a maternity leave, a return to further education, a sabbatical leave in mid-life, or a spell of part-time work to allow care for an older dependent family member. The flexible life-course might then become a reality, at least for those who had been able to save enough in the relevant account. But of course the price of "flexibility" and "choice" would be the loss of security and even of social cohesion, so beloved of social policy practitioners these days. Canada's key social insurance programs, represented by public pensions and unemployment insurance—to use its old name—are programs whereby the risks of providing for retirement income or for income support when a job is lost are pooled among all members of society to ensure that all citizens are equally protected. That equality and security are no longer assured when the risks are transferred from society as a whole to the individual.

There are other concerns, too. Tax incentives for such accounts generally give the greatest benefits to those with the highest incomes. In effect, they represent a transfer from lower-income to higher-income people. For example, since RRSP contribution limits are based on a percentage of income, those with higher incomes may contribute more in dollar terms than those who earn less. As well, the progressive income tax system means the same dollar contribution generates a higher rebate for those at higher marginal tax rates. A $1,000 contribution made by someone in a 30% tax bracket would result in a tax refund of $300, while a $1,000 contribution made by someone in a 50% tax bracket results in a refund of $500. In addition, lower-income earners generally can't afford to contribute to RRSPS, although the income taxes they pay must finance the tax deductions claimed by those who do contribute. In 1999, for example, of taxpayers eligible to make an RRSP contribution, 79% of those earning $80,000 or more contributed, but only 21% of those earning less than $20,000 did so.[93]

However, while the flexible life-course people seem to be intrigued by the idea of lifetime accounts, they also admit that the potential gains for such accounts would depend greatly on the particular designs adopted.[94] Some designs are highly redistributive; others are regressive. That, too, raises concern because either design might be adopted, depending on the political perspective of the government implementing the policy. There would be other difficulties. For instance, major issues of fiscal federalism would be raised; there are many social problems that can no more eas-

New Perspectives On the Aging Population

ily be addressed by lifetime accounts than by existing policies; we have no information about how people's behaviour might change as a result of particular design features; and transition to such a system would be difficult and probably costly.

Tax measures

Tax measures could also be designed to promote and encourage the flexible life-course option. Recent increases in the contribution limits for RRSPS, for example, were presented as helping more Canadians to save for their own retirement. But the higher limits, of course, were only of interest to higher-income individuals who believed their opportunities to save were restricted by the previous limits. Increases in 2003 affected only those earning more than $75,000 a year, who accounted for about 8% of tax-filers.[95] But limits were increased again in the 2005 budget. By 2010, RRSP contribution limits are scheduled to rise to $22,000. To make the maximum contribution then would require an income of more than $122,000, or roughly three times the average wage.

As noted earlier, Tax-Prepaid Savings Plans (TPSPS) have been proposed by the C.D. Howe Institute, among others, as a way of helping lower-income people save for their own retirement.[96] The federal government is said to be considering the introduction of such an option. The principle behind this idea would be that, since no tax deduction would be given for contributing to such a plan, funds would not be taxable when they are withdrawn. That would mean that lower-income people who may be eligible for income-tested benefits such as the Guaranteed Income Supplement (GIS) would not be deprived of such benefits when they withdrew their funds from a TPSP. They could also avoid the OAS clawback now applied to those whose income from other sources exceeds a certain threshold: in 2004, the threshold was $59,790, well above the average wage. In effect, the interest earned on amounts contributed to these plans would also be tax-free, so those with better investment skills or more money to invest would receive higher benefits.

But both these measures are essentially tax incentives for asset accumulation or lifetime accounts. Other types of tax measures might be required to support a flexible life-course option. The objective of such measures would be to reduce or eliminate tax measures that appear to favour pension income, thus reinforcing the objective of continuing to work over entering retirement. For example, the OECD suggests subjecting pensions to income tax in countries where this is not the case and reducing "excessive preferential tax treatment for occupational pension and individual retirement savings plans."[97] Special measures in the Canadian tax system directed at older people include the age credit and the pension income credit.

John Myles and Debra Street point out that tax deductions for RRSPS and Registered Pension Plans (RPPS) are tax expenditures directed at the working-age population to subsidize their savings for old age. Assuming one had decided to invent a new welfare state that invests more in the young in exchange for less income security in old age, these authors say, then an equitable solution would be to reduce tax expenditures for RRSPS and RPPS and use the savings for job retraining, job creation, public child care for young families, and other measures to enhance their earnings potential. They suggest that periods of labour market exit for purposes of training could be acknowledged in the CPP with an "educational drop-out" provision, just as child-rearing responsibilities are now taken into account through the child-rearing drop-out provision.[98]

It is not evident, however, that current policy objectives are intended to "invent a new welfare state." Instead, the initiatives being proposed seem to be designed to continue the move to the kind of "post-welfare state" model described by Ken Battle and others, referred to earlier.[99]

A flexible life-course for women

As we saw earlier, women have always had a very different and more complex life-course than men. It is now being suggested that female patterns are rapidly converging with those of men.[100] But, while it is true that women's participation in paid employment has continued to increase to levels rapidly approaching the participation rates of men, women are still largely responsible for unpaid work, particularly caregiving, in the home. Not only are they likely, early in their lives, to be primary caregivers for children, but increasingly they are responsible for care of elders at a later stage in their lives. Although this work is unpaid, it is still "work" and many women may never get to "retire" from it. Moving to a "flexible life-course" for women may therefore present particular challenges, and it is not clear at this point how the proponents of more flexibility in the life-course propose to address this concern. However, it is suggested that a life-course approach to social inclusion will also encompass newly emerging issues related to gender equality: time crunches and equality in the balance of time devoted to paid work, unpaid work, leisure, child-raising, and other caregving over a lifetime.[101]

The flexible life-course approach is very much directed at increasing the time spent in paid employment over the course of a lifetime, so encouraging women to spend more time working for pay seems to be integral to that approach. Hicks believes that, while the gap between women's and men's labour force participation may narrow further with the passage of time, it would be hard to imagine large gains beyond those that are already occurring. However, he says, "The most important policy levers to encourage higher participation would, in any event, be those that have already been identified: those related to life-course flexibility, to allow more choice in mixing work with caregiving and the other activities of life."[102] "Work," in this context, clearly implies paid work.

But Esping-Andersen argues that there are limits to the "masculinization" of women's life-course.[103] In his recent book *Why We Need A New Welfare State*, he argues that women's family responsibilities—particularly in relation to child care—make it difficult for women to change their life-course, even when there are incentive programs intended to encourage them to do so. Esping-Andersen notes that "Most countries have strengthened entitlements to child leaves, but crucial issues of day care provision for children and servicing the elderly have not been addressed seriously in the vast majority of welfare states."[104] The comment is certainly aptly applied to Canada. As we noted earlier, unpaid caregiving continues to be undertaken predominantly by women. Statistics Canada reported that, in 1996, almost one million women between the ages of 25 and 54, or 15% of all women in this age group, provided both unpaid child care and care or assistance to a senior.[105]

There is evidence that most caregivers have to adjust their participation in paid employment when they are responsible for providing unpaid care to other family members. Studies indicate that some caregivers have had to give up employment because of caregiving responsibilities; and there are indications that caregivers also make other adjustments to work schedules, such as switching from full-time to part-time work.[106]

One study of eldercare reported that women are much more likely than men to combine caregiving and employment responsibilities. As a result, they are also more likely to experience employment consequences. More specifically, female employees report more missed meetings, training sessions, business travel, or extra projects than their male counterparts. Women are also more likely than men to adjust their work schedules, utilize sick days and vacation days, and miss work-related social events because of eldercare demands. One study found that women are four times as likely as men to report having left a job because of eldercare demands. Women are twice as likely as men to report missed promotional opportunities.[107]

Similar constraints on paid employment are experienced by those who care for family members with disabilities. According to Statistics Canada's 1996 General Social Survey, for example, 20.3% of these caregivers had changed their hours of work because of their caregiving responsibilities; 34.5% had come late to work or left early; 31.2% had missed a day or more of work; 4.2% had turned down a job offer; and 16.0% said their caregiving responsibilities had affected their job performance.[108]

Changing or reducing participation in paid employment will almost certainly have an impact on the future pension income of the caregiver. As one recent study notes:

> Reductions in hours of paid employment or withdrawal from the labour force may also result in foregone employment-related benefits, such as extended health care insurance and future pension benefits, including both employer-provided pensions and Canada/Quebec Pension Plan benefits. Finally, future income may be lost when caregiving responsibilities hinder the acceptance of career-related opportunities, such as additional training, attending conferences, extra projects and promotions, which often lead to salary increases.[109]

New Perspectives On the Aging Population

Researchers note that part-time employment is a strategy caregivers use to meet competing work and family demands. But women are at greater risk than men of reduced current income and future pension income because of their greater propensity to decrease or cease paid employment in order to care for family members.[110]

Statistics Canada's LifePaths microsimulation model, referred to earlier, has been developed within a framework of "total work accounts" that take both paid and unpaid work into account. This model is one of the data tools being used in the PRI aging project. It is able to simulate basic individual and family choices, generating many of the events that, together, constitute an individual's life-course.[111] Analysts now use the term "total work retirement," meaning a shift from all forms of work, both paid and unpaid, to distinguish it from the more restrictive term "retirement," which is generally used to mean the process of giving up paid work.[112]

Women may have little choice about the timing of their caregiving activities. Caring for children, for instance, is probably most likely to happen between the ages of 25 and 44. But most women already "mix" their caregiving for children with their paid employment. For example, the majority of mothers with young children are in the paid workforce. In 2003, 63% of women with children under three and 69% of those whose youngest child was aged between 3 and 5 were in the paid workforce.[113] Only 23% of women with newborns in 2001 were not in the paid workforce. And among those mothers who had paid work prior to the birth of their child, 84% in 2000 and 82% in 2001 returned or planned to return to work within two years. Following the extension of the maternity benefits program from 10 weeks to 35 weeks in December 2000, the most common return time changed from five-to-six months in 2000 to between nine and twelve months in 2001.[114]

Of more concern, however, is the kind of jobs women in paid employment have. Many of those who must combine paid work with caring for children work shorter hours than men do, thus reducing their earnings and undermining both their current and future financial security. In 2003, for example, 21% of employed women compared with only 5% of employed men in the age group 25–44 had part-time jobs.[115] And just over 34% of women in this age group who had part-time jobs were working part-time because they were also caring for children. As well, many women who have paying jobs are employed in non-standard work arrangements. In 2003, for example, it was estimated that 40% of women's jobs compared with 30% of men's jobs fell into the category of non-standard work—including temporary or contract work, own-account self-employment, or multiple job holding, all of which may be either full-time or part-time.[116] While these types of jobs may give workers more "flexibility" to combine paid work with other activities, they are often low-paid, insecure, and without benefits, such as extended health care or pensions. And they are often not the kind of jobs women would choose to do if they had other options.

Women's caregiving for elders will inevitably occur later in life. For many women, it may be impossible to combine such unpaid work with paid employment. In fact, many women leave paid employment early to care for older family members, including their own spouses or partners. Far from wasting their time in "retirement," they continue to work, but without pay. Recent studies have shown that the years of transition to retirement from paid work for women are largely years in which women resume the behaviour patterns that come from life-long conditioning as society's primary caregivers. Although there has been an increase in the unpaid work done by older men in recent years, it is apparently not as systematic as it is for older women.[117] Eldercare is likely to become even more of an issue as the population ages and as pressure to cut back on social programs and state involvement continues to increase. But the emphasis of the flexible life-course approach on persuading people to work longer—meaning to continue longer in paid employment—is problematic where women are concerned, since it implies that the caregiving work women do, because it is unpaid, is perhaps not as "productive" as that done by people in paid employment.

Peter Hicks suggests a medium-term goal for a flexible life-course strategy would be more flexibility in how caregiving, including both child care and elder care, is mixed with work and learning, with most of the reallocated time coming from a reduction in leisure in retirement.[118] But the difficulty in making any of this a reality for women may prove insurmountable.

An Uncertain Future

The special concerns of women may also be heightened by the flexible life-course proponents' strong emphasis on equality of opportunity for the future, marking a shift from equality of outcomes for the present.[119] Following the Third Way approach—the "hand-up" rather than the "hand-out"—people would be given opportunities, for example, for access to education, help to accumulate financial assets or establish lifetime accounts, to make different choices and establish a more flexible life-course for themselves. Women have long been a disadvantaged group within society. And, like other disadvantaged groups and equality seekers, their long experience has taught them that providing "equal opportunities" for those who start from a disadvantaged position does not result in equality of outcomes. This is the very reason that affirmative action and head-start programs were initiated: so that those who start from behind can at least catch up to the starting line before the race begins, when equal opportunity for everyone has some meaning. There has been no indication so far as to how this issue would be addressed by the proponents of a flexible life-course.

Notes

1 Hicks 2003b: 12.

2 Hicks 2002: 2.

3 More details are available on PRI's web site at http://policyresearch.gc.ca

4 Ibid: 104.

5 Hicks 2003b: 12.

6 Ibid: 13.

7 Ibid.

8 OECD 1998: 13.

9 United Nations 2002: 2.

10 Ibid.

11 Hicks 2003b: 12.

12 United Nations 2004: 2.

13 OECD 1998: 3.

14 Ibid: 18

15 Ibid: 18–19.

16 Hicks 2003b: 13.

17 OECD 1998: 19.

18 Hicks 2003b: 13.

19 OECD 1998: 20.

20 Hicks 2003b: 14.

21 OECD 1998: 21.

22 Dodge 2004: 4.

23 Denton and Spencer 1999: 23.

24 Statistics Canada 2003f: 17.

25 Wolfson and Murphy 1997: 87.

26 Denton and Spencer 1999: 23.

27 OECD 1998: 23.

28 Hicks 2003b: 14.

29 OECD 1998: 25.

30 Boychuck 2004: v.

31 Martin 1994a: 10.

32 Ibid: 41.

33 Maxwell 2004: iii.

34 Ibid.

35 Jenson 2004: 13.

36 Ibid: 15.

37 Palier 2004: vi.

38 Ibid.

39 Ibid: 7.

40 Ibid: 8.

41 Ibid: 13.

42 Canadian Council on Social Development 2003: 1.

43 Canadian Council on Social Development 2004.

44 Jenson 2004: 2.

45 Béland and Myles 2003: 25.

46 Pawlick and Stroick 2004: 22.

47 Perry 2000: 45.

48 Battle 2001: 195.

49 Esping-Andersen 2002b: 4.

50 Ibid: 5.

51 Béland and Myles 2003: 25.

An Uncertain Future

52 Hicks 2002: 28.

53 Marshall and Mueller 2002: 2.

54 Ibid: 3.

55 Ibid: 4.

56 Myles and Street 1995: 354.

57 Ibid: 336.

58 Ibid. 345-346.

59 Ibid: 345.

60 Hicks 2002: 62.

61 Marshall and Mueller 2002: 37.

62 National Advisory Council on Aging 1999.

63 Myles and Street 1995: 353.

64 Hicks 2002: 3.

65 Hicks 2003a: 6, footnote 1.

66 OECD 2001b: 80.

67 Hicks 2002: 3.

68 Hicks 2003a: 4.

69 Ibid: 5.

70 Policy Research Initiative 2004b: 26.

71 Ibid: 28.

72 Ibid: 50.

73 Ibid: 6.

74 Ibid: 6.

75 Hicks 2004: Interview with author, October 22, 2003.

76 Hicks 2003b: 15.

77 Ibid: 16.

78 Policy Research Initiative 2005: 2.

79 Ibid.

80 Cheal 2003: 21.

81 OECD 1998: 15.

82 Myles and Street 1995: 354.

83 OECD 1998: 103.

84 Jackson 2004: 1.

85 Hicks 2002: 120.

86 Ibid: 121.

87 Ibid.

88 SEDI 2004: 3.

89 Policy Research Initiative 2003: 2.

90 Ibid: 4.

91 OECD 2003.

92 Hicks 2002: 5.

93 Frenken 2003: 90.

94 Hicks 2002: 71.

95 Yalnizyan 2004: 10.

96 Kesselman and Poschmann 2001: 1.

97 OECD 1998: 22.

98 Myles and Street 1995: 350.

99 Battle 2001: 195.

100 Hicks 2003a: 5.

101 Hicks 2002: 147.

102 Ibid: 52.

103 Esping-Andersen 2002a: 95.

104 Ibid: 73

105 Statistics Canada 2000: 114.

106 Keating et al. 1999: 61.

107 Ibid: 62.

108 Roeher Institute 2002: 55.

109 Fast et al. 2001: 3-4.

110 Ibid: 38.

111 Rowe 2003: 8.

112 Stone and Harvey 2001: 258.

113 Statistics Canada 2004d: 14.

114 Marshall 2003: 16.

115 Statistics Canada 2004d: 17.

116 Townson 2005: 45.

117 Stone and Harvey 2001: 267.

118 Hicks 2002: 62.

119 Ibid: 65

4

Raising the Age of Retirement

POLICY-MAKERS MAY BE fighting a losing battle in their efforts to get people to work longer. Not many people seem to be taking up the option. In Canada, as elsewhere, there is no law that sets a statutory retirement age. Traditionally, age 65 has long been considered the age of retirement, but most people have started on their pensions before they get to that magic number. Workplace pension plans generally allow for retirement with full benefits by about age 55. (Technically, it's when the person gets within 10 years of the "normal retirement age" provided by the pension plan). And, while Old Age Security is not available until age 65, CPP retirement pensions may be claimed at age 60, though with benefits reduced according to an actuarial formula for those who claim prior to age 65. (They are *increased* in the same way for those who postpone claiming benefits until after age 65.)

Talk about raising the retirement age tends to be confusing. To many people, it seems to mean raising the age of eligibility for public pension benefits, perhaps from age 65 to age 67 as the United States is now doing. Such a move would not prevent people from retiring prior to age 67, but for those who must rely on public pensions as a major source of income in retirement, it would make it very difficult to retire earlier. Public opinion polling in both Canada and Europe indicates that raising the age of eligibility for public pensions would be very unpopular.[1]

Canadians typically retire at about age 61. That's now the median retirement age, with half retiring earlier and half later. Persuading people, on a voluntary basis, to go on working until they reach age 64 or 65 would be another way of raising the retirement age: in this case, the average age at which people retire. Other options might include abolishing mandatory retirement, through which collective agreements or human resources practices of employers set a mandatory retirement age, generally at 65.

There's not much evidence that people want to go on working longer than they do now. But that could change if those who were counting on RRSPS to fund a comfortable retirement find they have not been able to save enough to reach their own "freedom 55." Failing workplace pension plans and a wholesale move by employers to replace their defined benefit plans with defined contribution plans could have the same effect. But so far, that hasn't happened. While pension coverage has been dropping over the past decade or so, the majority of pension plan members—82% at last count—still belong to defined benefit pension plans,[2] where pensions related to earnings and years of service are guaranteed by the plan sponsor. (Benefits from defined contribution plans depend on stock market returns, and no specific retirement age is required. The individual employee bears the entire risk and no particular pension is guaranteed.)

But there have been some recent developments that could signal change is on the way. For instance, pressure now seems to be building for the abolition of mandatory retirement. The practice is already banned in a number of provinces. The percentage of workers still in paid employment after age 65 has been creeping up. And a recent Statistics Canada survey found that a surprising 60% of new retirees—people aged 50 and older—would have liked to keep on working if circumstances had been different.[3] More on that later.

Why do governments want people to work longer?

There's no doubt that raising the age of retirement now seems to be a key preoccupation of policy-makers concerned about population aging, particularly in European countries. Why do governments want people to work longer? Is working longer the answer to the challenge of an aging workforce?

The Organization for Economic Cooperation and Development (OECD)—of which Canada is a member—takes the view that working longer will be crucial to address what it calls "the looming pension crisis." It has called on member countries to get rid of early retirement schemes and to make sure jobs are available for older workers. "If nothing is done quickly to extend working lives," the organization says, "living standards will fall in the course of the coming decades."[4] According to the OECD, the age at which workers retire is of critical importance to both future material living standards and to fiscal pressures. This organization maintains that, if people work longer, the output that can be shared among the population will be greater, the tax base will be larger, and there will be fewer dependent older persons receiving pensions. The implicit concern is that, given increasing life expectancy, the earlier people retire, the greater the chance that they will outlive their retirement savings and become a burden on the state.

The OECD has advised the British government to raise the pension age from 65 to 70 to keep more people at work.[5] And a government-appointed Pension Commission in the UK, reporting in mid-October 2004, also called for an increase in the average retirement age to close to 70.[6] The alternatives, said the Commission, were that pensioners will become poorer relative to the rest of society; or taxes and social insurance contributions devoted to pensions would have to go up; or savings must increase. But the UK Trades Union Congress says more than one in five people and nearly one in three men—higher in Britain's most deprived areas—will die before they get a pension if the government increases the retirement age to 70.[7]

That's an issue often overlooked in the debate about working longer. It's well-known that life expectancy is related to socioeconomic status. For instance, one study in the UK showed that people living in the poor-

Raising the Age of Retirement

est 10% of electoral wards in the north of England in the 1980s had death rates four times as high as people living in the richest 10%.[8] Raising the age of retirement may mean the government saves on the cost of public pensions because they're paid out for a shorter period of time. But the savings may come from public pensions that would otherwise have been payable to lower-income workers, who may have fewer years in retirement because of lower life expectancy. As well, of course, public pensions are a major source of retirement income for lower-income workers, who are less likely than higher-income earners to have other sources of retirement income and therefore little choice about when they retire. Any increase in the age of eligibility for public pensions is therefore likely to have a greater impact on lower-income workers than on higher-income earners.

Easing fiscal pressures

Sociologist Alan Walker, at the University of Sheffield in the UK, says that, on the basis of various institutional reforms in many of the European countries, there can be little doubt that pension expenditure has been stabilized. However, he says, "the mood for reform is nowhere near being assuaged." There is a new conventional wisdom among policy-makers in Europe, says Walker, that further change is required to ensure financial stability. Strong pressures for pension reform are coming from international economic agencies and from vested interests in the private pension world, he says.[9]

The United States is now gradually increasing the age of eligibility for Social Security benefits from 65 to 67. But, according to recently-retired Federal Reserve Chairman Alan Greenspan, there's still a need for policy changes to encourage a longer stay in the workforce to ease the burden.[10] And some observers believe the eligibility age in the U.S. will have to go past 67, perhaps reaching age 70 by about 2040.

In Canada, Old Age Security benefits have been around since 1952 and were originally only paid to those aged 70 or older—and that was when life expectancy was much shorter than it is now. But 65 has been the entitlement age for public pensions since 1970. More recently, the government was toying with the idea of increasing it again, at least for

Canada Pension Plan benefits. Life expectancy has continued to increase since the CPP was set up almost 40 years ago. When changes to the CPP were being discussed at the end of the 1990s, the government estimated that raising the age of entitlement to 67 would reduce the CPP's long-term costs by 4.2%.[11] In its 1996 consultation paper, issued for that round of reforms, the government also said that, if retirement benefits in 2030 were paid on average for the same period of time as in 1966 when the CPP began, the age of entitlement to full CPP pensions would have to rise from age 65 to almost 70. "This would be another way of dealing with the costs of rising life expectancy," the government said, "but many would consider this excessive."[12]

In the end, federal, provincial, and territorial finance ministers rejected the option of increasing the age of eligibility for public pensions. Instead, they chose to reduce some benefits and to jack up contribution rates quickly to build an investment fund. Earnings from the fund will be used to supplement contribution revenue, providing the money needed to finance the retirement of the baby boomers. The strategy is proving successful. The Chief Actuary's 21st Actuarial Report, issued in November 2004 and documenting the state of the plan at the end of 2003, was a good-news story. Earnings on the investment fund will not be needed until 2021.

Even by 2050, only 29% of the projected investment earnings will be needed to pay benefits. (The remaining funds needed to pay benefits will be generated by contributions made by those still in the workforce). These earnings, said the Chief Actuary, provide the plan with the capacity "to absorb a wide range of unforeseen economic or demographic fluctuations, which otherwise would have to be reflected in the legislated contribution rate." In spite of the projected substantial increase in benefits paid as a result of the aging population, he said, "the plan is expected to be able to meet its obligations throughout the projection period."[13] Given that the "projection period" he refers to is the next 75 years, it would seem the CPP is in good shape until well after all the boomers and their children and grandchildren have retired.

Canada has done more than many other countries to put its public pension plan on a sound financial footing. In fact, following the release of the latest CPP actuarial report in December 2004, Finance Minister

Raising the Age of Retirement

Ralph Goodale claimed that "Canada is one of the few countries in the world with a rock-solid public pension system."[14] That is why exhortations on pension reform by some international bodies don't necessarily apply to Canada. But it hasn't stopped some policy-makers from continuing to push the idea of getting people to work longer.

In a paper on Canada's pension system, issued in March 2004, the International Monetary Fund (IMF) praised the 1998 reforms, which it said "has put the CPP on a sound actuarial footing." But it suggested there was still scope for increases in the statutory retirement age.[15] Assuming that an increase in the eligibility age would apply to both OAS and CPP, and that the entry age for early retirement would also be shifted upward, the IMF claims there would be several advantages. The government would save money because it would be able to pay basic pension benefits over a shorter period of time; CPP contribution rates could be reduced; and people who work longer would be able to save more money for themselves, thus relieving pressure on the public pension system. There seems to be no clear reason why any of this is really necessary. But it's probably worth noting that all of the so-called advantages are directed at reducing the role of public pensions and transferring more risk and responsibility for generating a retirement income to individuals—probably not surprising given the IMF's well-known predilection for market-based policy alternatives. It's probably also significant that the IMF had to acknowledge that: "To ensure political acceptance and mitigate the impact on workers close to retirement age, any increase in the retirement age would need to be gradual and phased in over a longer time frame."[16]

More productive options for older workers

Still, the idea that people should work longer persists in Canada. Bank of Canada Governor David Dodge jumped on the bandwagon in a speech to the Montreal Board of Trade in early 2004, when he called for the removal of impediments for older workers who wish to remain in the labour force.[17] And in an appearance before the Senate banking committee in April 2004, Dodge pointed to the anticipated sharp increase in people in the age group 65 to 70 by the end of the next decade, which he said presented "a tremendous opportunity for greater participation, either in the market economy or in the voluntary, or third sector, by this very healthy, young-elderly part of the population."[18]

In this case, the emphasis seems to be less on fiscal issues and more on using the productive resources the aging population could potentially provide. That's also a preoccupation of the OECD and other international bodies which suggest that keeping older workers in paid employment will help supply the goods and services the aging population will need. The gender aspects of this approach don't seem to have been considered. It's apparently assumed that only paid employment will contribute to the support of the aging population. The many women who have had to take early retirement from paid employment to provide unpaid care for aging family members are apparently not considered to be making the necessary contribution.

Critics of the OECD's approach have also pointed to the value judgments that seem to form the basis of some of its policy proposals. For instance, in a comment on the absence of active ageing in retirement, the OECD complains: "Older people, it appears, are not living more active lives. The time that older people formerly spent in work is, for the most part, used passively after retirement—often in more television watching and sleep."[19] What priority, it asks, should be attached to "policies that support very long periods of passivity in the last third of life?" There seems to be a veiled threat implied here. Thoughtful commentators have pointed out that the danger in active aging policies is that they may become coercive. Sociologist Alan Walker calls for such policies to be responsive to age, gender, race, culture, and other differences. He also points out that, "in all this clamour for reform, the voices of current pensioners do not seem to be audible."[20]

Should mandatory retirement be abolished?

As part of the push to raise the age of retirement, there are now calls to abolish mandatory retirement. The issue was in the news again when the McGuinty government in Ontario reactivated the proposal by the former Conservative government to get rid of mandatory retirement in the province. While Ontario would not be the first jurisdiction in Canada to end mandatory retirement, with 39% of pension plan members and 38% of all pension plans, its laws regulate most of the pension plans covering most of the plan members in Canada. That's why observers are watching carefully to see how this all shakes out. Will pension plans in Ontario have to be amended? Would people who choose to go on working beyond 65 be able to add to the benefits they will receive from a workplace pension plan? What about the tax rules requiring individuals to start collecting pension benefits by the end of the year they turn 69—a requirement that also applies to RRSPS? And how would this change help those who don't have a pension plan at work and are saving for retirement through RRSPS?

Ontario introduced its legislation to end mandatory retirement in June 2005. It will come into effect one year after receiving royal assent. Among other things, the legislation would continue to allow mandatory retirement where it can be justified on "bona fide occupational requirement" grounds determined under the Human Rights Code—in other words, where there is a requirement or qualification necessary for the performance of essential job duties. A background paper released by the Ontario government explains that a "bona fide occupational requirement" is an employment requirement that is discriminatory on certain grounds, including age, but that is allowed under the Human Rights Code because of the nature of the employment.

Under the proposed Ontario legislation, the employer must establish:

- that the employer adopted the requirement for a purpose rationally connected to the performance of the job;

- that the employer adopted the requirement in an honest and good-faith belief that it was necessary to the fulfillment of that legitimate work-related purpose; and

- that the requirement is reasonably necessary to the accomplishment of that legitimate work-related purpose. It must be demonstrated that it is impossible to accommodate individual employees without imposing undue hardship in the employer.[21]

Under Ontario's proposed law, collective agreements would no longer be permitted to include provisions requiring mandatory retirement, except in those cases where mandatory retirement would be allowed under the Human Rights Code as a "bona fide occupational requirement." Unions and employers would still be able to negotiate voluntary retirement incentives—that is, early retirement packages. Mandatory retirement provisions in existing collective agreements would no longer be enforceable once the proposed legislation comes into effect, one year after Royal assent.[22]

Interest in proposals to abolish mandatory retirement is probably also heightened because of a perception that, where mandatory retirement remains in place, people may be forced to retire even if they have not been able to accumulate enough savings to do so comfortably, or if the value of their retirement nest egg has fallen with the volatile stock market.

Many people seem to believe there is some general rule requiring everyone to retire by age 65, but in fact there is no law in Canada that provides for mandatory retirement. Mandatory retirement is a matter of human resources policies set by employers, or is implied in workplace pension plan arrangements, or is provided for in collective agreements negotiated between the employer and the union.

Forcing an employee to retire at a particular age is considered a human rights issue and is regulated by human rights legislation. Generally speaking, it's a provincial or territorial concern, although federal government laws cover federal public sector workers and employers falling under federal jurisdiction, such as banks, airlines, and communications.

Provincial and federal laws on mandatory retirement

In Ontario, for instance, protection against age discrimination applies only to those aged 18 to 64, so a requirement to retire at age 65 would not contravene the law. Three other provinces—British Columbia, Saskatchewan, and Newfoundland—also have an age cap of 65 in their human rights legislation, effectively allowing for mandatory retirement. Of course, this restriction also means people aged 65 or older are not protected against other types of age discrimination in employment or services.

In a further six jurisdictions—federal, Alberta, Quebec, New Brunswick, Nova Scotia, and Prince Edward Island—the age cap in human rights legislation has been lifted. But all these jurisdictions exempt bona fide retirement or pension plans from the rule. In other words, while older workers are protected against age discrimination in employment, mandatory retirement is still allowed if it is part of such arrangements, which it generally is.[23] Only two provinces—Manitoba since 1982 and Quebec since 1983—specifically ban mandatory retirement, but even here there are exceptions. For example, in Manitoba, statutes governing individual universities provide exceptions for collective agreements negotiated between the university and its unions where a mandatory retirement age of 65 or over is imposed.[24] Quebec's legislation allows distinctions based on age in insurance contracts or pension plans "where the use thereof is warranted and the basis therefore is a risk determination factor based on actuarial data."[25]

Mandatory retirement at a specified age is permitted in all jurisdictions where age is deemed to be a "bona fide occupational requirement," such as firefighters and airline pilots. And some jurisdictions do not permit mandatory retirement unless it is contractual—that is covered by the terms of a collective agreement or pension plan.[26]

Past decisions by the Supreme Court of Canada have ruled that, while mandatory retirement does discriminate on the basis of age, it is a "reasonable limitation" of equality rights and therefore permissible under Section 1 of the Charter of Rights and Freedoms. But there is now pressure for the Court to revisit the issue and to reconsider its 1990 rulings allowing mandatory retirement.[27]

Who is affected by mandatory retirement?

It's estimated that about half the Canadian work force is employed in jobs where there are mandatory retirement provisions. According to economist Morley Gunderson, a professor at the Centre for Industrial Relations and the Department of Economics at the University of Toronto, mandatory retirement policies tend to cover advantaged workers who earn relatively high incomes in long-term employment positions, are male, covered by an employer-sponsored pension plan, and under the protection of a collective agreement or formal personnel policy.[28] He believes mandatory retirement should not be seen as blanket age discrimination, but rather as part of a mutually agreed company personnel policy, or collective agreement, generally negotiated by individuals with reasonable bargaining power. "It should only be banned if there are explicit reasons for governments to override such private contractual arrangements," Gunderson says.

But advocates for raising the age of retirement see the abolition of mandatory retirement as a key part of the picture. For instance, Jonathan Kesselman, a professor in the Public Policy Program at Simon Fraser University and a research fellow of the C.D. Howe Institute, argues that it's erroneous to assume collective agreements are equivalent to consensual agreements between the individual worker and the employer. Union members may be forced to go along with an agreement negotiated by the union leadership even if they don't agree with it, he claims.[29]

Gunderson maintains retiring because of mandatory retirement policies does not imply that the employer forced a person to leave involuntarily. While there is only limited evidence on this point, Gunderson suggests the number of employees who are involuntarily constrained by mandatory retirement is relatively small. Results from Statistics Canada's 2002 General Social Survey indicated that only about 12% of new retirees—people aged 50 or older who retired between 1992 and 2002 inclusive—would have continued paid employment if mandatory retirement polices had not existed.[30]

Women and mandatory retirement

According to Morley Gunderson, banning mandatory retirement should have less of an impact on women because they are less likely to be in jobs where retirement is mandatory.[31] But many of those who favour a ban on mandatory retirement suggest it would be particularly beneficial for women workers. Because of their family responsibilities, women may have only an intermittent record of paid employment. As a result, they've had less time to build up savings and fewer years of membership in both public and private pension plans. As well, since women can expect to live longer than men, on average, they must generally provide for a longer period in retirement, even where their retirement age is the same as that of men. Giving them the option to work longer—so the argument goes—would help them build up a better retirement nest egg and prevent poverty in old age.

Johanthan Kesselman notes[32] that women justices on the Supreme Court of Canada made this point in the landmark case of McKinney v. University of Guelph in 1990. They said:

> Women workers are unable to amass adequate pension earnings during their working years because of the high incidence of interrupted work histories due to child-bearing and child-rearing. Thus, the imposition of mandatory retirement raises not only issues of age discrimination but also may implicate other rights as well [that is, sex discrimination].[33]

On the face of it, the argument seems to make sense. But it is less convincing if we look at the reality of women's current experience in paid employment. Though we have no information on the percentage of women workers who are affected by mandatory retirement provisions, we do know that only 39% of women in paid employment belong to a workplace pension plan. We also know that, because of their low earnings, few women contribute to RRSPS. It may be doubtful that they could add significant amounts to their retirement savings if they continued to work in paid employment for longer than they do now.

Looking, for example, at Canadians aged 25 to 64 who filed tax returns in the period from 1995 to 2001, almost 37% had incomes of less than $20,000 a year, and 62% of people at this low income level saved nothing in RRSPS or pension plans during this period. For 2001, women accounted for 64% of those with incomes under $20,000 who had RRSP contribution room. But 88% of these women did not contribute to an RRSP. Interestingly enough, 91% of men with incomes of less than $20,000 who had RRSP room did not contribute, either. But men accounted for only 36% of taxpayers with incomes less than $20,000 who had contribution room.[34]

GROWING OLDER, WORKING LONGER

The growing trend to non-standard work arrangements—including part-time, temporary, and contract work, self-employment without employees, as well as casual work and multiple job-holding—also makes it difficult for women to accumulate retirement incomes from private pension arrangements such as workplace pension plans or RRSPS. About 40% of employed women now work in non-standard jobs. Many of these jobs are poorly paid and insecure, and they generally do not have pension coverage. Allowing women to go on working in these types of jobs beyond age 65 is most unlikely to generate more retirement income for them.

It's also worth noting that women no longer take long periods of time out of paid employment for child-bearing or child-rearing. Recent studies report the median time taken off work by women who give birth or adopt a child is now about 10 months. Over 80% of these women returned or planned to return to work within two years—a reflection of the importance of their earnings to the financial security of their families. There is a close correlation between the time taken off and eligibility for maternity and parental benefits through the EI program. Mothers who were self-employed and therefore not eligible for maternity or parental benefits were generally back at work within one month. One-quarter of those mothers who did receive benefits were back at work within eight months.[35] It should also be noted that 82% of women in the main child-bearing age group (25 to 44) now participate in the paid work force. Women are having fewer children, too—now averaging only 1.52 children per woman—a record low fertility rate.

Provisions in the CPP ensure that women who do take time off for child-bearing and child-rearing are not penalized. Through the so-called "child-rearing drop-out" a contributor may exclude years when she or he had a child under the age of seven from the average earnings calculation on which their retirement pension will be based. The low benefits many women receive from CPP retirement pensions are more likely a function of their low average earnings and also of the fact that a significant percentage of employed women are employed part-time, rather than the result of an interrupted paid work record.

The timing of retirement for women very often depends on their family situation. Many women are married when they reach retirement age,

Raising the Age of Retirement

and their spouses or partners are generally older than they are. Women often want to retire at the same time as their spouse or partner, which is a key reason why the retirement age for women is typically lower than that of men. As well, increasing numbers of women take early retirement so they can provide unpaid caregiving services for older and dependent family members. For these reasons, women do not necessarily want to work longer, and they may be unable to make that choice, anyway.

Finally, it seems somewhat invidious, to say the least, to imply that women's potential for accumulating an adequate income in their old age should depend on mandatory retirement being abolished so they can postpone their retirement and go on working. Surely a better option would be to improve the benefits under public pension programs on which the majority of women must rely for the bulk of their retirement income.

Unions and mandatory retirement

Unions have traditionally been strong supporters of mandatory retirement. The basis for their approach is summed up in a section of the brief prepared by the Ontario English Catholic Teachers Association in response to the Ontario Ministry of Labour's 2004 consultation paper on mandatory retirement:

> Our support for the concept of mandatory retirement is similar to our support for a 40-hour work week. In general, workers should be able to look forward to a secure retirement, normally at age 65, just as they look forward to two days of rest after five days of work. Regardless of decisions by some people to work more than 40 hours in the evening and on weekends, we continue to advocate for the 40-hour work week. We recognize that not everyone is ready and able to retire by age 65, but we believe, for the benefit of society, that it should continue to be a goal.[36]

In the past, without mandatory retirement, workers may have been forced to go on working virtually until they dropped—especially if they were not entitled to any pension benefits. Unions negotiated pensions for their members and included mandatory retirement in their collective agreements. Their continued support for mandatory retirement reflects—as the Ontario Federation of Labour puts it—"the right of unionized workers with pension plans to democratically negotiate the age at which they wish to retire."[37]

The labour movement's concern about the abolition of mandatory retirement is rooted in the fear that abolition may open the door to raising the age of eligibility for both public and private pensions, and to forcing workers to continue working against their will. While fewer and fewer jobs these days involve hard physical labour, there are still many jobs that do involve poor employment conditions. As economist Andrew Jackson, director of social and economic policy at the Canadian Labour Congress, has pointed out, they may include dirty and dangerous jobs; exposure to harmful substances; high levels of stress, because of the repetitive nature of the work or because of the exercise of arbitrary power in the workplace; jobs which are stressful because they do not meet human developmental needs; and jobs which are stressful because they are a source of conflict with the lives of workers in the home and in the community.[38]

It is also suggested that, as the large baby boom generation moves into retirement, there will be a shortage of skilled workers to take their place. This could lead employers to develop ways to persuade older workers to delay their retirement and go on working longer. Such efforts might become coercive if mandatory retirement is abolished.

It is understandable that unions want to protect their right to collectively bargain a retirement age for their members. A ban on mandatory retirement would effectively deny them this right. Perhaps that is why some Canadian jurisdictions that have banned age discrimination—including jurisdictions that specifically ban mandatory retirement—still allow some exceptions for mandatory retirement provisions in collective agreements.

There are also concerns that abolishing mandatory retirement could actually increase discrimination against older workers. Some observers suggest that employers who can no longer count on older workers terminating at age 65 will then have to figure out when these workers should retire if they don't voluntarily do so. That means giving them much more rigorous performance appraisals as they get into their 60s

Raising the Age of Retirement

and maybe even pushing them out *before* they get to 65. The end result of abolishing mandatory retirement may even be to *reduce* the retirement age rather than increasing it. In fact, Quebec—which has abolished mandatory retirement—has one of the lowest median retirement ages in Canada at 59.8 years.

Employers and mandatory retirement

The attitude of employers to mandatory retirement tends to reflect the particular approach they take to managing their workforce. Those who are concerned about a potential looming shortage of skilled workers may support the abolition of mandatory retirement because they want to retain skilled workers past the normal retirement age. Others may feel mandatory retirement is a relatively painless way to ease out older workers and open up jobs for younger employees. The differences were highlighted in a 2003 discussion paper on age discrimination, issued by the British government. On mandatory retirement, the government said:

> From our discussions with businesses it is clear that employers tend to adopt one of two approaches. Some see retirement ages as a way to manage their workforce sensitively and with the minimum of bureaucratic burdens. That reflects concern that some of them have about appraisal systems and the potential indignity of dismissing older workers on competence grounds at the end of their careers. Other employers see mandatory retirement ages as anachronistic and are moving away from using them. They prefer more flexible approaches to work and retirement to help retain valuable skills and expertise for longer—recognizing the indignity of requiring people to retire simply because they have reached a particular age.[39]

Public attitudes to mandatory retirement

There's evidence that the closer to retirement people get, the more they feel they should not be forced to retire. And with growing numbers of older people in the population, opposition to mandatory retirement has risen significantly. A public opinion poll, conducted in late 2003 by Decima Research for Investors Group, showed 33% of respondents thought mandatory retirement should be banned, up from 20% seven years earlier in 1996, when Gallup Canada conducted a similar poll for Investors Group. Among the over-50s, 39% would support a ban on mandatory retirement, compared with 24% of the under-30s who wanted it banned.

A spokesperson for the company said the findings reflect a growing desire for flexibility in planning for old age. While the survey indicated the percentage of people anticipating a retirement before age 60 had not changed much, the implication was that many more people are now saying they want a choice and the ability to be more flexible in when and how they retire. The number of people who said they wanted to work past 65—as long as they are able—had also increased, according to the survey. In 1996, 15% of those surveyed said they expected to retire some time after 65. That number increased to 26% in the 2003 survey.

The survey showed up some regional differences, and also suggested that many people don't know about mandatory retirement rules in their own provinces. For example, 52% of respondents in British Columbia did not want to see the abolition of mandatory retirement, while 44% of those in Quebec were opposed to a ban—even though mandatory retirement has been outlawed in Quebec since 1983. It seems some people may not be aware of a general mandatory retirement ban in a particular province, especially since it may still be permitted in some professions and in companies falling under federal jurisdiction, wherever they are located. Many people may just assume they have to retire at age 65, but they may not have checked to see if that is the case.

Mandatory retirement and pension plans

There seems to be a widespread perception that abolishing mandatory retirement would play havoc with pension plan arrangements. Pension experts point out that, regardless of whether or not mandatory retirement is permitted, provincial pension laws require pension plans to specify a "normal retirement age" (NRA) at which plan members are entitled to a benefit from the pension plan without any actuarial reduction. For actuarial purposes, there has to be a pivotal age around which to define a pension. The NRA is used to calculate the potential liabilities of the pension plan and to set contribution rates.

But the concept of the NRA tends to be confusing, and one expert suggests it might be better to call it a "normal pension commencement age," although the NRA is also generally treated either explicitly or implicitly as the end point in the employment relationship.[40] Pension plans generally allow early retirement for those who are within 10 years of the normal retirement age provided in the plan, or who meet certain requirements for age and years of service. The Ontario Pension Benefits Act specifies that the NRA cannot be later than one year after the plan member attains age 65.

Some pension plans allow employees to continue working and accruing benefits past the normal retirement age. And, when the amount of the pension is based on a percentage of average annual earnings—say, 2%—for each year of service, an employee who was hired later in his or her career could improve the amount of the pension by additional years of service beyond the NRA. However, some plans may put a cap on the number of years of service that can be accrued.

As one consultant explains,[41] defined benefit pension plans face a challenging actuarial balancing act. The pension benefits an individual receives are not directly related to their contributions, or to the contributions made by the employer on their behalf. Instead, benefits are generally related to final salary, or some other formulation of earnings, and years of service. The pension plan has to balance the total estimated potential liabilities, the current contribution rates for all members, and the residual liability of the employer to make up any difference.

The way in which defined benefit plans are structured means that individuals gain disproportionately from service close to retirement. Amounts contributed to the plan in the final year of service, for instance, can add a substantial amount to the pension in perpetuity. And, provided they draw a pension for a few years, older employees gain an amount which is more than actuarially fair, with the employer and the younger employees contributing to the fund making up the difference. The assumption is that younger employees will get their turn later when they are closer to retirement. But, as one expert explains:

> Since at any one point in time the balancing of assets and liabilities in defined benefit pension funds is not actuarially fair between the different parties, the existence of a normal retirement age beyond which no further benefits can be accrued sets a ceiling on the level of costs that individual employees can impose on others. If people in defined benefit pension schemes were able to choose to accumulate extra years of service beyond normal retirement age, this would essentially give them the right to take money from their employers and fellow employees.[42]

According to some experts, ending mandatory retirement would mean that members of both defined contribution (DC) and defined benefit (DB) pension plans who work after age 65 would have to be permitted to accrue benefits beyond their NRA, subject to any service or age-and-service caps on accrual in the plan text. As a result, according to pension experts, pension plan texts that do not already permit employees working beyond their NRA to accrue additional benefits would have to be amended. That doesn't mean pension plans should not be able to specify an NRA, though. In fact, experts argue they must be allowed to do so—and that it should continue to be not later than one year after the plan member attains age 65.[43] They also maintain that differentiations based on age should be acceptable where the differentiation is reasonable and based on actuarial risk factors—a practice permitted under Quebec's legislation.

Income tax rules and mandatory retirement

Income tax rules require a pension plan sponsor to start paying out benefits by the end of the year in which the employee turns 69 to ensure that the plan complies with the Income Tax Act (ITA). The same rules apply to RRSPS, which must be converted to a stream of income by the end of the year in which the holder turns 69. So far, it would appear there hasn't been any legal challenge to this provision. The ITA permits deferral of benefits until then, but the Act does not permit an individual to continue accruing benefits in a defined benefit pension plan while receiving benefits from that plan, so it is not possible to receive a partial pension while continuing to work. However, the Act does allow for a partial commutation of benefits from a defined benefit plan. And some provinces—notably, Quebec and Alberta—have relaxed their commutation rules, while remaining in compliance with the ITA, so that individuals may receive a lump sum benefit from their pension plan while continuing to work at reduced hours: in effect, taking a phased retirement. However, the eventual pension will be reduced accordingly.

In the ongoing debate about the abolition of mandatory retirement, it has been suggested that the Income Tax Act rules would have to be changed to accommodate those who want to go on working past age 69. Manitoba gets around this problem by recognizing that, since there is no tax advantage for anyone working beyond age 69 to continue making pension plan contributions, it is not unreasonable discrimination for employers to refuse to permit the active accrual of benefits of these employees in a pension plan. But one expert points out that employees choosing to work beyond age 69 potentially might challenge this because their total compensation would have been reduced once the employer's pension plan contributions cease.

The point at which pensions must be converted to benefits used to be age 71, and presumably it could be changed back to that again if necessary. But it's also worth noting that the government has an interest in taxing withdrawals from retirement savings plans and may not want to postpone receiving those additional tax revenues for another two years.

Potential impact on pension plan sponsors if mandatory retirement is abolished

Pension experts note there's nothing to prevent a 69- or 70-year old from continuing to work while drawing a pension, although there would be no further accrual of benefits. But once an individual reaches the age at which the pension plan allows for retirement with an unreduced benefit, there is no point in continuing to work—at least so far as the pension amount is concerned. While deferring the pension benefit by one year means losing one year of pension, the pension accrual gained by working an extra year will likely be worth less than the one year of pension that's lost—especially for older workers who may have many years of service. Of course, there may be other reasons for continuing to work. For example, the employee may not be able to live on the amount of the pension and would prefer to keep on working and getting paid a salary.

As for whether abolition of mandatory retirement would have a significant impact on employers who sponsor pension plans, most observers believe the overall impact on organizations is likely to be small. Of course, employers (and often employees) would have to go on contributing to the pension plan if workers continue working beyond the NRA, but the cost impact for employers is expected to be minimal. Experts believe few people will want to delay retirement beyond age 65, and, if they do so, in most cases they will not stay on for more than another two or three years. For the same reason, abolition of mandatory retirement would probably do nothing to alleviate predicted shortages of skilled workers in some sectors of the economy.

Will the abolition of mandatory retirement increase the average retirement age?

Some people apparently would like to go on working beyond age 65, but most are retiring before then. Clearly, most people don't want to work longer. In 2002, for instance, 60.6 years was the median age of retirement in Canada, with half retiring before that age and half later. And the numbers show that, even where people are not required to stop working at age 65, they generally choose to leave earlier. For instance, in Manitoba and Quebec, both of which have outlawed mandatory retirement, the median age of retirement is 59.8 in Quebec and 61.2 in Manitoba. In Ontario currently, it's 60.8.

In Manitoba, for instance, Dewar McKinnon, acting president and chief executive officer of the Manitoba Teachers' Retirement Allowances Fund (TRAF) in Winnipeg, says that, even though mandatory retirement does not apply, many teachers are opting for early retirement. In fact, the average retirement age for TRAF members is now 57.5 years, and it has been at that level for several years now. There has been no detect-

Raising the Age of Retirement

able change in the age of retirement over the past few years, McKinnon says.

It seems, then, that getting rid of mandatory retirement will be unlikely to have much of an impact on the average age of retirement. Some observers, however, suggest it may be too early to tell. It may be that, as the younger generation following the baby boomers approaches age 65, working longer will have become more attractive. And increasing longevity may be the trigger. As one financial advisor put it, "People don't want to outlive their money—and that becomes a bigger concern in light of the returns they've been getting on their investments over the past four or five years."

How to solve the mandatory retirement question

The ongoing debate on mandatory retirement has raised considerable controversy, but public perception of the issue still seems to reflect a lack of understanding of who is affected by the provisions and how or if their "freedom of choice" about retirement may be limited. Economist Morley Gunderson maintains: "The association of mandatory retirement with advantaged workers and good jobs lends credence to the notion that the system generally is not an arbitrary practice foisted on disadvantaged employees by a discriminating employer. Rather," says Gunderson, "it is part of a private contracting arrangement between consenting parties—employers and employees or their unions."[44] Banning mandatory retirement, says Gunderson, would be like "throwing out the baby with the bathwater."

But there is a solution that could address the concerns of the labour movement, while also helping those who do not have the benefit of a collective agreement or the protection afforded by union membership. Those provinces that have not already done so could remove the age cap in their human rights legislation, while exempting legitimate pension plans and collective agreements. This would provide people aged 65 or older with protection against age discrimination in employment. It's worth remembering here that the majority of Canadian workers do not have a workplace pension plan, but may still be subject to mandatory retirement if this is the practice of their employers. Banning age discrimination would protect these workers from being required to retire if they would prefer to go on working.

It would also protect older people against age discrimination in access to other services such as housing and social services—a protection that will become increasingly important as older people comprise a greater percentage of the population. Perhaps most important, this approach would strike a balance between combating age discrimination, while permitting mutually beneficial work arrangements between private parties with reasonable bargaining power.[45]

Attitudes to working longer or returning to work after retirement

At this point, it seems few people want to go on working much beyond their early 60s. One financial advisor says he's not seeing many clients who want to go on working in a structured job environment past 65. People may still continue doing something productive, he says, such as working part-time or running a small business. Echoing the view of an increasing number of people, this advisor says: "Retirement has to be a plan to start something else, not a plan to stop working." But his experience has been that people don't have the same level of commitment to saving that they once had, especially after they went through declining markets from 2000 to 2002. However, people are beginning to recognize they may have to go on working longer, he says. Many of those who thought they would retire at 55, or even 60, now realize that was a mirage. Lower investment returns have meant higher amounts are needed to finance a comfortable retirement, according to this observer.

It's suggested that most of those affected by mandatory retirement are likely to be working in the public sector with good pensions. But there may be people who came late into that environment who would be happy to work beyond age 65. As well, people brought up on the goal of "Freedom 55" may get to age 55, find they are enjoying what they do, and decide they want to continue doing it. According to some observers, as

Raising the Age of Retirement

people shake off the early retirement goal and realize they're going to live longer, later retirement may become more prevalent.

Apparently, some advisors are now using a retirement planning horizon of age 110 with their clients. But if people are going to work longer, they may also have to be encouraged to keep on saving to a longer time horizon, according to some financial experts. Not only will many people probably live longer than they think, but they will also likely get a lower rate of return on their investments than they hoped.

Attitudes to working longer may also be coloured by the way in which people are experiencing retirement. People who are not enjoying their retirement may wish they had continued in paid employment, especially if they took early retirement. Recent surveys provide evidence of this. For instance, data from Statistics Canada's 2002 General Social Survey (GSS) indicated that as many as 60% of recent retirees would have liked to go on working if circumstances had been different.[46]

Results were highlighted in a study, limited to recent retirees, defined as people who retired at age 50 or older during the years 1992 to 2002 inclusive, with the intriguing title *You can't always get what you want: Retirement preferences and experiences*. Respondents were asked to answer a series of nine questions about their willingness to continue working. But the authors of the study warn that responses to hypothetical questions should be treated cautiously. They may overstate the willingness of retirees to have continued working, especially if they've found their retirement less satisfying than they expected, these analysts say. "In such cases, the option of continued employment may look appealing in retrospect," they point out.[47]

Just the same, over one-quarter of recent retirees said they would have continued working if they'd been able to reduce their work schedule without affecting their pensions; 28% said they would have continued to work if they could have switched to part-time; and 26% would have gone on working if their health had been better. Perhaps surprisingly, in view of the current debate about the abolition of mandatory retirement, only 12% said they would have continued to work if mandatory retirement had not existed in their workplace.

It's clear from this study that retirement is not always the happy, relaxing time pictured in the ads—especially for those who have to stop working because of poor health or who are forced out because of downsizing or unemployment. People who have to retire against their will may not have had enough time to prepare for retirement, either financially or psychologically. Faced with a mismatch between their retirement preferences and their actual experience of retirement, it seems many people return to work after their initial retirement, and often it's for financial reasons. Almost one-third of those who found their retirement experience was not up to expectation went back to work, while only 16% of those whose retirement preferences were met by their retirement experience did.[48] The survey shows that about one-quarter of recent retirees left work in-

TABLE 4 Retirees would have continued paid work if...

Percentage of recent retirees who said they would have continued to do paid work if circumstances had been different

	% Total	% Men	% Women
Total	60	61	58
Would have continued to do paid work if...*			
Could work fewer hours without affecting pension	28	29	27
Could work shorter hours without affecting pension	26	26	25
Had more vacation leave without affecting pension	19	20	18
Any combination of above three reasons	30	31	30
Could have worked part-time	28	28	27
Personal health had been better	26	27	26
Salary was increased	21	22	20
Mandatory retirement policies had not existed	12	12	12
Could have found suitable caregiving arrangements	6	7	6
Other reasons	11	10	13

* Respondents could report more than one reason

SOURCE Statistics Canada General Social Survey, 2002.

Raising the Age of Retirement

voluntarily. And even those who left work willingly may not really have had much choice about it. They may have been faced with time-limited early retirement options, for instance.

Among retirees whose retirement experience generally met their expectations (what the authors of the study refer to as "high-congruence" retirees), financial considerations were the main reason they left the labour force. They had saved enough money to make retirement feasible, or they had accumulated enough years of service to qualify for a pension. Most said their financial situation after retirement was better than or the same as it had been in the year before they retired. Health problems were not a key factor in the retirement decisions of this group and very few of them had experienced downsizing or unemployment on their way to retirement, the authors say. Of the small percentage who decided to go back to work after retiring, few said it was for financial reasons. Most gave reasons such as "wanting something to do," "asked to help out," or "enjoyed the work."

Recent retirees who were only moderately satisfied with their retirement experience typically left the labour force at an earlier age than the high-congruence retirees. Although they left the labour force voluntarily, many would have continued working if circumstances had been different. Essentially, they left the labour force prematurely. This group was dubbed the "moderate-congruence" retirees, to highlight the partial mismatch between their retirement preference and experiences. Most of these people had first retired before age 60, and health considerations were a motivating factor in their retirement decisions for almost one-third of this group. While nearly three-quarters of the moderate-congruence group said their financial situation had made it possible for them to retire, 32% of them returned to the labour force after their initial retirement—double the rate of the high-congruence retirees.

About 27% of recent retirees surveyed were described as "low-congruence"—they had not wanted to retire, and 43% of them said health was the primary reason for retirement. The authors of this study note that most of these retirees perceived themselves to be in a weak financial situation, with only 34% saying retirement was financially possible. In terms of financial well-being, half of the "low-congruence" retirees felt worse off in retirement than they were in the year prior to retiring, compared with about one in five high-congruence retirees.

Whether or not retirement meets expectations may also depend on the type of job a person has before retiring. For instance, the study found self-employed workers were more likely than paid employees to be high-congruence retirees. That's probably because self-employed workers have more control over the timing and process of their retirement. Unlike paid employees, these authors note, the self-employed "do not typically face premature retirement because of organizational downsizing, mandatory retirement policies, or early retirement incentives."[49]

Finally, according to this study, the timing of retirement itself affects the match between retirement preferences and experiences. Those who first retired in their 50s were more likely to be moderate-congruence retirees than others who did so in their sixties or older because they may feel they had just reached their full earnings capacity or were not yet psychologically ready to withdraw from employment.

Retirement at age 70?

Given the median age at which Canadians now retire, the idea of age 70 eventually becoming the typical age of retirement seems particularly far-fetched. Yet that seems to be a potential retirement age target now being bandied about in some policy-making circles—although not yet in Canada.

The British government, for instance, proposed a "default age" of retirement of 70 in a 2003 discussion paper *Equality and Diversity: Age Matters.*[50] It was not suggesting people should wait until age 70 to retire, but rather that they should have the option of working until age 70, if they wanted to. The government was responding to an earlier European Union directive on age discrimination, issued in 2000, under which compulsory retirement ages will be unlawful unless employers can show they are objectively justified.

The government's proposal was that employers would no longer be able to force workers to retire before they reach age 70—although apparently there were to be exceptions for occupational pension plans that

Raising the Age of Retirement

set a normal pension age below that. The government emphasized that the "normal pension age" is not the same as a mandatory retirement age, that it is simply the age at which an employee is eligible to start receiving a pension. The government had already proposed allowing people to draw their occupational pensions while continuing to work for the same employer. However, critics said a default retirement age of 70 in Britain could be the first step to raising the state pension eligibility age to 70. Some also believed it would open the door to companies making their employees work for five more years by cutting back the pensions of those who choose to retire earlier.

The suggestion has nevertheless been floated that getting people to work until age 70 would be a simple way of dealing with the pension "crisis" posed by population aging. In fact, as we noted earlier, a government-appointed Pensions Commission in the UK, in its first report issued in October 2004, said that, to offset the rise in the dependency ratio solely by increasing the average age of retirement, it would need to rise from 63.8 for men today and 61.6 for women, to reach 69.8 for men and 67.4 for women.[51]

In the end, the British government backed off on making age 70 the default retirement age. In December 2004, it announced it would set the default age at 65. Legislation to come into effect in the fall of 2006 will provide for a national default retirement age of 65 and a right for employees to request working beyond the set retirement age, which employers will have a duty to consider. This right will follow the same approach as the right to request flexible working time for parents with young children, where, the government says, "it has been successful in changing the culture towards more family-friendly working." It will allow employers to objectively justify earlier retirement ages "if they can show it is appropriate and necessary," and pension schemes will be allowed to set normal retirement ages if they need to. The retirement age provisions will be subject to a formal review after five years. And the government says, "If at the point of review the evidence suggested that we no longer needed the default retirement age at 65, we would abolish it."[52]

In February 2005, however, the British government's Department of Work and Pensions released a *Five Year Strategy*[53] with the long-term objective of increasing the overall employment rate from 75% to 80% "by

tackling inactivity while still supporting those who are unable to work."
The three-pronged strategy includes changes to incapacity [disability]
benefits; measures to support lone parents in the paid work force; and
what was described as "increased opportunity to work longer and save
more for retirement." The "flexible retirement" proposals, aimed at ensuring that one million more older people are working, would provide a
one-off payment of over £30,000 after five years for people who choose to
take their state pension late. Alternatively, the deferred benefit can also
be taken as an increased weekly amount added to their pension when
they finally claim it. Since the state pension is payable at age 65 for men
(and age 60 for women, rising to age 65 by 2020), someone who is willing
to wait until age 70 would be eligible for a sizeable lump sum payment
or increased weekly benefits. Anyone who postpones claiming the pension until age 75 would be entitled to a lump sum payment of £77,090.
Interestingly, the proposals do not require the person to keep on working
while deferring the pension.

Retirement age in Canada

In Canada to date, there has been no suggestion that people should
continue working to age 70. However, CPP retirement pensions may be
claimed at any age between age 60 and 70. Those who postpone claiming
their benefits until after age 65 receive an actuarially enhanced benefit
and they may start receiving their CPP pension even if they continue to
work. However, once the pension is in pay, the individual may not make
any further contributions to the plan.

Still, actuary Robert Brown, a professor of actuarial science at the
University of Waterloo, says he has been claiming for the past 20 years
that people will have to work longer.[54] He believes the age of retirement
will increase, whether the government takes any action or not. He sees
potential labour shortages looming as the numbers of people leaving the
labour force exceed those who are entering. Employers in the private
sector will be looking for ways to persuade older workers to stay on, says
Brown. He says the motivation for the 62-year olds to continue working
will be a softening of the value of their assets—including their homes—in

Raising the Age of Retirement

the near future because the entire baby boom will be selling assets. "And who's going to buy them?" he asks.

But working longer, says Brown, will not necessarily mean another two or three years. He believes everybody staying in the labour force eight or nine months longer would be all it would take to bring the situation back into equilibrium. The calculation makes allowances for productivity improvements, otherwise another five years would be required, he adds. "My own studies tell me you don't have to shift to age 70," says Brown.

Increasing the age of eligibility for CPP retirement pensions

As for the CPP, Brown argues: "We don't have to raise the age of eligibility if we're happy with 9.9%"—the current combined employer/employee contribution rate. "That 9.9% will carry us through the baby boom bulge," Brown says. As well, the cost of other public pensions, such as Old Age Security and the Guaranteed Income Supplement, will be manageable because these benefits are indexed to the cost of living (prices), not to the standard of living (wages), he notes. This means that, as the economy expands, the relative cost of these programs will be cheaper, even though more people will be getting the benefits. (Of course, it also means the older population will fall further behind younger people as the value of their pensions declines in relative terms.)

Government surveys in 1995–96 found that Canadians did not want the age of eligibility to be raised, Brown adds. But the question that needs to be asked, he says, is: "Would you like to work a bit longer and have an 8.8% contribution rate?" People would probably go for that option, he believes. He also suggests the reward for staying beyond age 65 should be improved. Under current rules, anyone working to age 70 would get a pension equivalent to 130% of what's available at age 65, Brown notes. "That's unfair to the person who delays retirement," he adds.

Other observers also note that any increase in the age of eligibility for CPP at this point would mean existing contribution rates would generate more money than was needed to pay benefits. That could make it possible to reduce the contribution rate, but there has really been no pressure for a reduction. Most experts don't expect the age of eligibility will be increased now.

It's clear that, if the government did eventually decide to go that route, it would have to phase it in over a long period of time. In the United States, where the age of eligibility for Social Security is being raised from age 65 to 67, the change was legislated more than 20 years ago in a package of 1983 amendments to the Social Security Act. It will be phased in over the next quarter-century. Only those born after 1960 will be denied full benefits until age 67. However, observers of the U.S. scene are already suggesting the eligibility age will likely have to continue increasing, probably reaching age 70 by about 2040.

For many Canadians, the CPP and OAS public pension programs make up a significant chunk of their retirement income. Any move to increase the age of eligibility for these benefits would therefore probably have a marked impact on the age of retirement. But lower-income workers would be most affected, because they're the ones who are less likely to belong to workplace pension plans or to have other sources of retirement income. Workers with good pension benefits or substantial savings will always be able to retire when they like, and would probably not be deterred from doing so by an increase in the eligibility age for OAS or CPP.

Robert Brown suggests that, if Canadian policy-makers wanted to increase the age of eligibility for public pensions as a way of keeping older workers in the work force when the baby boomers retire, it would not need to be done until around 2016. However, it's also important to note that the vast majority of workplace pension plans are fully integrated with the CPP. Any change in the age of eligibility would therefore increase the costs of the private plans that make up the difference. One way of encouraging workers to work longer, says Brown, would be to allow them to resume contributions to the plan if they go back to work after starting their CPP benefits early—something early retirees are not allowed to do under the current system.

Changes in the benefit formula could also be used to discourage early retirement. As policy-makers increasingly focus on persuading people to work longer, this may well be an option they will consider, especially

Raising the Age of Retirement

since comments by the Chief Actuary, referred to earlier, have suggested that the CPP's early retirement provisions are too generous.

Persuading people to work longer

It's clear that the kind of jobs workers do will have an important bearing on the outcome of moves to encourage people to work longer. Those employed in physically demanding or stressful occupations will certainly not want to prolong their years of employment. And, under current rules, as we noted earlier, workers in a limited number of specific high-stress jobs are already allowed early retirement without penalty.

Some experts suggest that, if necessary, tax and pension laws could also be changed as a way of making early retirement less attractive. Companies that sponsor pension plans may also reduce early retirement incentives to cope with worker shortages. But some may see the best way of doing that is to switch from a defined benefit plan to a defined contribution plan where there is no early retirement incentive.

It must also be emphasized that, at the present time, a surprisingly high percentage of retirements seem to be involuntary. One study that tracked job separation and job acquisition of selected cohorts between the ages of 50 and 65 found the majority of separations involved a layoff—more often permanent than temporary—and a considerable number involved job-switching. Less often, job separations were associated with illness or disability, which would not necessarily have resulted in a permanent separation. Overall, according to this study, about 60% of all job separations, for both men and women, could be classified as involuntary.[55] The authors conclude that, in many cases, the job separation that ultimately ended a career must have been a layoff, an illness or disability, or a family event.

Phased retirement and other options

Other options, such as "phased retirement"—implemented some years ago in Quebec—could be designed to encourage people to keep on working, easing into retirement gradually. But Quebec's program, originally introduced in 1997, was designed to encourage early retirement to free up jobs for younger workers and address the problem of high youth employment. That's no longer the policy priority. Quebec has since emphasized changes to the QPP to penalize early retirement and encourage people to work longer.

However, policies that help people to ease into retirement gradually could still be used for older workers, perhaps as a reward for delaying full retirement. The 1997 Quebec phased retirement plan allowed people who would agree to reduce their hours of work to begin drawing on their workplace pension benefits while continuing to contribute to the Quebec Pension Plan as if they were still working full-time. Technically, the phase-in was accomplished by allowing a lump sum withdrawal from the pension plan, which could then be converted to an income stream without contravening income tax rules. But the effect of the withdrawal was to reduce the eventual pension to be received from the pension plan.

Those who believe the retirement of the baby boomers will trigger a shortage of skilled workers feel that employers will offer all kinds of incentives—including better pension benefits and financial rewards—to persuade older workers not to retire just yet.

Based on the responses to Statistics Canada's 2002 General Social Survey, referred to earlier, it's possible some workers would have postponed their retirement if they had been offered more flexible work arrangements such as part-time hours or fewer weeks of work in the year—particularly if they could have changed their work schedules without their pensions being affected. Willingness to continue working varied with level of education, occupation, industry, and other characteristics.[56] For example:

• Retirees with a university degree were among the most likely to have continued working under different working arrangements (with or without other factors). This could be because they have higher levels of job satisfaction and are more likely to have less physically demanding jobs. Employers who want to retain highly educated workers may therefore have to seriously consider alternative working arrangements for these workers.

Raising the Age of Retirement

• Retirees formerly employed in health care, social assistance, and education were the least likely to report preferences for continuing to work. That could mean there is less scope for retaining workers in these industries. (It may be significant that women predominate in these occupations, but the gender issue was not explored).

• For immigrants and retirees who had received early retirement incentives, willingness to continue working depended not just on alternative working arrangements but on other factors, too.

It must be noted that the General Social Survey did not address the extent to which job quality discourages older workers from remaining in the work force.

Advocates of working longer claim that moving away from early retirement shouldn't be seen as a threat to anybody. In policy terms, they maintain, they're not posing this as an issue of "work longer to get your pension." All they're really saying—at least according to them—is "let's increase choice and give people a better range of alternatives." But, as we've already seen, the QPP is already implementing measures designed to encourage people to work longer and penalizing those who want to retire early.

How the UK government plans to get people working longer

The UK government's plan to get people working longer, part of its *Five Year Strategy* mentioned earlier, includes rewarding those who delay claiming their state pension, a benefit worth about £105 (roughly $250) a week, including a basic benefit and a pension credit. They will be able to get a lump sum payment, the amount depending on how many years they postpone claiming it, or a 50% increase in their weekly pension for life. Although they're not required to go on working to get the reward, the incentive to continue working would likely be highest for lower-income workers who could not afford to quit work without getting their state pension. Of course, the risk these workers take would be that, the longer they postpone claiming their pension, the fewer years they will receive a state pension. In effect, they're also gambling on living long enough to claim enough additional benefits to make the postponement worthwhile. Presumably, for higher-income earners who have other sources of retirement income, postponing receipt of their state pension could provide them with a generous lump sum payment to form part of their estate, providing they live long enough to claim it.

While the UK government admits the average age at which people leave the labour market is no longer falling and the average retirement age has started to rise, "it will need to rise further if we are to meet the challenge of longevity," it says.[57] In 2006, the government will enact the European Directive on age discrimination, making it unlawful to discriminate on the basis of age in employment and vocational training. As well, changes to occupational pension plan rules from April 2006 will mean people will be able to draw their occupational pensions and continue to work for the same employer. The government also says: "We aim to explore how flexible working, financial incentives and information about retirement income can help older workers make sensible and supported choices about working, saving, and retirement."[58]

Using compulsion could hurt lower-income earners

It's worth repeating: trying to force people to work longer by raising the age of eligibility for public pension programs such as OAS and CPP would have particularly serious consequences for lower-income workers who are less likely to have other options, such as workplace pensions or private savings. Such workers are also more likely to be employed in precarious jobs or non-standard work arrangements where a requirement to work longer before being eligible for a pension could be a particularly punitive measure. The right to retire after a lifetime of hard work with a decent pension—essentially their deferred wages—is a right for which workers have fought and won. Attempts to undermine this right would undoubtedly be strongly resisted.

It has been suggested, however, that labour support for a later average age of retirement might be forthcoming if the objective were met through measures that result in the more complete utilization of older workers who are approaching "retirement age." That could involve more effective

Raising the Age of Retirement

adjustment programs for older workers; improvements to social services that reduce pressure on older women workers to leave paid work to care for family members; and general improvements in the quality of work that make paid work less burdensome.[59]

What recent trends show

Only 7% of men and 2% of women who are aged 70 or older participate in the paid work force. But the percentage of those who work past 65 has increased significantly over the past decade, and particularly over the past three or four years. In 2003, for example, 52.6% of men aged 60–64 were in the labour force, compared with 47.1% of men in this age group who were labour force participants in 1993. Among men aged 65–69, 21.0% were labour force participants in 2003, up from 16.0% in 1993, representing a 31% increase in the labour force participation of this age group over the decade. Labour force participation of older women experienced a similar increase. In 2003, 31.9% of women aged 60–64 were in the labour force, compared with 24.3% of this age group who were labour force participants in 1993. Few women work past 65, but even in this age group participation in the paid work force has increased. In 2003, 9.8% of women aged 65–69 were in the paid work force compared with 7.6%

TABLE 5 Older workers keep on working

Percentage of older workers in the labour force, Canada, 1993–2003

	1993	1994	1995	1996	1997	1998	1999	2000	2001	2002	2003
Men											
Aged 60–64	47.1	46.6	43.8	43.6	45.7	44.7	46.6	46.1	47.0	50.9	52.6
Aged 65–69	16.0	17.9	16.9	16.5	16.7	17.7	17.0	16.1	16.1	18.6	21.0
Women											
Aged 60–64	24.3	24.9	23.6	23.2	24.4	25.2	26.0	27.2	27.4	30.4	31.9
Aged 65–69	7.6	7.4	7.4	7.1	7.8	7.4	7.2	7.3	7.8	8.6	9.8

SOURCE Statistics Canada CANSIM.

GROWING OLDER, WORKING LONGER

in 1993, representing a 29% increase in the labour force participation of women in this age group over the period.[60]

It's probably significant that increased labour force participation among older workers—particularly among men—is most evident over the past few years, following closely on the heels of the stock market correction.

However, it has also been noted that the increased employment of older workers in the last couple of years seems to have been accounted for overwhelmingly by increased hiring, as opposed to a decrease in total separations from employment, including rates of retirement.[61] This is a development that underlines the importance of the overall demand for labour that would create job opportunities for workers of all ages, including older workers. In fact, observers maintain that the overall demand for labour will play a vital role in determining the actual age of retirement.[62]

Bob Baldwin emphasizes that important changes in the employment of older workers in evidence recently are not associated with any of the OECD prescriptions for increasing the labour force activity of older workers. It's also interesting to note that strategies to discourage early retirement by getting out of defined benefit plans with their early retirement incentives and converting to defined contribution plans could backfire. Future stock market booms that boost the value of investments in defined contribution plans and RRSPS could encourage workers in such plans to reactivate their dreams of early retirement. In other words, such strategies don't necessarily guarantee predictable patterns of labour force participation by older workers.[63]

When it comes right down to it, Canadians may already be moving to a form of phased retirement as they take up other forms of paid work following a first retirement from a career job. According to one study, estimates of job acquisition indicate that, by age 65, 14% of men and 7% of women had retired and then started a new job within a year. The numbers represent about 27% of male retirees and 23% of female retirees.[64] But the study also found that job changes at career-end suggest barriers or disincentives to re-employment for older workers should also be of concern. We return to that issue in the next chapter.

Raising the Age of Retirement

Notes

1 Baldwin 2004a: 9.

2 Statistics Canada 2004e: 11.

3 Schellenberg and Silver 2004: 3.

4 OECD 2004a: 1.

5 OECD 2004b.

6 United Kingdom Government 2004b: 44.

7 Trades Union Congress 2004b: 1.

8 Phillimore et.al, cited in Wilkinson 1996: 57.

9 Walker 2003: 11.

10 Kranc 2004:1.

11 Government of Canada 1997: 36.

12 Ibid:35.

13 Chief Actuary 2004:11.

14 Department of Finance 2004: 1.

15 International Monetary Fund 2004: 66.

16 Ibid: 66, footnote 20.

17 Dodge 2004a: 3.

18 Dodge 2004c: 15.

19 OECD 2000: 8.

20 Walker 2003:12.

21 Ontario Government 2005a: 2.

22 Ontario Government 2005b: 1.

23 Gunderson 2004: 5.

24 Smolkin 2004: 3.

25 Smolkin 2004: 7.

26 Kesselman 2004: 1-2.

27 Gunderson 2004: 5.

28 Gunderson 2004: 2.

29 Kesselman 2004: 4.

30 Schellenberg and Silver 2004: 3.

31 Gunderson 2004: 4.

32 Kesselman 2004:4.

33 McKinney v. University of Guelph, [1990] 76 D.L.R. (4th) 545, at 627.

34 Data from Statistics Canada Income Statistics Division.

35 Marshall 2003: 20

36 Ontario English Catholic Teachers Association 2004: 2.

37 Ontario Federation of Labour 2004: 3.

38 Jackson 2002: 1.

39 United Kingdom Government 2003: 21.

40 Meadows 2003: 3.

41 Ibid.

42 Ibid.

43 Smolkin 2004: 7,

44 Gunderson 2004: 2.

45 Gunderson 2004: 7.

46 Schellenberg and Silver 2004: 3

47 Ibid.

48 Ibid.

49 Schellenberg and Silver 2004: 6.

50 United Kingdom Government 2003.

51 United Kingdom Government 2004b: 44.

52 United Kingdom Government 2004c: 2 & 4.

53 United Kingdom Government 2005.

54 Interview with author, August 12, 2003.

55 Rowe and Nguyen 2003: 56.

56 Morissette, Schellenberg and Silver 2004: 18.

57 United Kingdom Government 2005: 52.

58 Ibid: 55.

59 Baldwin 2004a: 15.

60 Data from CANSIM, Statistics Canada.

61 Baldwin 2004a: 6.

62 Ibid: 17.

63 Ibid: 6.

64 Rowe and Nguyen 2003: 56.

Year:				Month:			MORNING		AFTERNOON		OVERTIME	
	MORNING		AFTERNOON		OVERTIME		IN	OUT	IN	OUT	IN	OUT
	IN	OUT	IN	OUT	IN	OUT						
MON												
WED								257	602			

5

Protecting Older Workers

INCREASING LONGEVITY and declining fertility rates have combined to produce Canada's ageing population. Just as older people will account for an increasing percentage of the population, so older workers will form a growing percentage of the workforce. That trend is evident over the past 10 years. In 1994, for example, men aged 50 to 64 held 17.5% of all jobs held by men in the Canadian economy. By 2004, men in this age group accounted for 22.7% of all male employment. Similarly, older women account for a growing percentage of female employment. In 1994, women aged 50 to 64 comprised 14.6% of all employed women. By 2004, women in this age group accounted for 21.4% of all employed women [*Table 6*].

These trends will continue regardless of whether or not Canadians are persuaded to delay their retirement and go on working. In fact, if there is any significant movement to later retirement, older workers will account for an even greater percentage of total employment. Regardless of how new concepts of retirement emerge and are adopted, protection of older workers will become an issue. We will have to look at how older workers are treated by employers and, in particular, we will need to make sure older workers are not forced to keep working against their will.

As we have seen, the push to persuade people to delay their retirement and go on working is viewed as a way to ease the pressure on pension systems that results from population aging. Then there's the argument that early retirement represents a huge waste of human capital, as older citizens spend long years in retirement when they could be continuing in paid employment and fuelling economic growth by contributing to the production of goods and services. In another version of this view, the workforce will shrink when all the boomers retire, so strong measures will be needed to prevent this from happening, otherwise economic growth could also shrink.

TABLE 6 Employment of older workers is increasing

Percentage of jobs held by older workers in Canada

Age group	1994	1995	1996	1997	1998	1999	2000	2001	2002	2003	2004
Males											
45–49	11.4	11.7	11.9	11.8	11.9	12.0	12.0	12.1	12.5	12.5	12.8
50–54	8.4	8.7	9.0	9.5	9.7	10.1	10.5	10.7	10.5	10.7	10.7
55–59	5.6	5.7	5.8	5.9	6.0	6.3	6.5	6.7	7.1	7.6	7.9
60–64	3.5	3.2	3.2	3.3	3.2	3.3	3.3	3.4	3.7	3.9	4.1
65–69	1.2	1.1	1.1	1.1	1.2	1.1	1.0	1.0	1.1	1.3	1.3
50–64	17.5	17.6	18.0	18.7	18.9	19.7	20.3	20.8	21.3	22.2	22.7
65 +	2.0	1.8	1.8	1.9	2.0	1.9	1.8	1.8	2.0	2.2	2.3
Females											
45–49	11.5	12.0	12.1	12.3	12.5	12.6	12.7	12.8	13.1	13.3	13.4
50–54	7.6	7.9	8.2	8.8	9.2	9.7	10.0	10.5	10.6	10.6	10.9
55–59	4.7	4.7	4.8	4.8	5.2	5.3	5.7	5.9	6.2	7.1	7.3
60–64	2.3	2.2	2.1	2.2	2.2	2.3	2.4	2.4	2.7	2.9	3.2
65–69	0.7	0.6	0.6	0.7	0.6	0.6	0.6	0.6	0.7	0.8	0.8
50–64	14.6	14.8	15.1	15.8	16.6	17.3	18.1	18.8	19.5	20.6	21.4
65+	1.0	1.0	1.0	1.1	1.0	1.0	1.0	1.0	1.0	1.2	1.2

SOURCE Statistics Canada CANSIM Table 282-0002.

GROWING OLDER, WORKING LONGER

Business advocates will likely argue that government policies should make it easier for them to hang on to their older workers—or, at the very least, should not bar or frustrate their efforts to do so. But, from the point of view of individual workers, age discrimination will be given increasing attention. In Canada, this is dealt with by federal and provincial human rights legislation. As we saw earlier, however, human rights laws in some provinces prohibit age discrimination only between ages 18 and 64. Discrimination against workers aged 65 or older would not be contrary to the law in these jurisdictions—although that could be remedied if the age cap in human rights laws were lifted, as we suggested in Chapter 4. Even so, however, enforcement of such laws might prove difficult.

At the international level, other countries are already trying to address the problem of age discrimination, but there seem to be rather wide loopholes in some of the proposals. The British government's 2003 paper *Equality and Diversity: Age Matters*,[1] with its suggestion of age 70 as a "default age of retirement," ostensibly was looking at ways to implement a directive of the European Union prohibiting discrimination against older workers. The "default age"—which was subsequently lowered to 65—would simply mean an employer could not force workers to retire prior to that age. But it was proposed to allow exceptions where employers could come up with a reasonable justification for continuing to discriminate on the basis of age.

The European Union in particular has been calling for a comprehensive active aging strategy to increase the employment of older workers. "Older workers must not be perceived as just another vulnerable group meriting special attention," says the EU, "but as a core component of the labour supply and a key factor for the sustainable development of the European Union."[2] The EU takes the position that the low employment of older workers in Europe represents "a waste of individual life opportunities and societal potential."[3]

As we noted earlier, European views about working longer seem to have spilled over into Canada, although it's not clear why this is so since Canada is doing much better than European countries in keeping older workers in paid employment. For instance, the federal government's PRI research project on aging is looking at how older workers might be persuaded to accept different kinds of work. In actual fact, however,

Canada has already exceeded the targets set by the EU for the employ-ment of older people in member countries of the EU. The 2001 Stockholm European Council agreed that half the EU population in the 55–64 age group should be in employment by 2010. But by 2004, 54% of people aged 55–64 in Canada were in the paid work force. The EU has also complained that the employment of women aged 55–64 is only around 30% (based on 2002 data). Labour force participation of Canadian women in this age group in 2004, at 46.2%, was much higher than in Europe [*Table 7*]. But it's worth repeating here that increasing numbers of women in this age group may have been forced to retire from paid employment because of family caregiving responsibilities, which don't seem to be acknowledged in the push to keep older workers in paid employment.

The second part of the EU's active aging strategy, adopted in 2002, is gradually to increase the effective age at which people in the EU stop working, so that it is about five years higher by 2010. On this one, Canada may be making progress, although it is perhaps too early to tell. The median age of retirement for men, which stood at 61.8 years in 2000, had had risen by 1.5 years to reach 63.3 in 2003. However, for women, the median age of retirement in 2003, at 60.4, was essentially the same as it was in 2000, when it stood at 60.3.

Some observers believe the retirement of the baby boomers will trig-ger such a shortage of skilled workers that employers will look for ways to encourage older workers to stay on. According to this school of thought, financial bonuses, better pensions, and other kinds of incentives will all be part of the arsenal employers will use to hold on to their long-term skilled employees. In theory, all this could make it so attractive for older workers to keep on working that there would be no need to resort to such harsh tactics as raising the age of eligibility for public or private pensions or changing the rules on RRSPS so people would just have to postpone their retirement.

But extending paid employment—whether on a voluntary or man-datory basis—raises a range of issues that need to be addressed. In this chapter, we will try to deal with some of the key concerns:

• Can we count on a shortage of skilled workers to persuade older work-ers to delay their retirement voluntarily?

- Are jobs available for older workers and what can be done to ensure they have the skills needed to fill these jobs?

- Is phased retirement becoming more popular, and what issues does it raise?

- What exactly is "active aging" and should we be encouraging it?

- What can be done to ensure older workers are protected and that they are not forced to continue working against their will?

Will a shortage of skilled workers keep older workers working?

For those people who like to promote cataclysmic views of the demographic "time bomb" about to explode when the baby boomers retire, Canada will face a major labour market crisis over the next decade or so. For the demographic doomsayers, voluntary methods of raising the age of retirement seem likely to fail. They argue there will be such a shortage of skilled workers that action must be taken now to raise the retirement age and keep older workers working. They also suggest that, with a smaller generation following the baby boomers, the workforce will shrink when the boomers retire—another reason for trying to keep them working, even if it means employers must invest in retraining their older workforce.

William Robson of the corporate-funded C.D. Howe Institute, in a 2001 report on *Aging Populations and the Workforce: Challenges for Employers,* talks about helping employers prepare for "the more chronic shortages that loom ahead."[4] "The more public policy encourages earlier retirement, shapes income support for senior citizens in ways that discourage work, or mandates the receipt of pension benefits by certain ages," says Robson, "the less sense it will make for employers to provide older workers the training opportunities that would keep them happy and productive."[5] He claims reforms to pension regulations and the taxes and transfers that encourage later exit from the workforce would make investments in training older workers more attractive. Robson's report was an official statement by the British North American Committee—a

Protecting Older Workers

group of senior business executives from the UK, the U.S. and Canada—sponsored by the British North American Research Association, the Center for Strategic and International Studies in the U.S., and the C.D. Howe Institute in Canada. However, critics note "these organizations are well known for promoting a view of population aging that is apocalyptic in tone."[6]

While Robson admits "the wheels of demographic change grind slowly," he believes "even slow-moving changes can surprise with their impact."[7] Cyclical downturns may cool the demand for workers, he suggests, but when the economy and financial markets pick up again, "the demographic trends prefigured here will become more than lines on a page. For many employers, they will be little less than a crisis." Robson maintains that labour shortages will simply put more of a premium on practices that make good business sense anyway: attracting and retaining people with key knowledge, skills and aptitudes, and ensuring that valuable prospective or current employees are not screened out by the use of inappropriate markers, such as age. Employers who do not adapt to a changing workforce will lose their edge in recruiting, he says, and find frustrated younger workers and pensioned older workers leaving for competitors. And "governments whose policies frustrate these adaptations will hurt their citizens' living standards."[8]

Some observers believe the need to attract and retain older skilled workers will motivate employers voluntarily to adopt enlightened policies, even to the extent of moving back to defined benefit pension plans in an effort to keep older workers happy. But, while it seems to be widely accepted that there will be a shortage of skilled workers when the baby boomers retire, recent studies imply that will not necessarily be the case. Like the demographic time bomb scare, it seems the coming "crisis" over the shortage of skilled workers may have been considerably overblown.

For example, a 2004 study from the Canadian Policy Research Networks (CPRN) concludes that "there is no evidence that Canada is facing a looming general shortage of skilled labour as a direct result of demographic aging."[9] It also concludes that skill shortages are not so much a looming "crisis" as a challenge that can be managed with careful planning by employers and policy-makers. The authors of this study suggest employer surveys frequently identify shortages of skills, in part, because it is in their interest to do so, as a larger pool of better-trained workers often leads to lower wages. It may be that an employer experiences difficulties filling positions, but this typically means that employees with the required skills are hard to find *at the wage the employer is offering.*[10] (*Emphasis added by the authors of the study*).

It is also important to note that the characteristics of some occupations and industries may make it difficult to attract or retain workers. Where the work environment is poor, the work is stressful or offers little flexibility, workers will not be interested in delaying their retirement. In other words, it's not just labour force aging that affects the supply and demand for labour. More important is the nature of the work itself.[11] That suggests employers who want to hang on to older workers may have to make concerted efforts to improve job quality, where there is room for improvement.

There may be other reasons why the labour market is slow to adjust to perceived skill shortages. For example, there may be a "credential gap" between the stated requirements of the work and the real skills needed to do the job. People with a high school education may be perfectly able to work as bank tellers, for instance, yet many banks now require new employees for these jobs to have a university degree.[12]

Looking at different industries and occupations in more depth, it is possible to see which ones have a high percentage of older workers. The study concludes that older occupations are spread across industries, suggesting that all industries have the potential to be affected by an aging labour force. But whether or not there will be a skill shortage when these older workers retire depends on the type of skill involved in the industry. In general, occupations requiring longer training or more experience tend to have older age structures, putting them at greater risk of large-scale retirement. Managerial and professional occupations, particularly in health care and education, are examples of this.[13]

Predictions of skill shortages as a result of the aging workforce apparently misunderstand the ways in which the economy will seek equilibrium.[14] In fact, some economists argue that shortages of labour in relation to physical capital will lead to higher wages. According to economist Marcel Mérette of the University of Ottawa, there will be greater incentives for investment in human capital, "whose importance as an engine of

Protecting Older Workers

growth is increasingly being recognized as industrialized countries shift away from resource-based and toward knowledge-based economies."[15] Mérette suggests that, if the investments in human capital materialize, population aging may stimulate economic growth in the context of a knowledge-based economy and increase the living standards of young and future generations.[16]

Summing it all up, the CPRN study emphasizes that labour force aging is only one of many factors that affect the supply of and demand for labour. There is a whole range of complex factors that interact and issues that need to be explored to see what is really going on in a particular industry or occupation. For example, has there been a lot of international competition in the industry that has led to a rationalization and reduction in the number of workers? Is the industry growing? Are there age-related barriers in a particular occupation that push older workers out? Is the length of training required to do a job reasonable, given the nature of the job itself?[17]

Job prospects for older workers

Policies to persuade older workers to continue in paid employment will not be effective if employers refuse to hire or train older workers. Many employers are still unwilling to promote older workers or to invest in their training, perhaps believing the return on their investment will not be great enough because the worker has fewer years left to work. But research shows that older workers are less likely than younger workers to change employers, and the retention rate for workers aged 45 or older seems to be as high or higher than for younger workers.[18] In other words, employers who invest in training younger workers have no particular guarantee those workers will stay with the employer long enough to make the investment pay off. Given the rapid changes in some skill requirements, it has been suggested that there could be significant economic benefits for employers offering training to older workers if those benefits can be accrued within a short period of time.[19]

Labour representatives point out that an important part of the trade union response to the suggestion that older workers need to be utilized more fully is a concern that any increase in the supply of older workers needs to be matched with an overall increase in the demand for labour. They argue that measures to increase the employment of older workers "should not create a zero sum relationship with other age groups."[20] But, regardless of what happens to the age of retirement, job prospects for older workers will become an important issue, if only because—as we noted earlier—older workers will account for an increasing percentage of the work force.

TABLE 7 **Older workers in the paid work force, Canada, 2004**

	Unemployment rate	Participation rate	Employment rate
	%	%	%
Both sexes			
Aged 45–64 years	5.4	73.6	69.6
45–54	5.1	85.0	80.7
55–64	5.9	57.4	54.0
65 years and over	3.2	7.7	7.5
55 years and over	5.6	30.8	29.1
Men			
Aged 45–64	5.5	80.1	75.7
45–54	5.2	89.9	85.3
55–64	6.1	66.0	62.0
65 years and over	3.1	11.8	11.4
55 years and over	5.6	38.4	36.2
Women			
Aged 45–64	5.2	67.2	63.7
45–54	5.0	80.1	76.2
55–64	5.7	49.0	46.2
65 years and over	3.3	4.5	4.3
55 years and over	5.4	24.1	22.8

SOURCE Statistics Canada (2005) Labour force characteristics by age and sex. At http://www. statcan.ca/english/Pgdb/labor20b.htm

Protecting Older Workers

Some observers argue that this fact alone will mean employers will be more favourably inclined to hiring, training, and promoting older workers. But even though older workers may be highly skilled with long years of experience, they are still often thought of as less productive and less amenable to training and retraining. However, research suggests there is no clear relationship between "trainability" and age. The ability of older workers to acquire new skills apparently depends on the design of the training. As well, it has been suggested that workers who receive training throughout their working lives may be better able to absorb it when they are older.[21] This is the familiar argument for lifelong learning that is a key part of the flexible life-course movement discussed in Chapter 3.

Ageism may keep older workers out of some occupations. For example, the age structure of information technology occupations is younger than the overall labour force. While this implies there will not be a danger of skill shortages in these occupations as a result of baby boomer retirements, if also suggests an over-valuation of youth in IT work that may present barriers to older workers interested in these occupations.[22]

Employers have often dealt with economic downturns by promoting early retirement or laying off older workers. Increasingly, employers are using contingent workers instead of establishing full-time permanent jobs. This change in employment relationships simply adds to the vulnerability of older workers. As well, the shift to a knowledge-based economy, and the technological changes that have accompanied it, have in many cases reduced the relative value of the previous skills and experience of many older workers, necessitating retraining for those who want to remain employed.[23]

It is also important to note that older workers do not form a homogenous group. Older women, for example, have particular needs and interests that are different from those of older men. As well, older workers in different occupations and different economic sectors will be faced with different issues and problems. A blue-collar industrial job is significantly different from a job in the retail sector, for example. Workers employed in occupations requiring strenuous physical work may face premature aging and become disabled at a much higher rate than those working in less stressful and demanding positions. But workers in low-paying service sector jobs with few benefits may face greater economic hardship after retirement.[24]

Widespread characterization of older workers as being less productive and less adaptable may make it difficult for older workers to find work if they are laid off. Some may decide to give up and simply retire. Workers over age 55 are much less likely to be in the paid workforce. For example, only 57.4% of workers aged 55–64 participate in the paid workforce, compared with 85% of those in the age group 45 to 54 [*Table 7*]. But, among those in the 45–64-year age group who are labour force participants, workers aged 55–64 have higher rates of unemployment than those aged 45–54 [*Table 7*]—perhaps suggesting these older workers who lose a job may have more difficulty than somewhat younger workers in finding another one.

It is worth noting, as Bob Baldwin has pointed out, that Canada is one of several countries to experience increased employment of older workers in the face of somewhat looser labour markets in the early years of the 21st century. Between the fall of 2001 and 2002, labour force participation of 60-to-64-year-old men and women each increased by roughly five percentage points, from 48% to 53% in the case of men and from 27% to 32% in the case of women. Baldwin notes that this kind of change usually takes some years to accomplish. Of particular interest is the fact that the increased employment of older workers seems to have been accounted for overwhelmingly by increased hiring, as opposed to a decrease in separations from employment, including rates of retirement. He calculates that, expressed as a percentage of the employed population aged 55–64, the hiring rate in 2002 jumped to 18% from a steady rate of about 11% in the previous few years.[25]

Baldwin also points out that these important changes in the employment of older workers were not associated with any of the OECD prescriptions for increasing the labour force activity of older workers. The stabilization of labour force participation rates in the mid-1990s, says Baldwin, provides a reminder of the importance of the overall demand for labour.[26]

Unions have been instrumental in negotiating pensions for their members, so that most union members now belong to workplace pension plans. In fact, 80% of union members, compared with 27% of non-union members, belong to a workplace pension plan.[27] But unions have also negotiated a variety of other provisions in their collective agreements that relate to older workers, ranging from anti-discrimination clauses to seniority-based systems for allocating access, to lighter work and the right to refuse or accept overtime.[28]

In an analysis of *Collective Agreements and Older Workers in Canada*, analysts from Human Resources Development Canada (HRDC) point out that, while only about one-third of Canadian workers are unionized, employers in non-unionized firms have historically often based their human resources policies on contract clauses found in collective agreements. As well, they note, federal and provincial legislation on employment standards, occupational health and safety, and various social programs have in many instances been inspired by practices stemming from the collective bargaining process.[29]

Some collective agreements contain affirmative action clauses that benefit older workers. (In this study, "older workers" are defined as those aged 45 or older). For instance, hiring quotas may be designed to guarantee employment opportunities for older workers—particularly in the construction industry where employers tend to prefer hiring younger workers due to the physically demanding nature of the work. For example, a clause in the collective agreement of the Construction and Labour Relations Association of B.C. and United Association of Journeymen and Apprentices of the Plumbing and Pipefitting Industry, Local 170 (1994–1998) states:

> It shall be the policy of the Employer to endeavour where there are five (5) or more journeymen employed by an Employer, that every fifth journeyman shall be fifty (50) years of age or over if available.[30]

But other clauses in collective agreements may potentially lead to age discrimination and make it difficult for older workers to find or retain employment. For example, some agreements give employers some flexibility in setting special wage rates—essentially lower wages—for older and/or partially disabled workers. As the authors of the HRDC study point out, although the intent is to make the hiring of older workers more attractive, and therefore increase their chances of finding and maintaining employment, the effect may be the institutionalization of wage discrimination on the basis of age.[31] Such provisions are clearly based on the stereotype that older workers are less productive.

Medical certificates and examinations may be required on hiring or on return to work following illness, to determine whether a worker is able to perform certain functions. But this system is open to abuse because it may disguise age discrimination in human resource management and have demoralizing effects on employees.

Mandatory retirement provisions, common in many collective agreements, are also viewed by some as discriminating against older workers. It could also be argued, however, that such provisions, freely entered into, in fact *prevent* the exploitation of older workers who might otherwise be forced to continue working against their will.

As the HRDC study notes, although many of these provisions are designed to guarantee that older workers are given the same opportunities as other workers, "employers and unions must remain mindful of the way in which certain potentially discriminatory clauses are used."[32] The collective agreements analyzed in this study were agreements that were in effect in January 1998. As the percentage of older workers in the paid workforce continues to increase, we can expect to see even more attention paid to the needs of these workers in future collective agreements.

Phased retirement

Governments, employers, and the other social partners are being urged to encourage phased retirement as a way of mitigating the impact of the aging population. Labour ministers of the G-8 countries, meeting in Turin, Italy, in November 2000, issued their Turin Charter, *Towards Active Aging,* which urged a comprehensive policy approach to deal with demographic trends. "To successfully utilize the huge potential for increased labour force participation among older workers," they said,

Protecting Older Workers

"we must make use of their talents and experience." Among other recommendations, the ministers said that "gradual retirement schemes, in which part-time job income is supplemented by a partial accrual of pension entitlements, should be further explored as means to increase participation rates."[33]

But it would seem phased retirement has not yet risen very high on the list of possible solutions to the anticipated shortage of skilled workers in Canada. A 2002 survey of business, public sector, and labour leaders conducted by the Canadian Labour and Business Centre found that phased-in retirement was not prominent on the list of possible solutions cited to apprehended skill shortages. For example, 48% of private sector managers cited skill shortages as a serious problem, but only 14% considered phased-in retirement as a "very important" option. In the public sector, 57% of managers cited skill shortages as a serious problem, but only 28% considered phased-in retirement a very important option, ranking sixth on a list of possible remedies. It may be significant that the CLBC survey found the strongest support for phased-in retirement came from public sector unions, 48% of whom cited this option as "very important" in meeting the skill shortage challenge.[34] Skill shortages seem to be most evident in public sector occupations such as nursing, where pubic sector unions have already taken the initiative to negotiate phased retirement arrangements.

While most Canadians apparently do not want to go on working until much older ages, more and more people do seem to be interested in phasing into retirement gradually—either because they can't afford to stop working completely, or because they simply want to remain active. In some cases, this may mean leaving a long-term permanent "career" job to become self-employed, or switching from full-time to part-time or contract work with the same employer. For many older workers, such non-standard work arrangements are a way of easing into a full retirement from paid employment. But for those whose pension income is inadequate, such jobs may be a vitally important lifeline. In 2001, while 38% of all employed Canadians aged 16 to 69 held some form of non-standard job (including part-time work, temporary jobs and self-employment), almost half (49%) of those aged 55 to 69 were in non-standard jobs.[35]

It is important to note that older workers who decide to work beyond the normal retirement age, or to phase into retirement by switching from full-time to part-time work, may lose out on certain employee benefits that come with being a full-time worker. For example, provisions in some collective agreements specify that a number of employment benefits are no longer available to older workers once they reach normal retirement age or become eligible for a pension. This is almost always the case for long-term disability insurance, since a pension is presumed to offer an adequate replacement income to disabled employees.[36] The HRDC study, referred to earlier, points out that the potential loss of benefits when a worker changes status from full-time to part-time may constitute a serious disincentive for older workers who wish to reduce their working time. The authors suggest that clauses in collective agreements that specifically grant part-time employees access to various benefits, even if they are pro-rated, can offer aging workers more flexibility and possibly improve their working lives.[37]

It is worth noting here that Ontario's new legislation banning mandatory retirement will still allow workers aged 65-plus to be denied other workplace benefits. For example, employers will still be able to discriminate on the basis of age in providing benefits to workers aged 65 or older. As well, entitlements under the Workplace Safety and Insurance Act will not change and injured workers aged 63 or more at the time of injury will only be able to receive loss of earning benefits for up to two years—as they did previously.

Recent surveys show a growing interest in phased retirement. For instance, one survey conducted for Desjardins Financial Security in December 2003 showed 61% of Canadians aged 40 or more were planning to phase into retirement, mainly by becoming self-employed and reducing their weekly hours of work.[38] Wanting to remain active was the main reason for planning a phased-in retirement, but maintaining the standard of living and getting additional income were also cited as key reasons.

Another survey, conducted by TD Waterhouse Canada Inc. in December 2004, found that one-third of those surveyed planned to go on working either part-time or full-time past the normal retirement age. One-quarter of those not yet retired said they planned to go on working part-time beyond age 65, while another 8% planned to be working full-

Protecting Older Workers

time past age 65. Among those who saw their working lives stretching out indefinitely, the survey found almost three-quarters plan to continue working out of choice rather than necessity. Men are more likely than women to continue working past 65. However, women who are working past 65 are more likely than men to do so because they have to, as opposed to wanting to.[39]

It's worth noting that, while almost everyone eventually stops working—at least working for pay—only about half of men and one-third of women ever "retire" from paid employment. Job separations that ultimately end a career are often the result of a layoff, an illness or disability, or a family-related event. Overall, as many as 60% of all job separations for women and men between ages 50 and 65 could be classified as involuntary. But most instances of involuntary job separation were followed by a job acquisition within 12 months.[40] Estimates of job acquisition indicate that 27% of men and 23% of women who had left the labour force for retirement had found another job.[41]

According to one study, job changes at career-end reveal barriers or disincentives to re-employment for older workers, and should raise some concern. Since only a bare majority of men and a minority of women explicitly retire, many older workers seem to be interested in continued employment[42]—although that may depend on the kind of job they had and the kind of job they are able to find once they have left a career job.

Phased retirement may be complicated for workers who are members of a pension plan. For one thing, defined benefit pension plans generally specify a "normal retirement age" at which the employee becomes eligible for an unreduced benefit based on years of service. Once that point is reached, there is little financial incentive to go on working because it will not increase the pension benefit—although a worker may prefer to continue working because earnings from wages or salary are higher than income that would be received from a pension.

Tax rules do not allow an employee to start drawing a pension while continuing to contribute to the pension plan. However, some phased retirement programs have been established that manage to avoid that problem through a rather creative technical manoeuvre. Lump sum withdrawals from a pension plan are allowed, (payment of a lump sum from a pension plan is not considered a pension under the Income Tax Act), so it is apparently possible to structure a phased retirement program that allows the employee to receive annual lump sum amounts from the pension plan while continuing to work and contribute to the plan.

In 2003, for example, the New Brunswick government and the provincial nurses' union negotiated a phased retirement plan with the consent of Canada Revenue Agency (CRA) that conformed to the Income Tax Act. Nurses who are aged 56 and older may work part-time and receive 85% of their full-time income. Some of the income will come from salary and some from pension pre-payments. Nurses who take the phased retirement option will continue to contribute to the pension plan, so their pension will not be reduced when they decide to fully retire.[43] Alberta's pension standards legislation also provides for phased retirement.

Quebec introduced a phased retirement program as long ago as 1997. At that time, the intention was to ease older workers out of the work force and create jobs for younger workers, who were facing high rates of unemployment. The program was only available to members of workplace pension plans who were between the ages of 55 and 69. (Actually, the program could be used by anyone who was less than 10 years away from the normal retirement age—generally age 65—under the pension plan. If the normal retirement age was 60, for example, a plan member who was aged 50 would have been eligible for a phased retirement arrangement.)

Under the program, an eligible pension plan member can agree with the employer to reduce his or her hours of work and start receiving part of their pension, known as a "temporary pension." In the meantime, the employee can continue contributing to the pension plan and can also contribute to the Quebec Pension Plan as if she or he is employed on a full-time basis.

Technically, the scheme is in compliance with the Income Tax Act because it is accomplished through a partial commutation of the accumulated pension benefits, providing a lump sum which constitutes the "temporary pension." However, the eventual pension the employee can receive from the pension plan is reduced accordingly, which means workers will receive a lower pension when they eventually retire from paid work.

Quebec's phased retirement program has been criticized by some observers because it is only available to the minority of workers having

Protecting Older Workers

a workplace pension plan. Apparently, it has also had a very low take-up rate. According to benefits consultants Watson Wyatt Worldwide, there are several reasons for this:

- Individuals who opt for phased retirement lose any early retirement subsidies that would otherwise have been available had full-time early retirement been chosen instead of electing to work part-time. In a plan with a generous early retirement provision, this represents a huge potential loss.

- Under CRA rules, the lump sum withdrawal from the pension plan may only be made annually, but most people would prefer to draw income monthly. (However, it may be of interest to note that, in the case of the New Brunswick nurses' phased retirement program, CRA has apparently said that administratively it will allow annual withdrawals from a pension plan to be paid out in equal monthly amounts to nurses taking phased retirement.[44])

- There is a cap on the lump sum withdrawal equal to 40% of the QPP's Year's Maximum Pensionable Earnings (YMPE)—equivalent to $16,440 at 2005 rates—which can create a potentially large drop in cash flow for higher-income earners.[45]

More recently, Quebec has proposed to allow workers who want to claim their QPP retirement pensions prior to age 65 to start receiving benefits while continuing to work—a measure intended to encourage workers to stay in paid employment longer and one likely to be implemented in the CPP as well. (Under current rules, anyone claiming a CPP retirement pension prior to age 65 must have substantially ceased working. Effectively, that means earning less than the maximum monthly CPP retirement pension—$828.75 a month in 2005—in the month before the pension begins and in the month it begins. After that, there are no restrictions on earnings, although the individual may no longer contribute to the plan.)

Quebec has also proposed to require workers who continue to work while collecting a QPP retirement pension to continue contributing to the plan. These additional contributions will increase the QPP retirement pension until the maximum is reached.[46]

It seems almost inevitable that interest in phased retirement will grow as the population ages. We may expect calls for pension legislation to be amended and for income tax rules to be made more flexible to accommodate phased retirement schemes. But special attention will have to be paid to the impact of phased retirement on the benefits coverage of older workers who decide to ease into retirement.

Active aging: The new buzz words for policy-makers

"Active aging" has become the key for policy-makers concerned about population aging. The new buzz words are supposed to reflect the more positive approach to population aging we discussed in earlier chapters. Instead of the demographic time bomb "aging crisis" view common just a few years ago, the emphasis now is on older people as an "asset to society." As the G-8 labour ministers put it in their 2000 Turin Charter, "They should have the possibility of developing and using their potential to lead active, independent, fulfilling lives."[47]

In fact, the World Health Organization (WHO) adopted the term "active aging" in the late 1990s. It says the term was meant to convey a more inclusive message than "healthy aging." Here's how the WHO describes its approach:

> The active aging approach is based on the recognition of the human rights of older people and the United Nations Principles of independence, participation, dignity, care and self-fulfillment. It shifts strategic planning away from a "needs-based" approach (which assumes that older people are passive targets) to a "rights-based" approach that recognizes the rights of people to equality of opportunity and treatment in all aspects of life as they grow older. It supports their responsibility to exercise their participation in the political process and other aspects of community life.[48]

That all sounds well and good, implying that older workers should be treasured and protected and helped to make the most of their potential. They should be fully included in cultural and social activities. But it's

Protecting Older Workers

the underlying hint of coercion that rings the alarm bells. Here's how the Turin Charter puts it:

> The rising ratio of elderly to working-age people will be associated with increased expenditures in areas such as pensions and health care. These increased costs may put growing pressure on the public finances of many countries in the next decades. If the economic impact is to be contained, the employment rate of all working-age people must be raised as much as possible.[49]

Active aging, as the OECD sees it, refers to the capacity of people, as they grow older, to lead productive lives. According to the OECD, "This means that people can make flexible choices in the way they spend time over life—learning, working, and partaking in leisure activities and in giving care."[50] Choices may be constrained in a number of ways: from ill-health in old age to lack of wheelchair ramps in buildings, to workplace inflexibilities and public policies "that have not kept up with changes in demography, families and employment." Active aging reforms, the OECD says, "are those that remove these undesirable constraints on life-course flexibility and that strengthen support for citizens in making lifetime choices."[51]

In other words, we are back to the flexible life-course approach discussed in Chapter 3. Active aging in this context is not just something that happens after age 50; it starts much earlier in life. Hence the focus on lifelong learning and ways in which people can change the balance between work, learning, leisure and caregiving throughout their life-course.

But active aging, as the G-8 labour ministers saw it, seems to focus much more on older workers. "To successfully utilize the huge potential for increased labour force participation among older workers," the labour ministers said, "we must make use of their skills, talents and experience." To pursue this goal, they agreed in their Turin Charter that:

> • Governments and social partners should facilitate the ability of older workers to continue to make an active contribution to the economy, capitalizing on the benefits of increased health and life expectancy.

• Investment in knowledge and lifelong learning is vital to prevent the skills of older workers from becoming obsolete and to maintain their competitiveness in the labour market. In this context, they renewed their commitment to lifelong learning as embodied in their 1998 G-8 Charter of Lifelong Learning.

• Active labour market policy measures should be reviewed in order to be tailored better to the needs of older workers. These measures should include action to improve information technology literacy and skills and to prevent the "digital-divide."

• Any existing incentive deriving from the tax and benefits systems needs to be carefully examined, with the view of enabling older workers to remain in the labour market.

• Gradual retirement schemes, in which part-time job income is supplemented by a partial accrual of pension entitlements, should be further explored as means to increase participation rates.

• Innovative programs should be supported in order to promote appropriate organizational restructuring of workplaces, including a review of management practices, to make them more friendly for older workers.

• Policies and practices which counter age prejudice and discrimination should be pursued.

• The promotion of the quality of jobs and occupational health and safety in the workplace is important to maintain employability and reduce involuntary withdrawal from the labour force.[52]

It's not clear to what extent policy-makers in Canada have climbed on the active aging bandwagon, but the concept seems certain to become a growing preoccupation as the population ages. Many older workers will no doubt want to remain active, and some may want to delay their retirement to continue working for pay or to phase out of their paid employment gradually. The challenge will be to make sure those who advocate pursuing a policy of active aging do not impose their own concepts and value judgments of what is appropriate activity for older people.

Protecting Older Workers

When the OECD suggests retirees would be better off working for pay than sitting at home wasting their time watching TV, that's a value judgment that implies older people have no right to decide how they wish to spend their time. Progressive policies on active aging would make sure older workers have a real choice about how and when to withdraw from paid employment. They would also recognize that the unpaid work of older people, such as caring for frail elderly or family members with disabilities—or even caring for grandchildren—also makes an invaluable contribution to the economy and society. "Active aging" cannot simply be defined as continuing to work for pay.

Active aging will not necessarily be something all older people can easily embrace. As the United Nations points out:

> ...while society embraces "active" aging and all its obvious benefits, care must be taken to recognize the diversity of interests and abilities that can characterize "active," and not to disregard those older individuals who are unable physically to join in the same activities as their peers. Reflections, wisdom and experience cannot always be portrayed in physical terms or even words, and no matter the situation, older persons must not be left out of the relative and participatory process.[53]

Protecting older workers

Research has shown that age-based discrimination in the workplace and in the labour market can limit the employment prospects of older workers. Stereotypical views of older workers abound. They are often characterized as being less productive, less flexible, unable or unwilling to adapt to new technologies or to upgrade their skills, prone to absenteeism and less capable of engaging in physically demanding or stressful work. Although studies have shown such generalizations are inaccurate and certainly do not reflect the working capacity of older workers, unjustified stereotypes may often lead to discriminatory practices that negatively affect older workers in terms of hiring, promotions, job security, access to training and other benefits, and remuneration.[54]

Some younger workers may wish older workers would leave paid employment because they believe older workers take jobs away from younger workers. This view was particularly prevalent some years ago when Canada was experiencing high rates of youth unemployment. Quebec's phased retirement program, referred to earlier, was even based on this premise and presented as a way to address high youth unemployment. In fact, there is no empirical evidence that younger workers and older workers are interchangeable. Exits of older workers from the workforce and inflows of younger workers apparently do not occur in the same sectors of the economy. And, according to the European Union, experience from several member states demonstrates that growth in the employment rate of older workers goes hand-in-hand with growth in that of younger workers.[55]

Many collective agreements include provisions designed to protect older unionized workers against discriminatory practices and harassment. For example, seniority-based systems included in many collective agreements allow workers with the greatest seniority—often older workers—certain rights such as the right to refuse overtime, to take part in voluntary workload reductions, or to benefit from various vacation entitlements. But labour representatives have pointed out that the potential usefulness to any particular older worker of some of these provisions depends on the range of employment options within a bargaining group.[56] Bob Baldwin of the Canadian Labour Congress says that contracting-out in both public and private sectors tends to limit the range of choice that is open to older workers, and this has been a collective bargaining issue in sectors such as garbage collection and auto assembly. Also, to the extent that older workers might wish to use seniority-based claims to ameliorate their work situation, he says, their scope for choice is also limited by the fact that many workplaces have quite compressed age structures because early retirement programs have led older workers to retire and there has been no new hiring.[57]

According to the HRDC study referred to earlier, there are also some contract clauses in collective agreements that may be considered discriminatory or that may have an unintended adverse impact on older workers. Lower wages for older workers and medical certificates and examinations are two examples referred to earlier.

Protecting Older Workers

Preventing discrimination against older workers is an integral part of the EU strategy on older workers, but this issue does not seem to have had much attention so far in Canada. According to the Ontario Human Rights Commission, age cases tend to be treated differently than other discrimination cases, particularly where the case involves retirement issues. The most noticeable difference from a human right perspective, says the Commission, "is the lack of a sense of moral opprobrium linked to age discrimination which, in comparable circumstances would generate outrage if the ground of discrimination were, say, race, sex, or disability."[58]

The Ontario human rights legislation prohibits discrimination and harassment on the basis of age in all social areas covered by the Human Rights Code. However, in employment, there is a maximum age for discrimination of 65. In other words, *in employment only,* the Code does not protect against discrimination on the basis of age where the individual is 65 years of age or more. All other Canadian jurisdictions provide protection for discrimination in employment on the basis of age, but in British Columbia, Newfoundland and Labrador, and Saskatchewan, as in Ontario, the maximum age limit for a claim of discrimination in employment on the basis of age is 65.[59]

It is widely recognized that age is a barrier for individuals trying to get a job. In fact, the Ontario Human Rights Commission says the problem is so prevalent that the Supreme Court of Canada has taken judicial notice of it. In the case of *Law v. Canada (Minister of Employment and Immigration)* [1999] 1 S.C.R. 497, the Court said:

> It seems to me that the increasing difficulty with which one can find and maintain employment as one grows older is a matter of which a court may appropriately take judicial notice. Indeed, this Court has often recognized age as a factor in the context of labour force attachment and detachment.[60]

But even the Supreme Court seems to have fallen victim to the stereotype of failing powers and declining skills as workers grow old. In the 1990 case of *Stoffman v. Vancouver General Hospital* [1990] 3 S. C. R. 483, it found that a regulation which took away doctors' hospital privileges at age 65, in effect forcing them to retire, was justified under Section 1 of the Charter of Rights and Freedoms. The Court apparently accepted the view that older persons "are not on the cutting edge of new discoveries and ideas" and that, at age 65, doctors are "less able to contribute to the hospital's sophisticated practice." Although it recognized there will be considerable variety between individuals as to the rate at which the skills and aptitudes essential to the practice of medicine deteriorate, the Court rejected skill-testing or performance evaluations as an option.[61] The dilemma, of course, is that such tests and performance evaluations may also be used to force older workers out—a concern of many of those who are opposed to the abolition of mandatory retirement.

As long ago as 1982, the United Nations World Assembly on Aging, meeting in Vienna, adopted the *Vienna International Plan of Action on Aging,* which included recommendations on the employment of older workers, as well as changing attitudes about aging and combating some of the stereotypes about older people.

Recommendation 37 stated:

Governments should eliminate discrimination in the labour market and ensure equality of treatment in professional life. Negative stereotypes about older workers exist among some employers. Governments should take steps to educate employers and employment counselors about the capabilities of older workers, which remain quite high in most occupations... The right of older workers to employment should be based on ability to perform the work rather than chronological age.[62]

The EU's Employment Directive, establishing a general framework for equal treatment in employment and occupation, issued in 2000, prohibits age discrimination—a prohibition which it says is "an essential part of meeting the aims set out in the Employment Guidelines and encouraging diversity in the workforce."[63] Member states have until the end of 2006 to implement the Directive, under which compulsory retirement ages will be unlawful, unless employers can show they are objectively justified.

But Article 6 of the Directive lists a number of situations under which there may be justification of differences of treatment on grounds of age, and seems to open up some potential loopholes. Differences in treatment based on age may not be considered discrimination if, "within the context of national law, they are objectively and reasonably justified by a legitimate aim, including legitimate employment policy, labour market

Protecting Older Workers

and vocational training objectives, and if the means of achieving that aim are appropriate and necessary."[64] For example, exceptions to the general non-discrimination rule may be permitted where fixing a maximum age for recruitment is based on training requirements of the post in question or the need for a reasonable period of employment before retirement.

The UK government's 2001 consultation on equality and diversity revealed how common age discrimination was. Fifty per cent of respondents believed they had either suffered age discrimination at work or had witnessed someone else suffering from it. They reported that discrimination took a variety of forms: 22% said it was being forced to retire after reaching a certain age; 18% said it was not being given a job they applied for; 17% said it was being prevented from attending training courses; 17% said it was being told their age was a barrier to general advancement; 15% said it was assumptions being made about abilities due to age; and 13% said it was being selected for redundancy because of age.[65]

In its 2003 age consultation, the government said it was determined to tackle age discrimination "through effective legislation implementing the European Employment Directive—legislation which will introduce important new and enforceable rights for individuals, but which will allow businesses to continue effectively without stultifying bureaucratic burdens."[66] In the end, it had to back down on its proposal to set age 70 as a "default age of retirement," moving that back to age 65. In its Five Year Strategy, announced in February 2005, the government said it was implementing a new high-profile national guidance campaign, providing practical guidance on adopting flexible approaches to work and retirement in relation to age, and supporting preparations for the implementation of age discrimination legislation.

In 2006, the UK government plans to enact the European Directive on age discrimination, making it unlawful to discriminate on the basis of age in employment and vocational training. As part of this legislation, employers will be able to set a compulsory age of retirement below 65 only if they can objectively justify it. Employers will also be required to consider formal requests from employees to work beyond 65. After five years, the government plans to conduct an evidence-based review of the legislation and consider whether compulsory retirement ages are required.[67]

Much of the debate about age discrimination in employment seems to refer to workers aged 65 or older. It may be that age discrimination has not yet become a serious policy issue in Canada because most workers now retire well before reaching that age. But as older workers account for an increasing percentage of the paid workforce, it will be important to make sure they do not face barriers to hiring, access to training, or discrimination in other employment-related areas. It could also be that unions will find that issues of concern to older workers feature more prominently in collective bargaining as older workers form an increasing percentage of their membership.

Clearly, we need a more positive image of aging, and the WHO believes older people themselves and the media must take the lead in developing this image. Political and social recognition of the contributions older people make and the inclusion of older men and women in leadership roles, says the WHO, "will support this new image and help debunk negative stereotypes. Educating young people about aging and paying careful attention to upholding the rights of older people will help reduce and eliminate discrimination and abuse."[68]

Notes

1 United Kingdom Government 2003.

2 European Union 2004: 13.

3 Ibid. 3.

4 Robson 2001: 4.

5 Ibid. 38.

6 McMullin, Cooke and Downie 2004: 20.

7 Robson 2004: 58.

8 Ibid. 59.

9 McMullin, Cooke and Downie 2004: 38.

10 Ibid. 3.

11 Ibid. 32

12 Ibid.3.

13 Ibid. 19.

14 Ibid. 20.

15 Mérette 2002: 3.

16 Ibid. 7

17 McMullin, Cooke and Downie 2004: 32.

18 Ibid. 37.

19 Ibid. 37.

20 Baldwin 2004a: 9.

21 McMullin, Cooke and Downie 2004: 37

22 Ibid. 29.

23 Fourzly and Gervais 2002: 2.

24 Ibid. 3.

25 Baldwin 2004a: 7.

26 Ibid. 8.

27 Akyeampong 2002: 43.

28 Baldwin 2004a: 17.

29 Fourzly and Gervais 2002: 3.

30 Ibid. 151.

31 Ibid. 154.

32 Ibid. 159.

33 G8 Information Centre 2000: 2

34 Wortsman 2003: 2.

35 Kapsalis and Tourigny 2005: 36.

36 Fourzly and Gervais 2002: 175..

37 Ibid. 176.

38 Desjardins Financial Security 2004: 1.

39 TD Bank Financial Group 2005: 1.

40 Rowe and Nguyen 2003: 56.

41 Ibid. 56.

42 Ibid. 57.

43 McMullin, Cooke and Downie 2004: 36.

44 Smolkin 2004: 11.

45 Watson Wyatt Worldwide 2001: 353.

46 Régie des rentes du Québec 2003: 34.

47 G8 Information Centre 2000 1.

48 World Health Organization 2002: 13.

49 G8 Information Centre 2000 1.

50 OECD 2000: 126.

51 Ibid.

52 G8 Information Centre 2000: 2

53 United Nations 2001: 7.

54 Fourzly and Gervais 2002: 147.

55 European Union 2004: 8-9.

56 Baldwin 2004a: 17.

57 Ibid. 17–18.

58 Ontario Human Rights Commission 2000: 39.

59 Ibid. 23.

60 Ibid. 28.

61 Ibid. 25.

62 Ibid. 38.

63 European Union 2000a: 1.

64 Ibid. Article 6.1.

65 United Kingdom Government 2003: 9.

66 Ibid. 9.

67 United Kingdom Government 2005: 54.

68 World Health Organization 2002: 44.

6

Where Do We Go From Here?

S INCE THE EARLY 1980S, pensions and pension policy have been the subject of hot and often acrimonious debate. From the National Pensions Conference in 1981 to the ill-fated proposals for a new "Seniors Benefit" in 1996 and the consultations on CPP reform that followed, we have been preoccupied with fixing our pension system. But we haven't had much discussion of retirement policy. Looking back on the pension debate, it seems odd that we haven't given much thought to how inextricably pension issues are linked with retirement policies, and vice versa.

As sociologist John Myles describes it, "Pension policy has to do with the ways we design and finance the accumulation of our pension benefits, the retirement wealth that will get us through our retirement years. Retirement policy, *per se,* has to do with the age of eligibility and other requirements that regulate how we can access this wealth."[1] But both are strongly influenced by politics: as Myles defines it, "the political behaviour and the forces that shape policy."

There's no doubt that some policy-makers would now like to turn the spotlight on retirement policy, whether that's getting people to work longer, abolishing mandatory retirement, or promoting active aging and phased retirement. While we need to look at these key issues raised by our aging population, the danger is that many of those same policy-makers seem to think we have already fixed the pension problem. Past debates about pensions and retirement incomes emphasized designing a "fix" for Canada's public pension programs, and particularly the CPP. But, as we have seen, it is now the privately administered parts of the system that are currently cause for concern. There's also evidence that incomes of the elderly are still inadequate compared with those of the working-age population. But whether there's the political will to address these concerns is another question.

Retirement issues not yet on the policy radar screen

Even before the advent of minority government in Ottawa in 2004 and the highly volatile political situation that continued through 2005, retirement issues were not on the policy radar screen. Yet there are signs many Canadians would like to see politicians turn their attention to this important issue. Surveys conducted for the Canadian Labour Congress in 2004, for instance, showed worries about retirement incomes ranked way up there with health care among the issues causing most concern for Canadians.

The CLC's first survey, conducted by Vector Research of Toronto in March 2004, asked 1,003 adult Canadians to rate 12 public policy issues on a scale of 1 to 10, indicating priority. Seventy-two per cent of respondents ranked "protecting retirees' pensions and retirement income" as priority level 1, 2 or 3, second only to concerns about health care, which was ranked by 82% of respondents at priority level 1, 2 or 3. The poll found that 73% of a cross-section of Canadians—not limited to union members—worried about not having enough money to live on in retirement. That was up from 54% just two years earlier. The poll is considered accurate to within 3.1 percentage points 19 times out of 20.

A second poll, conducted by Vector in May 2004, asked 1,131 Canadians to pick from a list of "what should be an absolute priority for the federal government or what can be delayed for another year?" The CLC says that, while some hot-button election issues—for example, government scandals—spiked during the pre-election political debates, bypassing "retirement security" and shooting to the top of the list, retirement security still continued to be a concern. In the May poll—that is, just a month before the election—73% of respondents identified "protecting pensions and retirement incomes" as an absolute priority for the government, almost exactly the same result as in the March poll, when 72% ranked retirement security among the top three most urgent public policy issues. The May poll is considered accurate to within 2.9 percentage points 19 times out of 20.

The third poll, conduced by Vancouver-based IdeaWorks Consulting in mid-August, was based on a very small sample, so has a wider margin of error. Only residents of Ontario, Alberta, and British Columbia were questioned, with the objective of finding out if the degree of concern expressed in the spring about retirement security still existed. Sixty-nine per cent of respondents said they were concerned about having enough money to live on when they retired, and 65% ranked retirement security as a high priority for the federal government, compared with 35% who gave the same high ranking to cutting taxes.[2]

In a letter to the Prime Minister in August 2004, CLC President Ken Georgetti said the polling results took the CLC "completely by surprise." An overwhelming majority of Canadians are worried about retirement security, Georgetti said. But it seems the politicians haven't yet registered that concern. Retirement security is "a public policy issue that appears to have more urgency in individual Canadian households than within national institutions like the federal government," Georgetti said.[3] Policy-makers pay very little attention to retirement security, he noted. He observed that none of the political parties made retirement security a major election issue [in the June 2004 federal election], while all parties focused a great deal on "fixing health care." In focus groups conducted by the CLC, some participants suggested the topic is ignored because it's "too scary" to bring it out in the open.

Georgetti said Canadian labour organizations had some specific concerns about issues such as the regulation of company pension funds, protection of pension plan members, and mandatory retirement. "Right now, we don't have anyone in government looking at the big picture," he said. "That's why we want a minister of state to create a table where

Where Do We Go From Here?

labour, business, and all interested Canadians can bring their concerns," Georgetti said. "We have ministers of state looking out for infrastructure and communities and for families and caregivers. They give voice to concerns that cut across several federal departments, and that's exactly what we need for retirement security." With a minister of state championing these issues in Parliament and at the cabinet table, Georgetti said, "the government will start looking at these concerns with an eye for solutions."

Needless to say, his call went unheeded, even though industry spokespersons seem to agree with him, at least at some level. For example, the Association of Canadian Pension Management (ACPM), an industry group describing itself as "the national voice of corporate and public sector pension plan sponsors in Canada, as well as of the professional firms they retain," says no Canadian cabinet includes the position of "Minister of Pensions." Writing in the December 2003 issue of ACPM's Newsletter, Stephen Bigsby, executive director of ACPM, noted that responsibility for pensions is folded into a major portfolio like Finance or Labour. "These ministers face agendas crowded with pressing issues, such as provincial deficits, credit rating reviews, or looming labour disputes threatening to shut down a key industry or essential public service," he said.[4] In other words, they're too preoccupied with other issues to pay much attention to retirement concerns. So far, it would seem, efforts by the labour movement and others to push the issue further up the policy agenda don't seem to be getting anywhere.

Will retirement policy be a major policy driver in the medium-term?

At this point, it's impossible to say for sure whether retirement policy will become the target of reform over the next decade in the same way that pension policy was in the last.[5] But some experts believe it will. Peter Hicks, now Assistant Deputy Minister, Strategic Direction, at Social Development Canada, believes policies that affect the work-retirement transition will be at the centre of the medium-term policy agenda over the next five to 10 years.[6] He was writing in 2002, but his timing implies priority would be given to retirement issues by around 2007 to 2012, when the first waves of baby boomers will be retiring.

According to Hicks, the OECD has noted that policy-making in Canada may be lagging behind other countries in recognizing the importance of the work-retirement balance. In Canada, he says, this issue is usually considered as one element in a work-life balance policy agenda, where the main focus is on child care and gender equality, on the role of quality workplaces as the missing link in human resources policies, and as the main determinant of productivity and on reducing time crunches and thereby increasing health and subjective well-being.[7] While these are certainly important issues that probably have not been given enough attention in policy-making, says Hicks, taken in isolation, "a focus on work-life balance would seem to miss the work-retirement tidal wave that is rolling in."[8]

There are signs, however, that policy-makers within key federal departments are now turning their attention to this issue. For example, the Minister of Labour, through Human Resources and Skills Development Canada, requested the organization of a roundtable in the fall of 2005 to discuss the theme of work-to-retirement transition, focusing on the aging workforce and developments in the workplace involving the transition from work to retirement.

Hicks articulates two key concerns:

• Everyone participates in the consumption of goods and services, but only a portion of the population contributes to their production. With the aging of the population, there will be a large shift in the ratio of producers to consumers. The only large pool of unused labour supply is among older people. By far the greatest effects on the producer-consumer ratio would come through increases in the effective age of retirement.[9]

• "In the absence of a shift to later retirement, there will be continued growth in the extraordinarily large pool of leisure that has been building up among retirees, where it is mainly passive, unhealthy and often unwanted—and a growing source of social exclusion. There would be many potential gains if people had the choice to spread work, learning, caregiving, and leisure more rationally over their lives."[10]

Where Do We Go From Here?

Three forces are likely to dominate policy-making in about five years' time, says Hicks, writing in 2002. They are: "a continuation of the competitiveness and social cohesion pressures that have resulted in today's preoccupation with lifelong learning; a new concern about a decline in the percentage of the total population that will be employed; and a new shift towards incentives to later retirement."[11]

But John Myles argues that the sorts of pressures and political controversy that put big pension reform at the top of the political agenda elsewhere in the OECD countries were weak or absent in Canada. The past two decades of pension politics can be summed up in two, or maybe three words, says Myles: "(Almost) nothing happened."[12] From the vantage point of retirees, Myles argues, the system in place today scarcely differs from the design that was in place in 1980. Given our recent history with the reform of pension benefits, then, we might reasonably ask why we should expect the future of retirement policy to be any different, he says. While Hicks seems to be suggesting that, with continued improvements in health and longevity, pressures for a more rational reallocation of work and leisure will grow, Myles points out that this would be "a remarkable turnaround from past experience."[13]

It may be correct that the changing ratio of producers to consumers is the big issue and that the impact on the public budget is only a derivative problem, says Myles. But he questions whether the appeal of a strategy to get people to work longer is sufficient to make it a major policy driver. "Where will the political pressures and the political coalitions required to sustain policy reforms that might lead to later retirement come from?" he asks.[14] Raising the age of eligibility for CPP, for example, would have the greatest impact on lower-income—and presumably lower-productivity—workers. Getting low-income workers, who also have shorter life expectancies, to work longer hardly satisfies anyone's criterion of distributive justice, says Myles.

As he points out, in nations like Germany, Italy or Sweden, where most pension "wealth" is stored inside public retirement schemes, policymakers have considerable discretion over the age at which individuals can gain access to that wealth. But Canada's public pension system is much more modest and provides a comparatively much smaller share of retirement income. The effects of raising the age of entitlement, says Myles,

GROWING OLDER, WORKING LONGER

are likely to be modest and perhaps even perverse, for both distributive and macroeconomic reasons.[15]

But if it is the better-educated and more productive employees we want to go on working longer, then the most important policy levers are the rules governing the age and conditions under which they can access the most significant part of their retirement wealth: their occupational pension plans and RRSPS.[16] It seems most unlikely there would be political coalitions or support for restrictive changes to be made here.

Nevertheless, it's worth pointing out that, because of the generous tax assistance directed to private retirement savings plans such as Registered Pension Plans and RRSPS, these arrangements represent a form of social program, too. Since these plans receive public subsidies, it could be argued that they should also be expected to contribute to realizing social goals. The official justification for subsidizing RPPS and RRSPS is that there's a need to help people save for retirement. Replacement rates for the CPP, for instance, were deliberately set low to allow the private retirement income system to flourish and take up the slack. (The fact that it hasn't done so is another question). But—at least in the case of RRSPS—there is nothing to prevent the beneficiary from using the funds for any other purpose long before reaching retirement age. The only stipulation is that funds released when a plan is cashed in must be declared as income and may be subject to income tax. In fact, using RRSP funds for buying a home or paying for post-secondary education now receives official blessing and can be done without tax consequences, as long as the funds borrowed from an RRSP for these purposes are paid back within a certain period of time.

If policy-makers wanted to encourage people to delay their retirement, there's no reason why they couldn't decree that RRSP funds could not be accessed until the holder reaches a certain age, just as funds transferred from an RPP when the beneficiary changes jobs must be transferred to a locked-in account where they must be used to provide a lifetime income for the holder at retirement age and may not be withdrawn in a lump sum, except under certain very limited circumstances. Such restrictions would almost certainly prove highly unpopular with RRSP holders. In fact, there is already strong pressure on pension regulators—to which some have already succumbed—to eliminate locking-in provisions for

Where Do We Go From Here?

funds transferred out of RPPS. Holders of these funds apparently feel they should be able to access their "wealth" at their own discretion, perhaps forgetting that tax subsidies, paid for by all taxpayers, helped them accumulate their so-called "retirement" savings.

As we have seen in earlier chapters, most workers see being able to retire as a benefit of having a decent retirement income. As national wealth has increased in the more affluent democracies, workers have chosen to use some of their increased productivity to purchase more years of retirement. Myles reminds us that the main objective of the "life-course flexibility" approach is not simply to reallocate work and leisure over the life-course, but to change the balance of work and leisure in favour of more work. There's nothing new about social policy strategies that give high priority to full employment, he points out. After all, that was the first objective of Keynes, Beveridge, and the Swedish social democrats in the 1940s. "Full employment was the precondition for a luxurious welfare state." But the example of the French workers, who took to the streets in June 2003 to demonstrate against proposals that would force them to work longer for a full pension, reminds us that the issue is about politics and not about who is correct on normative grounds, Myles observes.[17]

It would appear that there is not much support at the moment for a movement to get people to work longer. But Hicks argues that we need "a major consultation process that builds understanding of the issues and the possible effects of a range of policy options."[18] No doubt the PRI research project on *Population Aging and Life-Course Flexibility* has been designed to form the basis for such a consultation. Its report on *Population Aging and Older Workers* was due in the spring of 2005, but subsequent reports and roundtables were scheduled for the winter of 2005/2006, so it would appear the research is still ongoing. Whether there's any chance the federal government will take the initiative and proceed with consultations remains to be seen. Somehow, in the current volatile political situation in Ottawa, it seems unlikely—especially since the January 2006 federal election intervened before the completion of the aging research project. It also seems unlikely that a strategy of persuading people to shorten their retirement in favour of working longer would have such public appeal that politicians would happily make it their key policy issue over the next few years.

In the meantime, the concept of "retirement" will continue to evolve, with or without government intervention. People are phasing into retirement gradually, many are continuing to work, maybe switching from full-time to part-time. "Retirement" has become a process. For most people, it is no longer a point in time when paid employment ceases and full-time leisure begins. But the policy discourse has been slow to change. We still seem to think about retiring as the point at which people stop working at a career job, even though they may then start thinking about alternative ways of continuing to earn. In the not-too-distant future, we may see new policies and programs to match what is already happening. But policy changes would almost certainly have to be phased in gradually. And the politics of retirement policy will demand that changes address the priorities Canadians have identified, not necessarily the paths to which policy-makers would like to direct them.

More and more Canadians near retirement

With the leading edge of the baby boom generation entering their late 50s, we are faced with the prospect of more and more Canadians within 10 years of what has traditionally been thought of as "retirement." It's possible many of these individuals, especially the older boomers, may represent a transition to a new way of looking at retirement, or whatever new term we choose to use for easing into old age. If we do start to implement policies and programs to persuade people to prolong their paid employment and to raise the average age of retirement, it may well be the younger boomers who will pioneer this brave new world.

Recent studies from Statistics Canada have developed a way of calculating the percentage of workers who are within 10 years of retirement. The percentages are not simply a calculation of how many people are within a decade of turning 65. Instead, StatsCan estimated a median retirement age—the point at which half of the individuals are older and half are younger—for various occupations, industries and provinces, then calculated what percentage of individuals in the relevant category were within 10 years of that. The result is a "near-retirement rate."[19] Not only has the median retirement age been dropping in most occupations and

Where Do We Go From Here?

industries, but the numbers of older workers has also been increasing, so near-retirement rates have jumped from 11.4% in 1987 to 19.8% in 2002. The agency explains that the near-retirement rate indicates potential employment shortages, but does not predict precise numbers of future retirees. It simply identifies the proportion of workers nearing the median retirement age for their industry, occupation, or province.

Most of the increase in the near-retirement rate between 1987 and 2002 can be attributed to the public sector, where the median retirement

TABLE 8 Industry differences in near-retirement rates

	Near-retirement rate		Median retirement age	
	1987	2002	1987	2002
	%	%	Years	Years
Industry	11.4	19.8	64.3	60.6
Agriculture	24.7	23.0	64.9	66.0
Forestry, fishing, mining, oil and gas	13.9	25.7	61.7	59.4
Utilities	15.5	27.5	60.3	58.9
Construction	13.4	14.5	63.2	64.3
Manufacturing	13.0	16.4	63.2	61.7
Trade	8.8	14.7	64.8	62.0
Transportation and warehousing	13.5	26.7	62.7	60.3
Finance, insurance, real estate and leasing	10.6	20.9	64.4	61.1
Professional, scientific and Technical	5.1	19.8	69.1	61.2
Management, administrative and Support	14.7	12.9	62.7	65.3
Educational services	14.8	39.3	62.0	57.3
Health care and social assistance	9.2	24.7	64.8	60.2
Information, culture and recreation	7.8	16.0	64.6	60.4
Accommodation and food services	8.6	11.2	61.6	61.3
Other services	13.8	17.2	65.0	63.8
Public administration	14.7	32.1	62.4	58.2

SOURCE Statistics Canada Labour Force Survey

age dropped dramatically over much of the 1990s and into 2002. In 1987, when the median retirement age for public sector workers was 62.8 years, only 13% of public sector workers fell in the near-retirement group. But by 2002, the median retirement age had dropped to 58.1, and one in three workers was within 10 years of retirement.

There are significant differences between industries and occupations. For instance, the median retirement age in finance, insurance, real estate, and leasing dropped from 64.4 years in 1987 to 61.1 in 2002. But the near-retirement rate jumped from 10.6% in 1987 to 20.9% in 2002 [*Table 8*].

It may be of interest to note that the median retirement age in some industries—for example, agriculture, construction, and management, administrative, and support—actually increased between 1987 and 2002. The table also indicates dramatic increases in the near-retirement rates of workers in some jobs, particularly those in the public sector such as educational services, health care, social assistance, and public adminis-tration, where the median age of retirement has tended to be lower than

TABLE 9 **Near retirement rate by province**

	Near-retirement rate		Median retirement age	
	1987	2002	1987	2002
	%	%	Years	Years
Canada	11.4	19.8	64.3	60.6
Newfoundland & Labrador	9.6	21.6	63.3	59.6
Prince Edward Island	10.0	24.9	65.7	59.4
Nova Scotia	10.2	21.6	63.7	59.8
New Brunswick	9.2	20.9	64.6	59.6
Quebec	10.4	21.6	64.0	59.8
Ontario	10.8	19.6	64.7	60.8
Manitoba	11.5	20.3	64.6	61.2
Saskatchewan	15.3	13.8	64.1	65.1
Alberta	11.4	15.0	63.1	63.4
British Columbia	11.3	23.6	64.3	60.3

SOURCE Statistics Canada Labour Force Survey

Where Do We Go From Here?

in the private sector. Pressure for workers to delay their retirement may well be stronger in these occupations.

Wide differences also emerge in near-retirement rates by province, ranging from a low of 13.8% in Saskatchewan to a high of 24.9% in Prince Edward Island. Most provinces had near-retirement rates of about 20% in 2002. But Alberta and Saskatchewan were exceptions, with Saskatchewan's rate at only 13.8% the lowest in the country [*Table 9*]. The median retirement age in both these provinces actually increased over the period, which StatsCan says was undoubtedly partly because of the rise in the retirement age in agriculture during this time.

It's important to note that these near-retirement rates are based on past patterns in various industries, occupations, and provinces. They also reflect retirement from a career job and don't capture other alternatives such as continuing to work in another type of job or work arrangement. These options may become increasingly prevalent, particularly for workers who are not covered by a workplace pension plan, or who have inadequate retirement incomes.

Incomes of older Canadians still need attention

As we noted earlier, many policy-makers who are now advocating delayed retirement tend to assume that pension issues have been addressed and nothing further needs to be done about the incomes of older Canadians. Certainly, it is true that low-income rates among Canadian seniors have been reduced significantly over the past two decades, thanks largely to the maturing of the Canada Pension Plan. Using the yardstick of Statistics Canada's before-tax Low Income Cut-Off (LICO), the percentage of seniors with low income fell from 33.9% in 1980 to 16.8% in 2001. In the same period, low-income rates for senior couples dropped from 20.1% to 6.3%. But low-income rates for older women *on their own* remain stubbornly high. Measured by the before-tax LICO, the poverty rate for unattached women aged 65 or older fell from 71.7% in 1980 to 45.6% in 2001—still a higher rate even than for single-parent mothers with children under 18.[20]

While taxes and transfers help to reduce poverty rates among older women, there are signs that more needs to be done to ameliorate the poverty of this disadvantaged group. For example, almost 19% of unattached women aged 65+ remained in low income in 2003 after taxes and transfers were taken into account. In fact, since 1998, the low-income rate of this group, based on Statistics Canada's after-tax LICO, has fluctuated between 18% and 22%, with no noticeable downward trend. Statistics Canada estimated the average income gap in 2003—that is, the amount by which these individuals fell below the after-tax LICO—was $2,300, more than it was in 2002 and even greater than it was 10 years earlier in 1994, when just over 25% of older women on their own remained in low-income after taxes and transfers.[21]

In the past, many women elders spent most of their lives as full-time homemakers and were not able to accumulate pensions in their own right. But increasingly, these women will have been in paid employment, with relatively brief interruptions for child-bearing, for most of their adult lives. At the very least, they will be entitled to Canada Pension Plan benefits in their own names, and some may have benefits from workplace pension plans. But low earnings and lack of pension coverage will mean they may still end up with inadequate incomes of their own in old age, and a strong likelihood of falling into poverty when left on their own after the death of a spouse or partner.

It is clearly unacceptable to suggest—as some have done—that delaying retirement from paid employment will help these women avoid poverty when there is no longer a spouse or partner around to provide them with some financial support. Policy-makers will have to address the income needs of this demographic group more directly. The most effective way would be to look at how public pension benefits—particularly OAS and GIS—could be improved. A family responsibility dropout from the CPP would also make sure that those women who must leave paid employment early to care for frail elderly or disabled family members do not face reduced CPP retirement benefits as a result.

Where Do We Go From Here?

Cultural differences in attitudes to old age and retirement

Cultural differences in attitudes to aging, retirement, and family care for elders play an important role. In a country with such a diverse population as Canada, these differences may also be manifested. A 2004 report from the HSBC Bank on the future of retirement around the world says that in 1900 the average length of retirement throughout the world was just over one year. By 1980 it had risen to 13 years, and by 1990 to 19 years. In the future, says the report, retirement is expected to span two decades or more. The Chinese expect it to last, on average, more than a quarter of a century. The report looked at 10 diverse countries and territories representing about 50% of the global population, from Brazil, China, France, India, Mexico and Hong Kong, to the U.S., UK, Canada, and Japan.[22]

When asked which factors are important for a happy old age, "not having to worry about money" ranked in the top three in seven of the 10 countries and territories studied. While countries in the group had very different attitudes to aging, what most societies have in common, says the report, is that people tend to retire and plan to retire before the age at which they say old age typically begins. The Chinese believe old age typically begins at 50, the study found, while the French say 71.

But the idea of age itself has grown old, says the report. In the past, people thought of the onset of old age as being marked by an event such as a 65th birthday, retiring, or collecting a pension. According to the report, "people now see old age as beginning with the decline of personal abilities, such as memory, eyesight, and energy." This is a much more personal and individualistic definition, the report notes. It means people become old at different ages: a 60-year-old may be "old," while an 85-year-old remains youthful.

The report says Canada is unusual in that over one-third of people have consulted a financial advisor, whereas India is more typical with just 5%. But the report also says Indians view later life as a time to live with and be cared for by their families. They do little to plan or prepare for retirement. Of all the nations studied, the researchers found Canada was the best prepared for retirement. The survey also found Canadians don't expect their families to take care of them, either. In fact, older people are more likely to take care of the younger generation than the other way around.

Increasingly, people have a second life after they retire from their main job, but before they believe themselves to be old. Different countries and territories have different preferences about what they do in this second life, says the report. Paradoxically, people in more affluent societies want to carry on working in retirement, even though they may have less financial need to do so. But the report says most people in most countries want a balanced lifestyle that includes periods of work, leisure, and education—or a blend of all three at once, with the proportions altering to take account of the interests and demands of the moment.

The report says Canadians view their later years as a time of motivation, ambition, and close relationships with friends and family. They see retirement as a new chapter of life, a time for personal challenges (including work and careers), and taking risks. But, according to the report, most young people do not prepare adequately for old age. Most also underestimate how long they are likely to live and what their financial needs will be in retirement, says the report. Many think they will live no longer than the older people who are alive today, which most experts think is highly unlikely, the report notes.

The potential for inter-generational conflict

Fairness between the different generations has provoked heated debate in some countries as policy-makers grapple with the problems of their aging populations. In the United States, where inter-generational equity fuelled a backlash against seniors in the debate over privatization of Social Security, observers say the backlashing and scapegoating directed toward the elderly has been relentless.[23] They also suggest that the issue of inter-generational equity in the U.S. has come to serve a dual purpose: one as an approach to framing policy questions, the other as a provocative political slogan.[24] While the U.S. debate over inter-generational equity has been around for at least two decades, it intensified during the 1980s, when opponents of Social Security characterized the issue as one of "kids vs. canes."[25] By the 1990s, observers say what was once a model of

Where Do We Go From Here?

inter-generational trust had been transformed into a debate over fairness among age groups.[26] For those hoping to build a "society for all ages," this does not augur well.

Generational conflict does not seem to have been nearly as prominent in other industrialized counties as it has in the U.S. But the potential for its emergence is still there.[27] In some countries, the changing role of women may result in a different kind of inter-generational tension. In Japan, for example, the conflict between generations may be more of a debate over cultural values than a battle over the allocation of resources based on age, according to one observer. But the role of women is at the heart of that debate. Typically, wives are expected to stay home and raise their children with little, if any, assistance from anyone else, particularly the government, and then to devote their middle-age years to caring for their husband's parents as well. But as the trend of declining fertility and more women working outside the home continues, it is unlikely that families will continue to serve as caregivers and that the burden and responsibility will shift to the government. That could lead to a demand for higher tax revenues to support social services; younger generations would then be called on to support the old; and inter-generational conflict may take root.[28]

In the recent past, neo-liberal think-tanks and commentators in Canada did their best to whip up inter-generational conflict. In the overheated rhetoric about reforming the Canada Pension Plan in the late 1990s, advocates of privatization warned of a coming war between generations over mounting contribution costs. Pay-as-you-go pensions like the CPP—and most other public pension programs—are based on the principle that people in the workforce contribute to the plan to pay the benefits of those who have retired. Essentially, it's a contract between generations, where each new generation pays for the pensions of those who went before them, in the expectation that the generation that follows will do the same for them. But when the population is aging and the percentage of seniors is increasing, there are relatively fewer workers to pay into the plan, so contribution rates have to go up. Younger workers then have to pay relatively more into the plan than the previous generation did.

Contrary to widespread public misconception—fuelled by deliberate misinformation from those opposed to public pensions and dutifully repeated by a complicit media—the key policy issue in the reform debate was not that the CPP was "bankrupt," but that contribution rates, over the long run, would have to go up higher than policy-makers had anticipated. Canada solved the problem by jacking up rates quickly instead of over the longer term, thus generating surplus funds that could be invested in the market. Earnings on the new investment fund would be used to supplement future contribution revenues and pay the promised benefits. That enabled government to put a lid on contribution rate increases, holding them steady at a combined employer/employee rate of just under 10% of contributory earnings for the foreseeable future.

But privatization advocates argued that the CPP is basically unfair because it necessarily involves a transfer from the younger generation to the older. Young people should not be saddled with the increasing burden of paying for public pensions for a growing elderly population, they argued. Of course, inter-generational transfers occur throughout society, and not just in pay-as-you-go pension plans. Transfers are made from old to young as well as from young to old. And they take place in the private as well as in the public sphere. While younger people might be asked to contribute more to the CPP to pay the pensions of the elderly, older Canadians paid—and continue to pay—taxes to finance the building of infrastructure, such as schools, hospitals, transportation, and so on, and to fund the education of the young. They supported and actively participated in the war effort during the Second World War. They also bore the private costs of raising the baby boom generation.[29]

But, in spite of the changes to the CPP, the potential for generational conflict is still there and it is present in most countries with aging populations. It is worth noting here, however, that, as Bob Baldwin points out, the ability of societies to transfer increased income to the elderly without depressing the absolute standard of living of the working-age population is a direct function of labour productivity growth. In most countries, says Baldwin, it will be possible to keep up the transfers to a growing elderly population with no depression in the standard of living of the working-age population.[30]

Where Do We Go From Here?

Gerontologist Malcolm Johnson, Director of the International Institute on Health and Aging at the University of Bristol in the UK, observes that the recognition of a permanently changed world population structure dawned on those who make public policy just as the world economy went into a decline. According to Johnson:

> In the uncertainty about how to behave, two kinds of reaction emerged: one operational and the other rhetorical. The rhetoric declared a continuing commitment to older people, but one which had to be managed down because the financial and caring burden would be unmanageably great. Unrefined extrapolations of steeply rising pensions, housing, health, and other and social care costs produced by actuaries and statisticians fuelled a sense of political panic. Observing the consequences for national exchequers and therefore for taxation levels, a new vocabulary of individual responsibility grew in resonance with political shifts to the right. Within a remarkably short space of time, it became one kind of received political wisdom that making your own provisions for health care costs and for income later in life was a freedom.
>
> In practice, it meant two things: privatization of public services and cost-cutting. To bolster the logic, we were told the collectivism of state welfare undermined personal initiative. In its place we needed free market disciplines, entrepreneurship, and the cost efficiency which results from competition.[31]

Johnson also argues that the rapid impact of New Right thinking on services and income to the old was substantial. Restraints have been placed on state pension levels; encouragement to join private pensions schemes has massively expanded the personal financial service sector, and direct services have both been out-sourced and reduced. What began as a localized infection became an international epidemic, says Johnson. "Demographically induced gerontophobia began to manifest itself on an inter-continental scale."[32]

According to Johnson, in most of the countries in Europe, 50% or more of hospital beds were occupied by elderly people, in addition to the 5–9% of the retired population in long-stay accommodation. Community care policies were introduced to cut costs. Canada got into the act in 1992 when it declared that "community-based care should be the service of first option where appropriate," and continuing care should be used to "supplement or support, not replace family and community caregiving." Continuing care services, according to this policy statement, "should be developed to support the lowest cost alternative appropriate to the needs of the individual."[33]

But, while public services have been cut, community care facilities have often not expanded to replace them. In Europe now, according to Johnson, the evidence for economic rationing of care services is unequivocal. And, although official poverty rates for older people have declined in some countries, elders in many countries still have unacceptably high rates of low income. But Johnson believes there is now a hiatus in the willingness to further improve the financial lot of older people. Combined with the market shift away from state to private pension, he says, "it is possible to detect a re-formulation of the bond between generations which now requires further examination."[34]

The potential for generational conflict is also there in the labour market. Not too long ago, when younger workers couldn't find jobs and faced high rates of unemployment, it was felt that the huge baby boom generation was blocking their chances of advancement. Quebec's phased retirement program, for example, was introduced in 1997 with the objective of persuading older workers to retire and free up jobs for younger workers. Now the concern is more that there will not be enough younger workers to fill the jobs when the baby boomers leave their paid employment.

Some recent workplace trends could potentially cause problems, too. For instance, many employers have introduced two-tier pension plans in an effort to cut costs, closing their defined benefit pension plans to new hires—many of them younger workers—who may have the option of joining a defined contribution plan or group RRSP with no guaranteed benefits, while older workers remain in the more secure defined benefit plan. There may be differences in hours and wage rates between older and younger workers, too. Such polarization also raises the potential for inter-generational conflict. According to Peter Hicks, "If younger cohorts continue to be disadvantaged compared with older cohorts, there could be obvious consequences for policies—certainly bringing into question the inter-generational contract that underlies the tax-transfer system"[35]

Where Do We Go From Here?

But Hicks also believes there is too much uncertainty about future trends to consider these problems as clear policy pressures at this point. He suggests the generation that entered the difficult labour market of the 1990s will face a greatly eased situation once the existing baby boom generation moves into retirement.[36]

Referring to the interest in generational accounting techniques of the early 1990s, Hicks suggests that, while these showed how the tax and transfer system created generational winners and losers, they also "whetted the appetite for more sophisticated tools for exploring inter-generational distributional issues in a more realistic way—especially ones that took account of in-family transfers of income and services and the role of inheritances in a world with greatly reduced fertility and increased family instability."[37]

In the end, says Hicks, "The research task has proved too difficult." In particular, he notes, inter-generational fairness is greatly influenced by adjustment taking place within families, but existing data is not strong enough to show how families, markets, taxes, and transfers work together across cohorts and generations. Policy implications therefore still remain unclear."[38]

When it comes to retirement, however, Malcolm Johnson is more specific. "As an evangelist for the full citizenship of old people," he says, "I am now acutely aware that the contemporary patterns of retirement—beneficial as they are—are unsustainable in their present forms. More to the point, the life of extended leisure presently experienced by growing numbers of retirees is not what was ever meant in earlier conceptions of inter-generational support to the old. Such a contract must rest upon a principled reinterpretation of what is equitable and what is deliverable."[39]

According to Johnson, developed societies cannot afford to forgo the direct contribution of so large a segment of their adult populations. Between two and three decades of living outside of the mainstream of economic life is a breach of the contract, he says. The commitment younger generations have inherited is to support those who cannot support themselves, not to provide an ever-growing sabbatical in the third age. By the same token, he says, third age people will not tolerate exclusion from full citizenship. Nor will many of them be willing or able to exist economically on fixed and diminishing incomes.[40]

It will be imperative for older people—especially the "young old"—to continue to earn income, both to finance their current living needs and to avoid low income later in life, Johnson believes. So, in rethinking the generational contract, he emphasizes, it is essential that there be a reliable platform of services and pension provision for all. He says the post-60 phase of life will need to be greatly more flexible in offering flexible retirement between 55 and 75, and new opportunities for job changes in mid- and later career, possibly to lower-paying jobs, but ones which can go on much later, e.g., in the service sectors of industry and in the expanding realms of social and health care.

The care of the old, he notes, is increasingly the responsibility of over-55s, so mechanisms need to be found to include some of this in the formal economy. New generations must, as in earlier times, make provision for their old age through a lifetime investment. Johnson admits he says this "knowing all too well that there are structural inequalities which will make this difficult or impossible for some. It is properly within the Contract," he says, "for just and non-stigmatizing provision to be made for them."[41]

If societies are unable or unwilling to make adequate financial provision for the growing population of older people, says Johnson, those individuals must make greater provision for themselves. And there are only three ways in which this can be done:

1. greater lifetime investment in savings, investments and private pensions;

2. increased intra-family transfers to the old; and

3. continued earnings from employment or business activities.[42]

More emphasis on individual responsibility

Shifting responsibility on to individuals to provide for their own financial security in old age might be achieved through Johnson's first option of

Where Do We Go From Here?

greater lifetime investment in savings, investments, and private pensions. But, as we have seen, it's an approach that does not seem to be meeting with great success in Canada right now. Private pension coverage continues to decline, and unused RRSP contribution room is increasing exponentially. While many people seem to be worried about having enough to live on in retirement, they seem unwilling or unable to do much about the problem. Policy-makers may show signs of concern, but their efforts are generally focused on getting people to save more. Dealing with the problem by changing the pension system or by improving public pensions doesn't seem to be in the cards.

As the OECD puts it, "Like other countries, Canada's approach to managing the pressures of an aging society depends on its starting point." And one of the most important starting points for Canada is its multi-pillar retirement income system. According to the OECD, "The design of the system, which closely mirrors that advocated by the OECD, provides balance and flexibility."[43] While giving its stamp of approval to Canada, the OECD also says that Canada seems relatively well placed to manage the pressures of an aging population. The demographic trends are not as dramatic as in some countries, steps have already been taken to create a sound fiscal situation, and the labour market has flexibility to respond to changes in the workforce, says the OECD. Some "fine-tuning around the edges" may be required for the pension system, but no major reforms are anticipated now.[44]

However, in a 2005 publication, *Ageing and Employment Policies—Canada,* the OECD sets out what else it thinks Canada needs to do. "While the 1998 reform of the pension system may have ensured its long-term financial sustainability," says the OECD, "further reform is required to address the work disincentives inherent in the retirement system." Among other measures it believes Canada should take, the OECD says there should be more flexibility for combining pensions with work income; governments should move ahead with abolition of mandatory retirement; participation of older job seekers in employment programs should be increased; and self-employment among older workers should be facilitated as "an option for extending the working life of individuals." [45]

The fraying intergenerational contract suggested by Malcolm Johnson is already in evidence in Canada. It is clear that further improvements to the public pension system to help those who have fallen through the cracks are not likely to make it onto the policy agenda in the near future. As one federal policy-maker put it, "We sense there's no appetite for further changes to the CPP."[46] Instead, individuals will be expected to shoulder more of the burden of providing for their own financial security in old age.

From a policy point of view, efforts may be made to introduce new vehicles to help them do this. Tax-prepaid savings plans (TPSPS), lifetime accounts, and asset-based policies, discussed in Chapter 3, are all tools in the arsenal. Just how successful they will be remains to be seen. Lower-income earners, as we have seen, don't take advantage of existing programs such as RRSPS, generally because their low earnings don't leave them any spare cash to invest, even when there are tax incentives to do so. Just how they could be persuaded to save through a TPSP, for example, when the tax advantage doesn't appear until decades down the road is a mystery. Lifetime accounts may face the same problem, even when there is a matching government contribution to encourage savers. For instance, take-up rates for the government's Canada Education Savings Grant (CESG), introduced in the 1998 federal budget to provide a matching grant for those who save for post-secondary education through Registered Education Savings Plans (RESPS), have apparently been disappointing.[47]

With coverage of workplace pension plans declining, and increasing numbers of workers in defined contribution plans or group RRSPS that don't promise any particular pension, the outlook for improving financial security in this way as the population ages is not promising—to say the least.

Family care of elders: gender analysis is often missing

Increased intra-family transfers to the old—the second of Malcolm Johnson's possible ways to provide for the elderly—does not seem a promising prospect, either. He notes, for example, as the journey leads the older

Where Do We Go From Here?

generation to their last years, how the often unspoken dialogue of emotional support and services in kind in the unspecified expectation of inheritance is acted out. Empirical evidence of this, says Johnson, is to be found in long-term care where relatives seek to restrict expenditure to minimize diminution of their inheritance.[48]

But, in discussions about the possibility of families playing an increased role in the future as the population ages, the consequences for women are often overlooked. The intra-family transfers referred to by Johnson and others involve not just financial support, but unpaid eldercare: work that is still undertaken mainly by older women. The unspoken assumption that women will continue to shoulder this responsibility will continue to limit women's choices for retirement and how they spend their older years.

As the population ages, there has been a shift away from institutional care, leaving the bulk of care-giving duties to family and friends.[49] While many seniors in Canada live with their spouse or partner, men are far more likely than women to spend their senior years with a spouse or partner, because of their lower life expectancy and tendency to marry younger women. Older men are thus more likely to have a source of informal care.[50] In 2002, nearly half a million Canadians aged 45 and over provided personal care to a senior, and three-quarters of them were women. More than half of personal care providers were 45 to 54 years old, with proportions decreasing with age.[51]

When Johnson talks about the care of the old being increasingly the responsibility of over-55s, those providing the care are almost certain to be women. As we have seen, women often must retire early from their paid employment to care for older family members or those with disabilities. Many caregivers have to change their work patterns, perhaps working split shifts or leaving early and then making up the time. Statistics Canada's 2002 General Social Survey found that a change of work patterns was required by more than one-quarter of female caregivers aged 45 to 54. The proportion of men in this age group reporting work pattern impacts was about half that of women. Reducing hours of work was common for caregivers aged 45 to 54: 20% of women and 13% of men reported having done so.[52] All of these changes may affect the financial security of women as they grow older, and will almost certainly affect their own retirement decisions.

Of course, the fact that the vast majority of Canadian women in the pre-retirement age group are now in paid employment is also often overlooked. Unfortunately, a gender analysis of policies for retirement is often missing. Papers in the 2001 United Nations publication on *The World Aging Situation: Exploring a Society for All Ages* demonstrate that this problem is not confined to developed countries. Many developed countries assume the public sector should play an important role in care and support for elders, but virtually all countries in the developing world apparently assume that role will be played by the family, even though the domestic arrangements of the inter-generational family that tradition-ally supported older persons are themselves under threat. Ironically, as authors of one paper point out, "it is precisely those societies which are about to encounter the greatest change in their demography—and which therefore have experienced the greatest changes in family structure—that are advocating kinship as the solution."[53]

The importance of a gender analysis in developing a "society for all ages" is clearly critical, but it is not receiving the attention it deserves. In the developing world, analysts say gender and aging is an area that needs immediate attention from policy researchers and development agencies in poverty alleviation strategies. But the focus of development activities has been unambiguously on youth, and very often male youth, they note.[54] They also note that reductions in family size have positive consequences for women's health status and lifetime earning capabilities. But such reductions also have the consequences of spreading care among a smaller number of persons. Social changes that enable women to enter employment and take financial control of their own lives mean they are less dependent in their older years. But these same changes deplete the domestic workforce which has traditionally cared for the old.[55] Policy-makers in most of the developing countries—and in some developed countries, too—are still not addressing this crucial issue. Yet, unless they do, it is difficult to see how we might move to a "society for all ages."

Where Do We Go From Here?

Continuing to work in paid employment

Much of the emphasis in the new approach to aging populations is focused on persuading older persons to prolong their working lives. This is Johnson's third option for individuals to provide for themselves where societies are unable or unwilling to make adequate financial provision for the growing population of older people. But, as we have seen, "work" in this context is implicitly understood as paid work. Continuing to work for pay may not be possible for many women, who — whether in developed or developing countries — are still expected to be the major caregivers in the family. Proponents of the society for all ages often advocate raising the retirement age so that older people will continue to "contribute fully" to the economy and society. The implicit assumption seems to be that the unpaid caregiving work older women do in the home is not valued as a contribution in the way that paid work is.

There will certainly be adverse consequences if the policy emphasis is shifted more and more towards individual responsibility for retirement provision, and if working longer becomes the answer to a secure old age. What happens then to those who are not able to go on working for pay? Do we tell women that the answer to their high rates of poverty when they are left alone in old age is to keep on working in the paid work force? Are we willing to improve publicly-funded eldercare as the population ages, or will we continue to assume that older women will undertake this work without pay? What about workers in high-stress, physically demanding jobs? Will they be forced to go on working against their will simply to provide themselves with adequate financial support in retirement? What about those workers who become ill or disabled and are no longer able to work in paid employment? A policy based on individual responsibility for retirement provision would leave these workers unprotected. Ultimately, we may have to revisit the structure of our public pension programs and strengthen them to make sure these individuals are provided with adequate support for their older years.

Left on their own to provide for their future financial security, however, it seems almost certain that more and more Canadians will have to delay their full retirement from paid work. Some people may do so because they prefer to phase into retirement gradually; others may see it as a deliberate strategy they could employ if they haven't accumulated enough savings by the time they would ideally like to stop working. Increasingly, retirement will be seen as a process of easing out of paid employment, and not a point in time when all paid work suddenly ceases.

After almost a decade of decline, the median age of retirement stabilized in the mid-1990s. We may even see it start to creep up as the baby boom generation approaches its 60s. All this could happen without any direct intervention by governments to raise the age of retirement: for example, by raising the age of eligibility for public pensions. In fact, such a move seems unlikely, given the recent favourable actuarial reports on the CPP.

Building the society for all ages

Will we be able to build the kind of "society for all ages" that the United Nations has in mind? It seems almost like a kind of dream world—in the words of one writer, "rewriting life-maps: towards flourishing lives." She believes if we rewrite the scripts for living in late life in more expansive terms, encompassing "doing, becoming, and being," we will expand elders' choices and redefine the meaning of life's end-stage for humanity."[56] While these are overlapping conditions, she says, each has a distinctive character and a multiplicity of expressions according to age, temperament, and culture. "Doing" in late life can create a unique legacy for the next generations. "Becoming" through self-actualization may open up to us the true potential of late life; and "being," as experienced in the later years, may give access to a transcendent reality beyond ego consciousness.[57]

The current concentration of adult years on work, says this author, is a legacy of industrialization which segregated education, work, and leisure horizontally by age-set: education in youth, work in adult years, leisure in late life. A vertical distribution of these opportunities over the entire life-course, as is more common in pre-industrial societies, would give workers more time for continuing education (necessary to avoid social and skills obsolescence in a fast-changing world); more time for family and community life (necessary as women worldwide join men in

Where Do We Go From Here?

the paid workforce), and gradual and phased retirement (necessary as longevity extends this phase of life from a few years, when retirement was first introduced, to a few decades as is more often the case now).[58] It is urgent that adult years be restructured, says this author, allowing men and women alike the opportunities to accumulate stores of economic capital through work, human capital through continuing education, and social capital through cultivating family and social networks.[59]

It's a remarkably ambitious project. It's the same kind of approach now being developed by the federal government's Policy Research Initiative through its *Population Aging and Life-Course Flexibility* project, discussed in Chapter 3. The success of this effort will almost certainly depend on how the ideas are presented to the general public, and how people understand the objectives. Judging by focus group testing conducted as part of the PRI aging project, it seems that the idea of a "flexible life-course" is not well understood. As well, public support for the idea seems likely to fade quickly as long as it is associated with working longer or delaying retirement. Innumerable surveys have shown that people do not want to work longer if it can be avoided. They might be willing to do so in a job that they liked, but a good many people don't seem to like the jobs they are doing. As one focus group participant put it, "I love to work. It's just that I hate my job."[60] Other participants said, "We've worked hard all our lives. We deserve to retire. Why does the government want us to keep working?" The reality of the matter for some, says PRI, was that, "having toiled and struggled for most of their lives at mind-numbing and/or physically demanding jobs, the thought of choosing to work past retirement was not only anathema, but threatening." Reminding these participants that Canadians were living longer and healthier lives, and thus more able to work past retirement, "had little impact on their views," PRI says.[61]

PRI admits: "It is difficult for people to consider concepts in the abstract, without being distracted by thoughts of implementation mechanisms."[62] It is perhaps also significant that, when participants were asked to reflect on the relevance of what was being discussed to their own lives, and whether they would be willing to make now, or in hindsight, the hypothetical trade-off of greater flexibility (i.e., time off) during their prime working years in exchange for working later in life (i.e., remaining in the paid labour force past their expected age of retirement), the concept appeared to hold the greatest appeal to people described as being of "upper socioeconomic status." As we saw in Chapter 3, the concept held less appeal for lower socioeconomic status participants, particularly the pre-retirement segment. "Those who were attracted to it put forward the same reasoning as other supporters. Those who were not interested, or, in some cases opposed the idea," the report says, "could not see how they personally would benefit, and still harboured concerns about a possibly hidden government agenda to keep older people in the workforce more or less forcibly."[63]

It's worth repeating here that the PRI's mandate is to focus on the medium and longer-term policy agenda for the federal government. It seems evident that efforts to promote "life-course flexibility" are likely to require a very long-term perspective. In fact, it may well be that the United Nations goal of "a society for all ages" may be something of a fantasy. But it is worth noting here that, as elders form an increasing percentage of the population, their influence on public policy may well increase as they exercise their democratic options. In the meantime, the new face of retirement will continue to evolve—with or without government intervention. But we will need to keep a watchful eye on the process to make sure the much-vaunted freedom of choice about life-course and retirement really does offer the free choices Canadians want to have without replacing the collective responsibility that ensures all citizens are equally protected.

Notes

1 Myles 2003: 1

2 Canadian Labour Congress 2004: 1.

3 Geogretti 2004: 1.

4 Bigsby 2003: 1.

5 Myles 2003: 1.

6 Hicks 2002:104.

7 Ibid. 131.

8 Ibid.

Where Do We Go From Here?

9 Ibid. 44–46.

10 Ibid. 3.

11 Ibid. 2.

12 Myles 2003: 3.

13 Myles 2003: 16.

14 Ibid.15.

15 Ibid.

16 Ibid.

17 Ibid. 17.

18 Hicks 2002: 62.

19 Statistics Canada 2004f: 68.

20 National Council of Welfare 2004: 20–25.

21 Statistics Canada 2005: 124 and 146.

22 HSBC Bank 2005.

23 Wisensale 2001: 104.

24 Ibid. 103.

25 Ibid. 102.

26 Ibid. 104.

27 Ibid. 105.

28 Ibid.106.

29 Townson 2001: 51–52.

30 Baldwin 2004b: 28.

31 Johnson 2000: 4.

32 Ibid. 5.

33 Ibid. 6.

34 Ibid. 8.

35 Hicks 2002: 50.

36 Ibid.

37 Ibid. 149.

38 Ibid.

39 Johnson 2000: 10.

40 Ibid. 11.

41 Ibid. 12.

42 Ibid.

43 OECD 2000: 55.

44 Ibid.

45 OECD 2005: 11–17.

46 In a private conversation with the author.

47 Lefebvre 2004: 25.

48 Johnson 2000: 3.

49 Cranswick 2003: 8.

50 Ibid. 10.

51 Ibid. 15.

52 Ibid. 15

53 Grieco and Apt 2001: 22.

54 Ibid. 16.

55 Ibid. 25.

56 Donelan 2001: 112.

57 Ibid. 118.

58 Ibid. 112.

59 Ibid. 120.

60 Policy Research Initiative 2004b: 20.

61 Ibid. 25.

62 Ibid. 49.

63 Ibid. 28.

Bibliography

AccountancyAge.com (2002) "E & Y staff in pension row," by Michelle Perry, 24-01-2002. At http://www.managemnetconsutacy.co.uk (Accessed July 23, 2002).

Akyeampong, Ernest (2002) "Unionization and Fringe Benefits," in *Perspectives on Labour and Income*. Vol. 14, No. 3. Autumn 2002. Ottawa: Statistics Canada Catalogue no. 75-001-XPE.

Altmann, Ros (2002) "Retirement—a 'process' not an 'event'." At http://www. rosaltmann.com/retirementandpensionsprocess.htm. (Accessed January 14, 2004).

———. (2003) "Have Private Pensions Lost Their Credibility? Can Government do Better? London, England: UBS Pensions Research Programme: London School of Economics Pensions Debate, December 2, 2003. At http://www. rosaltmann.com (Accessed January 14, 2004).

Ambachtsheer, Keith (2005) "Pension autopilot: Private accounts are too risky. Indecisive, impulsive workers need to have retirement contributions invested for them" in *The Financial Post,* March 22, 2005.

American Association of Retired Persons (2004a) "Statement by AARP CEO in response to Fed Chairman Greenspan's proposal to cut future Social Security benefits." Washington: AARP, February 25, 2004. At http://www.aarp.org/research/press/presscurrentnews (Accessed March 23, 2004).

————. (2004b) "Statement of AARP Board of Directors in reaction to the Social Security and Medicare Trustees Reports." Washington: AARP, February 25, 2004. At http://www.aarp.org/research/press/presscurrentnews (Accessed March 23, 2004).

Amicus-MSF (2002a) *The Crisis in Occupational Pensions.* London, England: Amicus-MSF. At http://www.msf.org.uk (Accessed July 19, 2002).

————. (2002b) "Workers will strike to save pensions, says Amicus." News release issued June 8, 2002. At http://www.msf.org.uk/cgi-bin/news (Accessed July 19, 2002).

Ananova News Service (2002) "Big Food Group faces court action over pensions change," story filed July 3, 2002. At http://www.ananova.com/business/story (Accessed July 19, 2002).

Association of Canadian Pension Management (2003) *Are Defined Benefit Plans in Crisis?* Proceedings of a Forum held on May 23, 2003. Toronto: ACPM.

Baker, Dean (2005) "Bush's Numbers Racket," in *American Prospect* Online edition, February 2005. At http://www.prospect.org (accessed June 1, 2005).

Baker, Dean and David Rosnick (2004) "Basic Facts on Social Security and Proposed Benefit Cuts/Privatization," *Briefing Paper.* Washington, Center for Economic and Policy Research, November 16, 2004.

Baldwin, Bob (2004a) *Trade Unions, Older Workers and the Age of Retirement.* Ottawa: Canadian Labour Congress. Research Paper #29, April 2004.

————. (2004b) *Pension Reform in Canada in the 1990s: What Was Accomplished, What Lies Ahead?* Ottawa: Canadian Labour Congress. Research Paper #30, April 2004.

Baldwin, Bob and Pierre Laliberté (1999) *Incomes of Older Canadians: Amounts and Sources, 1973–1996.* Ottawa: Canadian Labour Congress. Research Paper #15, December 1999.

Bank of Canada (2003) *Financial System Review June 2003*. Ottawa: Bank of Canada.

Battle, Ken (2001) "Relentless Incrementalism: Deconstructing and Reconstructing Canadian Income Security Policy," in *The Review of Economic Performance and Social progress: The Longest Decade: Canada in the 1990s*. Montreal: Institute for Research on Public Policy.

————. (2003) *Sustaining Public Pensions: A Tale of Two Reforms*. Ottawa: Caledon Institute of Social Policy.

Baxter, David and Andrew Ramlo (1998) *What Can You Expect? Life Expectancy in Canada, 1921 to 2021*. Vancouver: Urban Futures Institute, Report 25.

Béland, Daniel and John Myles (2005) "Stasis amidst change: Canadian pension reform in an age of retrenchment," in Giuliano Bonoli and Toshimitsu Shikawa (eds), *Ageing and Pension Reform Around the World*. Cheltenham: Edward Elgar Publishing.

Bigsby, Stephen (2003) "If Pension Reform makes Sense, Why is it so Difficult?" in *ACPM Newsletter*. Volume 3, Issue 4. December 2003.

Blöndal, Sveinbjörn and Stefano Scarpetta (1997) *Early Retirement in OECD Countries: The Role of Social Security Systems*. OECD Economic Studies No, 29, 1997/II. Paris: OECD.

Boychuck, Gerard (2004) *The Canadian Social Model: The Logics of Policy Development*. Ottawa: Canadian Policy Research Networks. CPRN Social Architecture Papers Report F/36, Family Network.

Brooks, Richard, Sue Regan and Peter Robinson (2002a) *A new contract for retirement*. London, England: Institute for Public Policy Research.

————. (2002b) *A new contract for retirement. Modelling policy options to 2050*. London, England: Institute for Public Policy Research.

Brown, Robert (2002a) "An Argument for Higher RRSP Limits," in *Benefits Canada*, September 2002. Toronto: Rogers Media Inc.

————. (2002b) *Paying for Canada's Aging Population: How big is the problem?* Toronto Canadian Institute of Actuaries, March 2002.

Burtless, Gary and Joseph F. Quinn (2002) *Is Working longer the Answer for an Aging Workforce?* An Issue in Brief, December 2002, Number 11. Boston: Center for Retirement Research at Boston College.

Canadian Council on Social Development (2003) *Working Conference on Strategies to Ensure Economic Security for All Canadians. Proceedings and Final Report.* Ottawa: Canadian Council on Social Development. At http://www.ccsd.ca/events/2003/lerner.pdf (Accessed May 25, 2004).

———. (2004) *What Kind of Canada" A Call for a National Debate on the Canada Social Transfer.* Ottawa: Canadian Council on Social Development.

Canadian Labour and Business Centre (2001) *Where Did All the Workers Go? The Challenges of the Aging Workforce.* Ottawa: Canadian Labour and Business Centre: Analysis of the Viewpoints 2000 Leadership Survey.

Canadian Labour Congress (2004) *Backgrounder—Polling Details.* Ottawa: Canadian Labour Congress details provided to the author.

Canadian Union of Public Employees (2004) "CUPE Supports Stelco workers," CUPE News Release, March 19, 2004. At http://www.cnw.ca/fr/releases/archive/March2004 (Accessed March 30, 2004).

Casey, Bernard (1998) *Incentives and Disincentives to early and late retirement.* OECD Working Paper AWP 3.3. Paris: OECD.

Casey, Bernard, Howard Oxley, Edward Whitehouse, Pablo Antolin, Rornain Duval and Will Leibfritz (2003) *Policies for an Ageing Society: Recent Measures ad Areas for Further Reform.* OECD Economics Department Working Papers No. 369. Paris OECD.

Cato Institute (2003) *Ownership Society: Responsibility, Liberty, and Prosperity.* At http://www.cato.org/special/ownership_society/ (Accessed June 1, 2005).

Cheal, David, (2000) "Aging and Demographic Change," in *Canadian Public Policy,* XXVI, August 2000. Kingston, Ontario: Queen's University, School of Policy Studies.

———. (2002) Editor: *Aging and Demographic Change in Canadian Context.* Toronto University of Toronto Press.

———. (2003) "Aging and Demographic Change in Canadian Context," in *Horizons Volume 6 Number 2*. Ottawa: Government of Canada, Policy Research Initiative.

Chief Actuary (2002a) *Eighteenth Actuarial Report*. Ottawa: Office of the Chief Actuary.

———. (2002b) *Nineteenth Actuarial Report*. Ottawa: Office of the Chief Actuary.

———. (2003) *Canada Pension Plan Actuarial Adjustment Factors Study*. Ottawa: Office of the Chief Actuary, Actuarial Study No. 2.

———. (2004) *Actuarial Report (21st) on the Canada Pension Plan as at December 31, 2003*. Ottawa: Office of the Chief Actuary.

Compton, Janice (2001) *Determinants of Retirement: Does Money Really Matter?* Ottawa: Government of Canada: Department of Finance Working Paper 2001–2.

Cook, David T. (2002) "Delayed retirement is here to stay." New York: *Christian Science Monitor*. At http://www.csmoitor.com (Accessed January 14, 2004).

Cotis, Jean-Philippe (2003) "Population ageing: Facing the challenge," in OECD *Observer*, September 26, 2003. Paris: OECD.

Cranswick, Kelly (2003) *General Social Survey Cycle 16: caring for an aging society*. Ottawa: Statistics Canada Catalogue no. 89-582-XIE. September 2003.

Dean for America (2003) "The Bush Tax: How Much Is It Costing You?" At http://www.bushtax.com (Accessed April 2, 2004).

Denton, Frank T. and Byron G. Spencer (1999) *Population Aging and Its Economic Costs: A Survey of the Issues and Evidence*. Hamilton: McMaster University. SEDAP: A Program for Research on Social and Economic Dimensions of an Aging Population. SEDAP Research Paper No.1.

Department of Finance (2003) *Canada Pension Plan Actuarial Adjustment Factors Study*. Ottawa: Office of the Chief Actuary. Actuarial Study No. 2.

————. (2004) "Canada Pension Plan Financially Sound: Chief Actuary." Ottawa: Department of Finance Canada press release 2004-077, December 8, 2004 at http://www.fin.gc.ca/news04/04-077e.html (Accessed 12/9/04).

————. (2005) *Strengthening the Legislative and Regulatory Framework for Defined Benefit Pension Plans Registered under the Pension Benefits Standards Act, 1985.* Ottawa: Department of Finance, Financial Sector Division. May 2005.

Desjardins Financial Security (2003) "Canadians will not work to death." Toronto: Desjardins Financial Security media release, February 11, 2003. At http://www.Desjardinsfinancialsecurity.com (Accessed March 26, 2003).

————. (2004) "Canadians' Dream of Traditional Retirement Evaporate." Toronto: Desjardins Financial Security media release, February 16, 2004. At http://www.Desjardinsfinancialsecurity.com (Accessed February 16, 2004).

Dodge, David (2004a) "Adjusting to a Changing Economic World," Remarks to the Board of Grade of Metropolitan Montreal, 11 February 2004. Ottawa: Bank of Canada. At http://www.bankofcanada.ca/en/speeches/2004/sp04-1.htm. (Accessed 10/22/04).

————. (2004b) "Adjusting to Global Economic Change," Remarks to the Brazil-Canada Chamber of Commerce, São Paulo, Brazil, 10 March 2004. Ottawa: Bank of Canada. At http://www.bankofcanada.ca/en/speeches/2004/sp04-3.htm. (Accessed April 16, 2004).

————. (2004c) Proceedings of the House of Commons Standing Committee on Banking, Trade and Commerce, Issue 3—Evidence: April 20, 2004.

Donelan, Brigid (2001) "Rewriting Lifemaps: Towards Flourishing Lives," in *The World Ageing Situation: Exploring a Society for All Ages.* New York: United Nations Economic & Social Affairs.

Duschesne, Doreen (2004) "More seniors at work," in *Perspectives on Labor and Income.* Online edition, February 2004, Vol. 5, No. 2. Ottawa: Statistics Canada Catalogue no. 75-001-XIE.

Edwards, Laura, Sue Regan and Richard Brooks (2001) *Age old attitudes? Planning retirement, means-testing, inheritance and informal care.* London, England: Institute for Public Policy Research.

Erwin, Steve (2004) "Some steelmakers face doom if labour costs not cut, debt rating agency says," Canadian Press, March 25, 2004. At http://www.canada.com/components/printstory

Esping-Andersen, Gosta (2002a) "A New Gender Contract," in *Why We Need A New Welfare State.* Gosta Esping-Andersen with Duncan Gallie, Anton Hemerijck and John Myles. New York: Oxford University Press.

————. (2002b) "Towards the Good Society, Once Again?" in *Why We Need A New Welfare State.* Gosta Esping-Andersen with Duncan Gallie, Anton Hemerijck and John Myles New York: Oxford University Press.

Ettlinger, Michael and Jeff Chapman (2005) "Social Security and the Income of the Elderly," epi *Issue Brief #206.* Washington: Economic Policy Institute. March 23, 2005.

European Union (2000a) *Council Directive 2000/78/EC establishing a general framework for equal treatment in employment and occupation.* Brussels: European Community.

————. (2000b) *The Future Evolution of Social Protection from a Long-Term Point of View Safe and Sustainable Pensions.* Communication from the Commission to the Council, to the European Parliament and to the Economic and Social Committee. Brussels: Commission of the European Communities. com (2000) 622 final.

————. (2001) *Supporting national strategies for safe and sustainable pensions through an integrated approach.* Communication from the Commission to the Council, to the European Parliament and to the Economic and Social Committee. Brussels: Commission of the European Communities. com (2001) 362 final.

————. (2003) *Draft joint report by the Commission and the Council on adequate and sustainable pensions.* Report to the Council from the Economic Policy Committee and the Social Protection Committee. Brussels: Council of the European Union, ecofin 51 soc 72. March 3, 2003.

—————. (2004) *Increasing the employment of older workers and delaying the exit from the labour market.* Communication from the Commission to the Council, to the European Parliament and to the Economic and Social Committee. Brussels: Commission of the European Communities. COM (20040 146 final.

Foot, David K. with Daniel Stoffman (1996) *Boom, Bust & Echo.* Toronto: Macfarlane Walter & Ross.

Fourzly, Michel and Marc Gervais (2002) *Collective Agreements and Older Workers in Canada.* Ottawa: Human Resources Development Canada Labour Program.

Frenken, Hubert (2003) "Individual Programs—Registered Retirement Savings Plans," in *Canada's Retirement Income Programs: A Statistical Overview (1990-2000).* Ottawa: Statistics Canada Catalogue no. 74-507-XPE.

Furman, Jason and Robert Greenstein (2005) *An Overview of Issues Raised by the Administration's Social Security Plan.* Washington: Center on Budget and Policy Priorities.

G8 Information Centre (2000) *G8 Turin Charter: "Towards Active Ageing."* Labor Ministers Conference, Turin, Italy, November 10–11, 2000. Toronto: G8 Information Centre at http://www.g8.utoronto.ca/labor/ageingnov2000.htm. (Accessed April 28, 2005).

Georgetti, Ken (2003) Letter to Dean Conner, CEO of Mercer Consulting, provided to the author by the Canadian Labour Congress.

—————. (2004) Letter to The Right Hon. Paul Martin, Prime Minister of Canada, provided to the author by the Canadian Labour Congress.

Globe and Mail (2005) "How (not) to fix pensions," In *The Globe and Mail,* Toronto, February 5, 2005.

Government of Canada (1996) *An Information Paper for Consultations on the Canada Pension Plan.* Released by the Federal, Provincial and Territorial Governments of Canada. Ottawa: Department of Finance.

—————. (1997) *Securing the Canada Pension Plan: Agreement on Proposed Changes to the CPP.* Ottawa: Department of Finance.

Gower, Dave (1997) "Measuring the age of retirement," in *Perspectives on Labor and Income.* Summer 1997, Vol. 9, No. 2. Ottawa: Statistics Canada Catalogue no. 75-001-X P E.

———. (1998) "Retirement patterns of working couples," in *Perspectives on Labour and Income,* Autumn 1998, Vol. 10, No. 23 Ottawa: Statistics Canada Catalogue no. 75-001-X P E.

Grieco, Margaret and Nana Apt (2001) "Development and the Ageing of Populations: Global Overview by Experts on Ageing in Africa." In *The World Ageing Situation: Exploring a Society for All Ages.* New York: United Nations Economic & Social Affairs.

Gunderson, Morley (2004) *Banning Mandatory Retirement: Throwing Out the Baby With the Bathwater.* Toronto: C.D.Howe Institute Backgrounder No. 79, March 2004.

Habtu, Roman (2003) "Men 55 and older: Work or retire?" in *Perspectives on Labour and Income,* Spring 2003. Vol. 15 No. 1. Ottawa: Statistics Canada Catalogue no. 75-001-X P E.

Hamilton, Malcolm (2003) *Should the Pension "Deal" be Revisited?* Toronto: Mercer Human Resource Consulting, November 20, 2003.

Hauser, Richard (1998) *Adequacy and poverty among the retired.* O E C D Working Paper A W P 3.2. Paris O E C D.

Hicks, Peter (2001) *Public Support for Retirement Income Reform.* Paris: Organization for Economic Cooperation and Development. Labour Market and Social Policy—Occasional Papers No. 55.

———. (2002) *Preparing for Tomorrow's Social Policy Agenda: New Priorities for Policy Research and Development That Emerge From an Examination of the Economic Well-Being of the Working-Age Population.* Ottawa: Social Research and Demonstration Corporation.

———. (2003a) "New Policy Research on Population Aging and Life-Course Flexibility," in *Horizons Volume 6 Number 2.* Ottawa: Government of Canada, Policy Research Initiative.

————. (2003b) "The Policy Implications of Aging: A Transformation of National and International Thinking," in *Horizons Volume 6 Number 2*. Ottawa: Government of Canada, Policy Research Initiative.

HSBC Bank (2005) *The future of retirement in a world of rising life expectations*. London: HSBC Bank at http://www.hsbc.com/futureofretirement Accessed May 17, 2005.

Human Resources Development Canada (2001) *Income Security Programs Evaluation of Public and Private Financial Incentives for Retirement*. Ottawa: HRDC Strategic Policy. SP-AH087-05-01E.

Human Resources and Skills Development Canada (2002) *Challenges of an Ageing Workforce: An overview of the issue*. Ottawa: HRDC Labour Program. At http://www.hrsdc.gc.ca/en/lp/spila/wlb/pdf/overview-aging-workforce-challenges-en.pdf. Accessed March 1, 2005.

Institute for Public Policy Research (2001) *A new Contract for Retirement: an interim report. Incremental and Fundamental Reform Options for Pensions and Long-term Care*. London, England: Institute for Public Policy Research.

International Monetary Fund (2004) *Canada: Selected Issues*. Prepared by C. Towe, M. Mühleisen, R. Cardarelli, C. Faulkner-MacDonagh, R. Luzio, S. Swiston and A. Kose. Approved by the Western Hemisphere Development. Washington: International Monetary Fund, February 2, 2004.

Investors Group (2003) "Majority of Canadians plan to work during retirement." Winnipeg Investors Group Media Release, January 21.2003, at http://www.investorsgroup.com (Accessed March 26, 2003).

Jackson, Andrew (2002) *The Unhealthy Canadian Workplace*. Ottawa: Canadian Labour Congress. Research Paper Number 19. At http://action.web.ca/home/clcpolcy/attach/The%20Unhealthy%20Canadian%20Workplace1.pdf (Accessed 1/14/05).

————. (2004) "Asset-Based Social Policies—A 'New Idea' Whose Time has Come?" *Caledon Commentary, March 2004*. Ottawa: Caledon Institute of Social Policy.

————. (2005) *Work and Labour in Canada: Critical Issues.* Toronto: Canadian Scholars' Press.

Jackson, Richard and Neil Howe (2003) *The 2003Aging Vulnerability Index: An Assessment of the Capacity of Twelve Developed Countries to Meet the Aging Challenge.* Washington: Center for Strategic and International Studies and Watson Wyatt Worldwide.

Jenson, Jane (2004) *Catching Up to Reality: Building the Case for a New Social Model.* Ottawa: Canadian Policy Research Networks. CPRN Social Architecture Papers, Research Report F/35, Family Network.

Johnson, Malcolm L. (2000) *Generational Equity and the Reformulation of Retirement.* Hamilton: McMaster University. SEDAP: A Program for Research on Social Economic Dimensions of an Aging Population. SEDAP Research Paper No. 12.

Kaplan, Matthew (2001) "Rethinking 'Retirement': What's In a Word?" University Park, PA: PennState University: College of Agricultural Sciences. At http://www.aginfo.psu.edu. (Accessed January 14, 2004).

Kapsalis, Costa and Pierre Tourigny (2005) "Duration of non-standard employment" in *Perspectives on Labour and Income,* Vol. 17, No. 1 Spring 2005. Ottawa: Statistics Canada Catalogue no. 75- 001-XPE.

Keating, Norah, Janet Fast, Judith Frederick, Kelly Cranswick and Cathryn Perrier (1999) *Eldercare in Canada: Context, Content and Consequences.* Ottawa: Statistics Canada Catalogue no. 89-570-XPE.

Keenay, Gordon and Edward Whitehouse (2003) *Financial Resources and Retirement in Nine OECD Countries: the Role of the Tax System.* Paris: Organization for Economic Cooperation and Development. Social, Employment and Migration Working Papers No. 8.

Kesselman, Jonathan and Finn Poschmann (2001) *A New Option for Retirement Savings: Tax Prepaid Savings Plans.* Toronto: C.D.Howe Institute.

Kesselman, Jonathan R. (2004) *Mandatory Retirement And Older Worker: Encouraging Longer Working Lives.* Toronto: C.D.Howe Institute Backgrounder No. 200, June 2004.

Kranc, Joel (2004) "Greenspan: raise age for full retirement," in *Benefits Canada*. Online edition, August 27, 2004 , at http://www.benefitscanada.com/news/article.jsp?content=2004827_105648_5576 (Accessed 9/1/04).

Krugman, Paul (2003) *The Great Unraveling: Losing our way in the new century*. New York: W.W.Norton & Company.

Kuttner, Robert (2003) "Bush's 'ownership' scam: Why Bush's 'Ownership Society' is just another bait and switch," in *The American Prospect* Online edition, December 2003. At http://www.prospcet.org (Accessed June 1, 2005).

Labor Research Association (2005) "Workers Can't Afford Bush's 'Ownership Society'." *LRA Online*. At http://www.laborresearch.org/story2.php/379 (Accessed June 1, 2005).

LeBlanc, L. Suzanne and Julie Ann McMullin (1997) "Falling through the Cracks: Addressing the Needs of Individuals between Employment and Retirement," in *Canadian Public Policy*, XXIII, September 1997. Kingston, Ontario: Queen's University, School of Policy Studies.

Lefebvre, Sophie (2004) "Saving for post-secondary education," in *Perspectives on Labour And Income*, Vol. 16, No. 3. Autumn 2004. Ottawa: Statistics Canada Catalogue no. 75-001-XPE.

Leibfritz, Willi (2003) "Retiring later makes sense," Paris: Organization for Economic Co-operation and Development. *OECD Observer,* January 2003.

Le Pan, Nicholas (2003) "Notes for Appearance by Nicholas Le Pan, Superintendent of Financial Institutions to the House of Commons Standing Committee on Transport, Regarding the Regulation and Supervision of Air Canada's Pension Plan," April 3, 2003. Ottawa: Office of the Superintendent of Financial Institutions. At http://www.osfi-bsif.gc.ca (Accessed March 31, 2004).

Lise, Jeremy (2001) *Is Canada's Retirement Income System Working?* Ottawa: Government of Canada: Department of Finance.

MacKenzie, Andrew and Heather Dryburgh (2003) "The retirement wave, in *Perspectives on Labour and Income,* Spring 2003. Vol. 15 No. 1. Ottawa: Statistics Canada Catalogue no. 75-001-XPE.

MacNaughton, John (2004) *The Challenge of Investing CPP Assets*. Presentation to the Calgary Chamber of Commerce, January 20, 2004.

Marshall, Katherine (2003) "Benefiting from extended parental leave," in *Perspectives on Labour and Income*, Summer 2003, Vol. 15, No. 2. Ottawa: Statistics Canada Catalogue no. 75-001-X PE.

Marshall, Victor W. and Margaret M., Mueller (2002) *Rethinking Social Policy for An Workforce and Society: Insights From the Life Course Perspective*. Ottawa" Canadian Policy Research Networks. CPRN Discussion Paper No. W/18.

Martin, Paul (1994a) *The Budget Speech*. February 22, 1994. Ottawa: Department of Finance.

————. (1994b) *The Budget Plan*. February 22, 1994. Ottawa: Department of Finance.

Maser, Karen and Thomas Dufour (2001) *The Assets and Debts of Canadians: Focus on private pension savings*. Ottawa: Statistics Canada Catalogue no. 13-596-X IE.

Marshall, Katherine (2003) "Benefiting from extended parental leave," in *Perspectives on Labour and Income,* Summer 2003, Vol.15, No. 2. Ottawa: Statistics Canada Catalogue no. 75-001-X PE.

Maxwell, Judith (2004) "Foreword" in Jenson, Jane (2004) *Catching Up to Reality: Building theCase for a New Social Model*. Ottawa: Canadian Policy Research Networks. CPRN Social Architecture Papers, Research Report F/35, Family Network.

McDonald, Lynn (1997) "The invisible poor: Canada's retired widows," in *Canadian Journal on Aging*, 16 (3): 553–583.

McMullin, Julie Ann, Martin Cooke, with Rob Downie (2004) *Labour Force Ageing and Skill Shortages in Canada and Ontario*. Ottawa: Canadian Policy Research Networks Research Report W/24, Work Network.

Meadows, Pamela (2003) *Retirement ages in the UK: a review of the literature*. Employment Relations Research Series No. 18. London: Department of Trade and Industry.

Mercer Human Resource Consulting (2003) "Latest UK pension policies: an industry view Mercer." Press release of October 8, 2003, at http://www.mercerhr.ca, (Accessed March 15, 2004).

———. (2004) "Are pension plans at the dawn of a new era?" Release of March 3, 2004. At http://www.mercerhr.com (Accessed March 15, 2004).

Mérette, Marcel (2002) "the Bright Side: A Positive View on the Economics of Aging," in *Choices: Economic Growth,* Vol. 8, no. 1. March 2002. Montreal: Institute for Research on Public Policy.

Meyerson, Harold (2005) "Assault on Social Security," in *The American Prospect*, Online edition, 02.03.05. At http://www.prospect,org. (Accessed June 1, 2005).

Michalski, Joseph H. (2002) *What Matters to Canadian NGOs on Aging: An Analysis of Five Public Dialogue Discussions.* Ottawa: Canadian Policy Research Networks.

Monette, Manon (1996) *Canada's Changing Retirement Patterns: Findings From the General Social Survey.* Ottawa: Statistics Canada Catalogue no. 89-546-XPE.

Morissette, René and Xuelin Zhang (2004) "Retirement plan awareness," in *Perspectives on Labour and Income,* January 2004, Vol. 5, No. 1. Online edition. Ottawa: Statistics Canada Catalogue no. 75-001-XIE.

Morissette, René, Grant Schellenberg and Cynthia Silver (2004) "Retaining older workers," in *Perspectives on Labour and Income,* October 2004, Vol. 5, No. 10. Online edition. Ottawa: Statistics Canada Catalogue no. 75-001-XIE.

Myles, John (2000) "The maturation of Canada's retirement income system: income levels, income inequality and low income among the elderly," in *Canadian Journal on Aging.* 19 (3) 287–316.

———. (2002) "A New Social Contract for the Elderly," in G. Esping Andersen, D. Gallie, A, Hemerijck and J. Myles (2002) *Why We Need a New Welfare State.* Oxford: Oxford University Press.

————. (2003) *From Pension Politics to Retirement Politics.* Ottawa: Statistics Canada Symposium on New Perspectives on Retirement, September 5–6, 2003.

Myles, John and Paul Pierson (2001) "The comparative political economy of pension reform in Paul Pierson (ed) *The New Politics of the Welfare State.* New York: Oxford University Press.

Myles, John and Debra Street (1995) "Should the economic life course be redesigned? Old age security in a time of transition." In *Canadian Journal on Aging* 19 (3): 287–316.

National Advisory Council on Aging (1999) *1999 and Beyond: Challenges of an Aging Canadian Society.* Ottawa: Minister of Public Works and Government Services Canada.

National Council of Welfare (2004) *Poverty Profile 2001.* Ottawa: National Council Welfare, Autumn 2004.

New Democratic Party (2004) "NDP demands long-overdue federal pension protection for Canadian pensions," Press Release March 31, 2004. Ottawa: New Democratic Party. At http://action.web.ca/home/ndpnpd/en. (Accessed March 31, 2004).

Novelli, William (2002) "The End of Retirement." New York: American Association of Retired Persons. At http://www.aarp.org. (Accessed January 14, 2004).

Ontario English Catholic Teachers Association (2004) *Response (Revised) To the Ministry of Labour's consultation paper on Mandatory Retirement.* September 2004.

Ontario Federation of Labour (2004) "speakers Notes on the Mandatory Retirement Consultations." Toronto: Ontario Federation of Labour.

Ontario Government (2005a) *FAQ: Mandatory Retirement.* Toronto: Government of Ontario, Ministry of Labour. At http://www.gov.on.ca/LAB/english/news/2005/05-71faq.html (Accessed 6/29/05).

246 ————. (2005b) *Ending Mandatory Retirement: What it Means to You.* Toronto: Government of Ontario, Ministry of Labour Backgrounder. June 7, 2005. At http://www.gov.on.ca/LAB/english/news/2005/05-71b3.html (Accessed 6/29/05).

Ontario Human Rights Commission (2000) *Discrimination and Age: Human Rights Issue Facing Older Persons in Ontario.* Toronto: Ontario Human Rights Commission.

Organization for Economic Co-operation and Development (1998) *Maintaining Prosperity in an Aging Society.* Paris: OECD.

————. (2000) *Reforms for an Ageing Society.* Paris: OECD.

————. (2001a) "Maintaining the Economic Well-Being of Older People—challenges for retirement income policies." OECD *Observer, Policy Brief,* December 2001. Paris: OECD.

————. (2001b) *Ageing and Income: Financial resources and Retirement in Nine OECD Countries.* Paris: OECD.

————. (2002) "Increasing employment: The role of later retirement," Chapter V in *Economic Outlook No. 72.* Paris: OECD.

————. (2003) *Asset Building and the Escape from Poverty.* Local Economic and Employment Development Programme. Paris: OECD

————. (2004a) "Ageing Societies and the Looming Pension Crisis." Paris: OECD. Notes on the OECD web site at http://www.oecd.org/documentprint/0,2744,en_2649_201185_2512699_1_1_1_1,00.html (Accessed 6/8/04).

————. (2004b) *Ageing and Employment Policies: United Kingdom.* Paris: OECD.

————. (2005) *Ageing and Employment Policies: Canada.* Paris: OECD.

Osberg, Lars (1998) "Meaning and Measurement in Intergenerational Equity," in *Government Finances and Generational Equity.* Edited by Miles Corak. Ottawa: Statistics Canada Catalogue no. 68-513-XIB.

Palameta, Boris (2003) "Profiling R R S P contributors, in *Perspectives on Labour and Income*. Spring 2003. Vol. 15 No. 1. Ottawa: Statistics Canada Catalogue no. 75-001-X P E.

Palier, Bruno (2004) *Social Protection Reforms in Europe: Strategies for a New Social Model*. Ottawa: Canadian Policy Research Networks. C P R N Social Architecture Papers, Research Report F/37, Family Network.

Partridge, John (2004) "Investor to decide April 15 on Air Canada bailout," in *The Globe and Mail Report on Business*. Toronto: March 30, 2004.

Pawlick, Roxanne M. and Sharon M. Stroick (2004) *One Discourse, Three Dialects: Changing the Social Model in Australia, the United Kingdom, and the United States*. Ottawa: Canadian Policy Research Networks. C P R N Social Architecture Papers, Research Report F/38, Family Network.

Perry, Julia (2000) "One language, three accents: Welfare reform in the United States, the United Kingdom and Australia," in *Family Matters* No. 56 (Winter) 40–47. Melbourne, Australia: Government of Australia: Australian Institute of Family Matters at http://www.aifs.org.au/institute/pubs/fm2000/fm56/jp.pdf (Accessed May 25, 2004).

Phillimore, P., Beattie, A., and Townsend, P. "The widening gap. Inequality of health in northern England, 1981–1991." *British Medical Journal* 308:1125–8. 1994.

Policy Research Initiative (2003) *Exploring the Promise of Asset-Based Social Policies: Reviewing Evidence from Research and Practice."* Synthesis Report of a Conference on Asset-Based Approaches, December 8–9, 2003. Ottawa: P R I Project New Approaches for Addressing Poverty and Exclusion.

———. (2004a) *Population Aging and Life-Course Flexibility: The Pivotal Role of Increased Choice in The Retirement Decision*. Ottawa: P R I Project: Population Aging and Life-Course Flexibility, March 2004.

———. (2004b) *Views on Life-Course Flexibility and Canada's Aging Population*. Ottawa: P R I Project: Population Aging and Life-Course Flexibility, July 2004.

———. (2005) P R I *Update Spring 2005*. Ottawa: Policy Research Initiative.

Pyper, Wendy and Philip Giles (2002) "Approaching retirement," in *Perspectives on Labour and Income,* Winter 2002, Vol. 14, No. 4. Ottawa: Statistics Canada Catalogue no. 75-001-XPE.

Régie des rentes du Québec (2003) *Adapting the Pension Plan to Quebec's new realities.* Québec: Minister of Employment, Social Solidarity and Family Welfare.

Rix, Sara E. (2001) "Restructuring Work in an Aging America: What Role for Public Policy in *Restructuring Work and the Life Course.* Edited by Victor W. Marshall, Walter R. Heinz, Helga Krüger and Anil Verma. Toronto: University of Toronto Press.

Robson, William B.P. (2001) *Aging Populations and the Workforce: Challenges for Employers.* Toronto: C.D. Howe Institute, British-North American Committee.

Roeher Institute (2002) *Moving in Unison Into Action: Towards a Policy Strategy for Improving Access to Disability Supports.* Toronto: The Roeher Institute.

Rose, Geoff and Huan Nguyen (2003) "Older workers and the labour market" in *Perspectives on Labour and Income,* Spring 2003. Vol. 15 No. 1. Ottawa: Statistics Canada Catalogue no. 75-001-XPE.

Rowe, Geoff (2003) "Fragments of Lives: Enabling New Policy Direction through Integrated Life-Course Data," in *Horizons Volume 6 Number 2.* Ottawa: Government of Canada, Policy Research Initiative.

Rowe, Geoff and Huan Nguyen (2003) "Older workers and the labour market," *Perspectives on Labour and Income* Spring 2003. Vol. 15 No. 1. Ottawa: Statistics Canada Catalogue no. 75-001-XPE.

Sangster, Derwyn (2000) *Viewpoints 2000: Serious Economic Issues and Policy Solutions.* Ottawa: Canadian Labour and Business Centre Leadership Survey.

Sass, Steven (2004) *Reforming the Australian Retirement System: Mandating Individual Accounts.* Boston: Center for Retirement Research, Boston College.

Schellenberg, Grant (1994) *The Road to Retirement: Demographic and Economic Changes in the 90s.* Ottawa: Canadian Council on Social Development.

————. (2004) *The retirement plans and expectations of non-retired Canadians aged 45 to 59*. Ottawa: Statistics Canada Analytical Studies Research Paper series. Catalogue no. 11F0019MIE—No. 223.

Schellenberg, Grant and Cynthia Silver (2004) "You can't always get what you want: retirement preferences and experiences," in *Canadian Social Trends*. Winter 2004, No. 75.

Scherer, Peter (2001) *Age of Withdrawal from the Labour Force in OECD Countries*. Labour Market and Social Policy—Occasional Papers No. 49. Paris: OECD.

Schetagne, Sylvain (2001) *Building Bridges Across Generations in the Workplace: A Response to Aging of the Workforce*. Vancouver: Columbia Foundation.

Short, David (2003) "The Impact of Aging on Fully-Funded Pension Plans," in *Pension News Issue No. 3*. Ottawa: Canadian Labour Congress.

Smolkin, Sheryl (2004) *Providing Choice: A Consultation Paper on Mandatory Retirement* Toronto: Watson Wyatt Canada.

Social and Enterprise Development Innovations (SEDI) (2004) *learn$ave Backgrounder*. Ottawa: SEDI. At http://www.sedi.org. (Accessed April 23, 2004).

Spencer, Charmaine (2003) "Grey Power in Canada: Will Baby Boomers Become a Political Force As They Age?" in *GRC News, Vol. 22 No 2 2003*. Vancouver: Simon Fraser University Gerontology Research Centre.

Statistics Canada (1999) *A Portrait of Seniors in Canada*. Ottawa: Statistics Canada Catalogue no. 89-519-XPE.

————. (2000) *Women in Canada 2000; A gender-based statistical report*. Ottawa: Canada Catalogue no. 89-503-XPE.

————. (2003a) *General Social Survey Cycle 16: caring for an aging society*. Ottawa: Statistics Canada Catalogue no. 89-582-XIE.

————. (2003b) *2002 General Social Survey Cycle 16: Aging and Social Support—Tables*. Ottawa: Statistics Canada Catalogue no. 89-583-XIE.

———. (2003c) "General Social Survey: Social support and aging, 2002," in *The Daily,* September 2, 2003.

———. (2003d) "Fact-sheet on retirement," In *Perspectives on Labour and Income.* Online edition, December 2003. Vol. 4, No. 12. Ottawa: Statistics Canada Catalogue no. 75-001-XIE.

———. (2003e) *Canada's Retirement Income Programs: A Statistical Overview (1990-2000)* Ottawa: Statistics Canada Catalogue no. 74-507-XPE.

———. (2003f) "Canada's Retirement Income Programs: 1990 to 2001" in *The Daily.* November 17, 2003. Ottawa: Statistics Canada.

———. (2003g) *Profile of the Canadian population by age and sex: Canada ages.* Ottawa: Statistics Canada, Catalogue no. 96F0030XIE2001002.

———. (2004a) "Labour force characteristics by age and sex," at http://www.statcan.ca/engish/Pgdb/labor20b.htm, (Accessed on February 27, 2004).

———. (2004b) "Persons in low income before tax" at http://www.statcan.ca/engish/Pgdb/famil41a.htm, (Accessed March 29, 2004).

———. (2004c) "Proportion of labour force and paid workers covered by a registered pension plan," at http://www.statcan.ca/english/Pgdb/labor26a.htm (Accessed March 30, 2004).

———. (2004d) *Women in Canada: Work chapter updates, 2003.* Ottawa: Statistics Canada Catalogue no. 89F0133XIE.

———. (2004e) *Pension Plans in Canada—January 1, 2003.* Ottawa: Statistics Canada Catalogue no. 13F0026MIE.

———. (2004f) "The near-retirement rate." In *Perspectives on Labour and Income.* Vol. 16 No. 1, Spring 2004. Ottawa: Statistics Canada Catalogue no. 75-001-XPE.

———. (2005) *Income in Canada 2003.* Ottawa: Statistics Canada Catalogue no. 75-202-XIE.

Stein, David (2000) "The New Meaning of Retirement." ERIC Digest No. 217. Columbus, Ohio: Ohio State University: Center on Education and Training for Employment.

Stone, Leroy O. and Andrew S, Harvey (2001) "Gender Differences in Transitions to Total-work retirement," in *Restructuring Work and the Life Course.* Edited by Victor W. Marshall, Walter R. Heinz, Helga Krüger and Anil Verma. Toronto: University of Toronto Press.

TD Bank Financial Group (2004) "Generation Xers lack confidence in CPP, according to TD Waterhouse RSP poll," Toronto: TD Bank at http:www. newswire.ca/en/releases/archive/January2004/05/c7449.html, (Accessed January 6, 2004).

————. (2005) "Retirement, what retirement? According to TD Waterhouse RSP Poll ⅓ Canadians plan to keep on working." Toronto: TD Bank at http://www. tdassetmanagment.com/Content/InvResources/PressRoom/p_LibraryItem. asp?LIID=351&CAT=30 (accessed January 5, 2005).

Townson, Monica (1997) *Independent Means: A Canadian Woman's Guide to Pensions and a Secure Financial Future.* Toronto: Macmillan Canada.

————. (2001) *Pensions Under Attack: What's behind the Push to Privatize Public Pensions.* Ottawa: Canadian Centre for Policy Alternatives and James Lorimer and Company Ltd., Publishers.

————. (2003) *Women in Non-Standard Jobs: The Public Policy Challenge.* Ottawa: Status of Women Canada.

————. (2005) *The development of maternity and parental benefits in Canada.* Ottawa; Unpublished report prepared for Shields & Hunt, Barristers and Solicitors.

Trades Union Congress (2004a) "TUC to hold pensions demonstration," Press release of March 30, 2004. London: Trades Union Congress. At http://www. tuc.org.uk/pensions. (Accessed March 31, 2004).

————. (2004b) " One in five won't get pension if retirement age rises." London: Trades Union Congress. http://www.tuc.org.uk/pensions/tuc-8159-fo.cfm (Accessed 11, 2005)

United Kingdom Government (2003) *Equality and Diversity: Age Matters.* London Department of Trade and Industry: Age Consultation 2003.

———. (2004a) *Simplicity, security and choice: Informed choices for working and saving.* Presented to Parliament by the Secretary of State for Work and Pensions by Command of Her Majesty. London: Department of Work and Pensions.

———. (2004b) *Pensions: Challenges and Choices. The First Report of the Pensions Commission.* Norwich, England: United Kingdom Stationery Office.

———. (2004c) "Statement made to the House of Commons on age discrimination: treatment of retirement age." At http://www.agepositive.gov.uk/news-detail.cfm?sectionID=44&newsid=504 (Accessed 1/18/05).

———. (2005) *Department of Work and Pensions Five Year Strategy: Opportunity and security throughout life.* Presented to Parliament by the Secretary of State for Work Pensions by Command of Her Majesty. London: Department of Work and Pensions.

United Nations (2001) *The World Ageing Situation: Exploring a Society for All Ages.* New York: United Nations Department of Economic and Social Affairs.

———. (2002) *Report of the Second World Assembly on Ageing: Madrid, 8–12 April 2002.* New York: United Nations.

———. (2004) *Resolution adopted by the General Assembly 58/134. Follow-up to the Second World Assembly on Aging.* 77th plenary meeting, 22 December 2003.

United States Social Security Administration (2004) *The 2004 Annual Report of the Board of Trustees of the Federal Old-Age and Survivors Insurance and Disability Insurance Trust Funds.* Washington: Social Security Administration.

Van Dalen, Hendrik P. and Kène Henkens (20023) "Early retirement reform: can it and will it work?" in *Ageing and Society 22.* Cambridge, UK: Cambridge University Press.

Walker, Alan (2003) *The Policy Challenge of Population Aging.* Hamilton, Ontario: University: Program for Research on Social and Economic Dimensions of an Aging Population. SEDAP Research Paper No. 108.

Watson Wyatt Worldwide (2001) *Canadian Pensions and Retirement Income Planning.* Toronto: CCH Canadian Limited.

Weisbrot, Mark (2005) "Social Security: Another Media Failure." Washington: Center for Economic and Policy Research, column. At http://www.cepr.net/columns/weisbrot/2005_05_17.htm (Accessed June 1, 2005).

Wilkinson, Richard G. (1996) *Unhealthy Societies: The Afflictions of Inequality.* London and New York: Routledge.

Wisensale, Steven K. (2001) "Global Ageing and the Intergenerational Equity Issue," in *TheWorld Ageing Situation: Exploring a Society for All Ages.* New York: United Nations Economic & Social Affairs.

Wolff, Edward N. (2002) *Retirement Insecurity: The Income Shortfalls Awaiting the Soon-to-Retire.* Washington: Economic Policy Institute.

Wolfson, Michael and Brian Murphy (1997) "Aging an Canada's Public Sector: Retrospect and Prospect,' in *Reform of Retirement Income Policy: International and Canadian Perspectives.* Edited by Keith G. Banting and Robin Boadway. Kingston, Ontario: Queen's University School of Policy Studies.

World Bank (1994) *Averting the Old Age Crisis.* Washington: The World Bank.

World Economic Forum (2004) *Living Happily Ever After: The Economic Implications of Aging Societies.* Geneva: World Economic Forum.

World Health Organization (2002) *Active Ageing: A Policy Framework.* Geneva: World Organization.

Wortsman, Arlene (2003) *Phased-In Retirement Options Needed for Skill Shortage Challenge.* A CLBC Commentary. Ottawa: Canadian Labour and Business Centre. October 2003.

Yalnizyan, Armine (2004) *Squandering Canada's Surplus: Opting for debt reduction and "scarcity by design."* Ottawa: Canadian Centre for Policy Alternatives.

Yamada, Atsuhiro (2002) *The Evolving Retirement Income Package: Trends in Adequacy Equality in Nine OECD Countries.* Organization for Economic Cooperation and Development. Labour Market and Social Policy—Occasional Papers No.63.

254